MW01040829

The Rivers
North of the Future

Also by David Cayley

The Age of Ecology
Ivan Illich in Conversation
Northrop Frye in Conversation
George Grant in Conversation
The Expanding Prison

The Rivers
North of the Future

The Testament of Ivan Illich
as told to David Cayley

Foreword by
Charles Taylor

ANANSI

Copyright © 2005 David Cayley

All rights reserved. No part of this publication may be reproduced or transmitted
in any form or by any means, electronic or mechanical, including photocopying, recording,
or any information storage and retrieval system, without permission in writing from the publisher.

Published in 2005 by
House of Anansi Press Inc.
110 Spadina Avenue, Suite 801
Toronto, ON M5V 2K4
Tel. 416-363-4343
Fax 416-363-1017
www.anansi.ca

Distributed in Canada by
HarperCollins Canada Ltd.
1995 Markham Road
Scarborough, ON M1B 5M8
Toll free tel. 1-800-387-0117

Distributed in the United States by
Publishers Group West
1700 Fourth Street
Berkeley, CA 94710
Toll free tel. 1-800-788-3123

Permission is gratefully acknowledged to reprint excerpts from the following:

(p. vi) Muska Nagel, *A Voice . . . Translations of Selected Poems by Paul Celan* (Puckerbrush Press, 1998).
(The title of this book and p. vi) Paul Celan, "In den Flüssen," taken from:
Paul Celan, *Atemwende* © Suhrkamp Verlag, Frankfurt am Main, 1967.
(pp. 40–41) Maurice Merleau-Ponty, "Eye and Mind," trans. Carleton Dallery,
in *The Primacy of Perception*, ed. James M. Edie (Evanston: Northwestern University Press, 1964).

Every reasonable effort has been made to contact the holders of copyright for materials
quoted in this work. The publishers will gladly receive information that will enable
them to rectify any inadvertent errors or omissions in subsequent editions.

House of Anansi Press is committed to protecting our natural environment. As part of
our efforts, this book is printed on New Leaf EcoBook 100 paper: it contains 100%
post-consumer recycled fibres, is acid-free, and is processed chlorine-free.

09 08 07 06 05   2 3 4 5 6

LIBRARY AND ARCHIVES CANADA CATALOGUING IN PUBLICATION DATA

Illich, Ivan, 1926–2002.
The rivers north of the future : the testament of Ivan Illich /
edited by David Cayley.

Includes index.
ISBN 0-88784-714-5

1. Illich, Ivan, 1926–2002 — Views on Christianity. 2. Illich, Ivan, 1926–2002 — Views
on technology. 3. Christianity — Controversial literature. 4. Christianity — Philosophy.
I. Cayley, David II. Title.

BR85.I44 2004   230'.01   C2004-905560-7

Cover design: Bill Douglas at The Bang
Cover art: Peter Schumann
Typesetting: Brian Panhuyzen

Canada Council   Conseil des Arts
for the Arts   du Canada

ONTARIO ARTS COUNCIL
CONSEIL DES ARTS DE L'ONTARIO

*We acknowledge for their financial support of our publishing program
the Canada Council for the Arts, the Ontario Arts Council, and the Government of Canada
through the Book Publishing Industry Development Program (BPIDP).*

Printed and bound in Canada

To Barbara Duden

Into the rivers north of the future
I cast out the net, that you
hesitantly burden with stone-engraved
shadows

— Paul Celan

CONTENTS

FOREWORD

We all owe a debt to David Cayley for bringing to the public this statement of the core thinking of Ivan Illich. It is an understatement to say that those who have read the books for which Illich is best known, even those most enthused by them, have rarely seen into the rich and complex position which underlies them. But this position is extraordinarily fertile and illuminating. In a way, it sets some of our cherished commonplaces on their heads.

The place of Christianity in the rise of Western modernity has been under discussion for more than a century. Those who are sympathetic to religion tend, these days, to give it an important place, and those who are less so (such as Hans Blumenberg) tend to minimize its role. Thinkers with a basically favourable stance towards modernity see it as the realization of Christian ideals. Christian reactionaries who hate the modern world, in the tradition of Joseph de Maistre, define Christianity as its antithesis. But, either way, debate tends to be framed by certain familiar alternatives — for or against modernity, for or against religion — and these alternatives are mixed and matched in different combinations. Illich changes the very terms of the debate. For him, modernity is neither the fulfillment nor the antithesis of Christianity, but its *perversion*. The link between ancient religion and present reality is affirmed, but not necessarily to the benefit of either.

Illich, in this sense, is reminiscent of another great voice from the sidelines: Friedrich Nietzsche. Nietzsche also tried to transform the debate, but he found a Christian source for the things he most hated in modernity: equality, democracy, the concern for suffering. His picture of Christian faith was a caricature in which faith could not be distinguished from its perversions. Illich, on the other hand, speaks as a man of faith. (Certain modern Nietzscheans, in particular Michel Foucault, raise many of the same issues as Illich, however.)

Illich argues that Western modernity finds its original impetus in a mutation of Latin Christendom, a mutation in which the Church began to take with ultimate seriousness its power to shape and form people to the demands of the Gospel. I had been working for a number of years on a project to account for the rise of secular civilization, and the basic thesis of my account was similar to Illich's. But I had no idea of the parallels until David Cayley brought Illich's thought to public attention in a radio series a few years ago.[1] This helped both to inspire and to refocus my efforts.

What I call a "mutation" in Latin Christendom could be described as an attempt to make over the lives of Christians and their social order, so as to make them conform thoroughly to the demands of their faith. I am talking not of a particular, revolutionary moment, but of a long, ascending series of attempts to establish a Christian order, of which the Reformation is a key phase. As I see it, these attempts show a progressive impatience with older modes of religious life in which certain traditional collective, ritualistic forms coexisted uneasily with the demands of individual devotion and ethical reform which came from the "higher" revelations. In Latin Christendom, the attempt was made to impose on everyone a more individually committed and Christocentric religion of devotion and action, and to suppress or even abolish older, supposedly "magical" or "superstitious" forms of collective ritual practice.

Allied with a neo-Stoic outlook, this became the charter for a series of attempts to establish new forms of social order. These helped to reduce violence and disorder and to create populations of relatively pacific and productive artisans and peasants who were more and more induced/forced into the new forms of devotional practice and moral behaviour, be this in Protestant England, Holland, or later the

American colonies, or in Counter-Reformation France, or in the Germany of the *Polizeistaat*.

This creation of a new, civilized, "polite" order succeeded beyond what its first originators could have hoped for, and this in turn led to a new reading of what a Christian order might be, one which was seen more and more in "immanent" terms. (The polite, civilized order *is* the Christian order.) This version of Christianity was shorn of much of its "transcendent" content, and was thus open to a new departure, in which the understanding of good order — what we could call the modern moral order — could be embraced outside of the original theological, Providential framework, and in certain cases even against it (as by Voltaire, Edward Gibbon, and in another way David Hume).

The secularization of Western culture and, indeed, widespread disbelief in God have arisen in close symbiosis with this belief in a moral order of rights-bearing individuals who are destined (by God or Nature) to act for mutual benefit. Such an order thus rejects the earlier honour ethic which exalted the warrior, just as the new order also tends to occlude any transcendent horizon. (We see one good formulation of this notion of order in John Locke's *Second Treatise of Government*, in which he argued for a human origin of the authority to rule.) This understanding of order has profoundly shaped the modern West's dominant forms of social imaginary: the market economy, the public sphere, the sovereign "people."

This, in bare outline, is my account of secularization, one in which I think Illich basically concurs. But he describes it as the corrupting of Christianity. To illustrate he draws, again and again, on the familiar parable of the Good Samaritan, Jesus' story about an outsider who helps a wounded Jew. For Illich this story represents the possibility of mutual belonging between two strangers. Jesus points to a new kind of fittingness, belonging together, between the Samaritan and the wounded man. They are fitted together in a proportionality which comes from God, which is that of agape, and which became possible because God became flesh. The enfleshment of God extends outward, through such new links as the Samaritan makes with the Jew, into a network which we call the Church. But this is a network, not a categorical grouping; that is, it is a skein of relations which link particular, unique, enfleshed people to each other, rather than a grouping of people together on the grounds of their sharing some important property. Corruption occurs when the Church begins to respond to the failure and inadequacy of a motivation grounded in a sense of mutual belonging by erecting a system. This system incorporates a code or set of rules, a set of disciplines to make us internalize these rules, and a system of rationally constructed organizations — private and public bureaucracies, universities, schools — to make sure we carry out what the rules demand. All these become second nature to us. We grow accustomed to decentring ourselves from our lived, embodied experience in order to become disciplined, rational, disengaged subjects. From within this perspective, the significance of the Good Samaritan story appears obvious: it is a stage on the road to a universal morality of rules.

Modern ethics illustrates this fetishism of rules and norms, as Illich observes in Chapter 15. Not just law but ethics is seen in terms of rules — as by Immanuel Kant, for example. The spirit of the law is important, where it is so, because it too expresses some general principle. For Kant the principle is that we should put regulation by reason, or humanity as rational agency, first. In contrast, as we have seen, the network of agape puts first the gut-driven response to a particular person. This response cannot be reduced to a general rule. Because we cannot live up to this — "Because of the hardness of your hearts" — we need rules. It is not that we could just abolish them, but modern liberal civilization fetishizes them. We think we have to find the *right* system of rules, of norms, and then follow them through unfailingly. We cannot see any more the awkward way these rules fit enfleshed human beings, we fail to notice the dilemmas they have to sweep under the carpet: for instance, justice versus mercy; or justice versus a renewed relation, as we saw in South Africa with its Truth and Reconciliation Commission, a shining attempt to get beyond the existing codes of retribution.

Within this perspective, something crucial in the Good Samaritan story gets lost. A world ordered by this system of rules, disciplines, and organizations can only see contingency as an obstacle, even an enemy and a threat. The ideal is to master it, to extend the web of control so that contingency is reduced to a minimum. By contrast, contingency is an essential feature of the story of the Good Samaritan as an answer to the question that prompted it. Who is my neighbour? The one you happen across, stumble across, who is wounded there in the road. Sheer accident also has a hand in shaping the proportionate, the appropriate response. It is telling us something, answering our deepest questions: *this* is your neighbour. But in order to hear this, we have to escape from the monomaniacal perspective in which contingency can only be an adversary requiring control. Illich develops this theme profoundly in Chapter 3.

This is why Illich's work is so important to us today. I have found it more than useful, even inspiring, because I have been working over many years to find a nuanced understanding of Western modernity. This would be one which would both give a convincing account of how modernity arose and allow for a balanced account of what is good, even great, in it, and of what is less good, even dangerous and destructive. Illich's understanding of our modern condition as a spin-off from a "corrupted" Christianity captures one of the important historical vectors that brought about the modern age and allows us to see how good and bad are closely interwoven in it. Ours is a civilization concerned to relieve suffering and enhance human well-being, on a universal scale unprecedented in history, and which at the same time threatens to imprison us in forms that can turn alien and dehumanizing. This should take us beyond the facile and noisy debate between the boosters and knockers of modernity or the "Enlightenment project."

Illich, in his overall vision and in the penetrating historical detail of his arguments, offers a new road map, a way of coming to understand what has been jeopardized in our decentred, objectifying, discarnate way of remaking ourselves, and he does so without simply falling into the clichés of anti-modernism.

Codes, even the best codes, can become idolatrous traps that tempt us to complicity in violence. Illich reminds us not to become totally invested in the code — even the best code of a peace-loving, egalitarian variety — of liberalism. We should find the centre of our spiritual lives beyond the code, deeper than the code, in networks of living concern, which are not to be sacrificed to the code, which must even from time to time subvert it. This message comes out of a certain theology, but it should be heard by everybody. This rich book assembles countless reminders of our humanity, which we can all hear and gain from, regardless of our ultimate metaphysical perspective.

— Charles Taylor

PREFACE

The seed of this book was planted in the fall of 1988, during an extended radio interview with Ivan Illich that I was recording in the town of State College, Pennsylvania, for the Canadian Broadcasting Corporation. Every day, for eight days, Illich had set aside a couple of hours to talk with me, and I had led him, and he me, on a meandering journey through his life and work. Then, on my final day with him, he made a remark that took me by surprise:

> [M]y work is an attempt to accept with great sadness the fact of Western culture. [Christopher] Dawson . . . says that the Church is Europe and Europe is the Church, and I say *yes*! *Corruptio optimi quae est pessima.* [The corruption of the best is the worst.] Through the attempt to insure, to guarantee, to regulate Revelation, the best becomes the worst. . . .
>
> I live also with a sense of profound ambiguity. I can't do without tradition, but I have to recognize that its institutionalization is the root of an evil deeper than any evil I could have known with my unaided eyes and mind.[1]

Before coming to see Illich I had made a careful review of his published work, but here was an idea for which my research had not prepared me, and one which I could not quite grasp. This book is the result of my attempt to get to the bottom of it.

The following summer Illich stayed with me and my family for several days, while he was in Toronto for a conference. His visit allowed us many hours to talk, and our conversation soon returned to the idea he had surprised me with the year before: that the utter singularity of modern society can only be understood as the result of a perverse attempt to institutionalize the Christian Gospel, and that this corruption of the best produces a unique evil that only becomes fully intelligible when one grasps its origin.[2] The more we talked, the more I began to feel that this idea might provide a key to the whole of Illich's work. Shouldn't this become the subject of a book? I asked, as I drove him to the airport. The next time we meet, he replied, I'll bring you several chapters.

I saw Illich as often as I could in subsequent years, and our friendship grew, but I never saw those chapters. There were a number of possible reasons for this: other commitments, a painful illness that prevented the sustained effort that would have been required for such an ambitious new undertaking, and perhaps a certain reticence in the face of a theme potentially so explosive and so easily misunderstood. But, whatever the reasons, by the mid-1990s I had realized that the book I wanted to read might never be written. So I made a suggestion. I would tape record Illich's thoughts on this subject, with a view to producing both a radio series and a transcript which might then be developed into a book. This would allow him to take one step at a time, and to put a good deal of the responsibility onto me. After some consideration, he agreed.

Illich usually spent the spring and early summer of the year in the Mexican city of Cuernavaca. From 1961 to 1976 he had directed the Center for Intercultural Documentation (CIDOC)[3] there, and after closing the Center he had kept a place in the household of his former CIDOC colleague, Valentina Borremans, in the village of Ocotepec on the outskirts of the city. I spent two weeks with him there in June of 1997, and the first fourteen chapters of this book are edited, and slightly rearranged, transcriptions of what he said to me during those days. These were not interviews in the sense of interchanges in which the interviewer sets the agenda. For the most part Illich introduced and developed each topic on his own. I interrupted occasionally in order to clarify or refocus what he was saying, but often I had no idea where we were going or what was coming next, and more than once he declined a direction I proposed. I feel I have been faithful to the occasion, therefore, in eliminating myself and simply presenting these chapters as his uninterrupted talks.

Two years later I again visited Ocotepec, and we followed up many of the themes that Illich had introduced during our first session. These talks comprise the remainder of this book (Chapters 15–22); and, since they really were interviews, I have preserved their question-and-answer format. Excerpts from these two sets of recordings were incorporated in a five-hour radio series which I presented on CBC Radio in January of 2000 under the title *The Corruption of Christianity*.[4] I don't think Illich ever listened to those broadcasts — I certainly didn't expect him to — but he was interested in the effect they produced. He had sometimes joked with me that I was the only interlocutor he could find on this theme, and, while this was a characteristic exaggeration, it is certainly true that his efforts to provoke discussion among his fellow Roman Catholics, and even among Christians more generally, had found few echoes in recent years. So he took careful note of the lively interest with which *The Corruption of Christianity* was studied, particularly in Germany, where he taught at the University of Bremen during the fall and winter semesters, and where a study group had been formed to discuss a translation of the transcript. His sense of the promise this held eventually overcame his reluctance to release a vulnerable and unpolished draft of his ideas, and in the spring of 2002 he unequivocally blessed the preparation of the full transcript of our conversations for publication.

Ivan Illich died in Bremen in December of 2002. We had intended to meet that winter to go over the manuscript, and that would certainly have produced a more complete and more refined book than the one I now have to offer. But, even as it is, with all the limitations of an oral, off-the-cuff presentation, I am convinced that this is an invaluable work, not just for the light it sheds on Illich's life and teaching, but even more for the insight it offers into the origin and coming to be of the uncanny world in which we live.

I have taken the title for this book from a poem by Paul Celan, who was a German-speaking Jew from the city of Czernowitz in

Bukowina, a community to which Illich also had ancestral connections. During the Second World War, Celan's parents were deported
and murdered in a Nazi concentration camp in the Ukraine. He was
forced into a labour battalion but survived. Until he drowned himself
in the Seine in 1970, at the age of forty-nine, Celan wrote poetry in
German. He explained his approach to the language of the Holocaust
in a speech in Bremen in 1958, after he had been given the city's
Literature Award.

> . . . Reachable, near and not lost, one thing remained in the midst of all
> losses: language.
>
> Yes, language was not lost, yes, notwithstanding. But it had to go
> through its own incapacity to find answers, go through the terrible
> silencing: go through the thousand darknesses of death-bringing talk. It
> went through and gave no words for what had happened: went through
> and was allowed to reappear: enriched from all that.
>
> In this language I have tried, in those years, and since then, to write
> poetry . . .[5]

Illich felt a strong connection with Paul Celan. German was the language, among the many Illich spoke, in which he was most "poetically
involved" — at fourteen, he told me, he had tried to write like Rilke
— and he had himself lived in Nazi-occupied Vienna, where he had
been paraded in front of his class while a school official pointed at his
nose and remarked to the other students that this was "a typical
Jewish profile."[6] So, when Illich returned to Germany to live and
teach in the late 1970s, and had to find his way back into a language
that had been deformed not just by Nazism but also by the plastic
coating applied during the years of the *Wirtschaftswunder*, the post-
war "economic miracle," Celan was one of his inspirations.

Celan's poems enact what he calls the reappearance of language
— in words that have been through the purgatorial fire of "terrible
silencing." Illich too knew something of the silence imposed by a
corrupted language, and he struggled life-long for fresh and surprising ways of speaking and writing. Of Celan's poems, Illich
particularly admired "The Rivers North of the Future." It speaks of a

hoped-for "not yet," a time and place which cannot be reached by simply projecting from the present, since it lies north of the future. And, even in these inaccessible waters, the nets that can be cast out are "burdened with stone-engraved shadows," the weight of all that has been. This seems to me a suitable image to stand for the place that Ivan Illich conjured for himself and for those lucky enough to have met him on their way, a place heavy with history but still reaching out of time into mysterious and refreshing waters. I have chosen it in preference to a reflection of the book's main theme — that the corruption of the best is the worst — because I believe that hope, however chastened, is Illich's fundamental note, even when he is talking about the gathering darkness of our world.

In an interview that Illich recorded with his friend Douglas Lummis in Japan in the winter of 1986–87, Lummis asks him about a "possible future." "To hell with the future," Illich replies. "It's a man-eating idol. Institutions have a future . . . but people have no future. People have only hope."[7] Since there obviously was, and will be, a tomorrow, I interpret this curse in two ways. First, it points to the fact that no sane person can project the future of the economic utopia of endless growth in which we live as anything but catastrophe, sooner or later. Second, and even more important, the future as an idol devours the only moment in which heaven can happen upon us: the present. Expectation tries to compel tomorrow; hope enlarges the present and makes a future, north of the future.

My chosen subtitle refers to what follows as Illich's testament. By this term I hope to imply both a testimony and a bequest. Illich registered the changes through which he lived with extraordinary sensitivity, and this makes him, in my view, an invaluable witness to his times. But he also opened many more paths than he was himself able fully to explore, and in this sense the book is a bequest to those interested in fleshing out the many ideas that he has only sketched in these pages.

I have dedicated this work, with love and admiration, to Barbara Duden, who kept her door open for Illich's far-flung fellowship, and keeps it open still, despite the demanding pace of her own teaching and writing. It was to her house in State College, Pennsylvania, and to her house in Bremen in northern Germany, that Illich invited the many friends, colleagues, and students who wanted to talk with him. And it was her generous hospitality that helped to give so many of Ivan's gatherings their special flair. I would also like to acknowledge several people who counselled and corrected me during the preparation of the manuscript: Jutta Mason, Lee Hoinacki, Sebastian Trapp, Klaus Baier, Lenz and Ruth Kriss-Rettenbeck, Sajay Samuel, and again Barbara Duden. My thanks finally to CBC Radio, to my executive producer, Bernie Lucht, and to my colleagues at *Ideas* for their support and encouragement.

INTRODUCTION

Ivan Illich believed that the puzzling and unprecedented character of modern society makes sense only when it is recognized as a mutation of Christianity. This hypothesis formed and matured throughout his career as a priest and itinerant scholar. His exposition of the idea here draws on a lifetime's effort to probe and to bear this mysterious and consequential deformation of faith; and so it seems best, before discussing this theme explicitly, to begin with a brief account of the course of his public life.

He was born in 1926. His father, Piero, came from a landed family of Dalmatia, with property in the city of Split and extensive wine and olive oil producing estates on the adjacent island of Brac.[1] His mother, Ellen, belonged to a family of converted German Jews. Her father, Fritz Regenstreif, had made his fortune in the lumber trade in Bosnia, where he owned sawmills, and had built a handsome *art nouveau* villa in the outskirts of Vienna. The alliance between Piero and Ellen was affectionate but ill-starred. During the early years of their marriage, anti-foreigner and anti-Jewish sentiment was rising in Yugoslavia, and the Yugoslavian government was pursuing a claim against Fritz Regenstreif's holdings in Bosnia at the International Court in the Hague. In 1932 Ellen Illich left the home she had established with her husband in Split and returned with her three children to her father's house in Vienna. Piero Illich died of natural causes during the Second World War.

After their return to Vienna in 1932, Ivan and his twin younger brothers never again saw their father.

In 1942 Ellen Illich and her children left Vienna for Florence. Fritz Regenstreif had died the year before, and his magnificent house had been taken over by the Nazis. Ellen, though Christian, was in danger as an ethnic Jew, and the children, following the death of their father, were now classified as half-Jewish rather than half-Aryan.[2] Ivan finished his schooling in Florence, played a small part in the Italian Resistance,[3] and then, after the war, did advanced studies in philosophy and theology at the Gregorian University in Rome and in history at the University of Salzburg, where he obtained a Ph.D. In Rome Illich was also ordained a priest. He said his first Mass in the catacombs where the early Roman Christians had hidden from their persecutors.

Illich was apt in every way for a career as a prince of the Church. He came from an aristocratic family with old connections to the Roman Church, and he was charismatic, intellectually brilliant, and devout. Amongst those who pressed him to remain in Rome were Giovanni Montini, who later became Pope Paul VI. But Illich had no liking for the papal bureaucracy and, at the beginning of the 1950s, left for the United States with the idea of studying the alchemical works of Albertus Magnus (1206–1280) at Princeton. Shortly after his arrival in the U.S., during a visit to a friend of his grandfather's in Manhattan, he was told of the Puerto Rican migration to New York which was then transforming northern Manhattan and unsettling the older European immigrants who comprised the vast majority of New York's Roman Catholics. Illich was intrigued, and he spent the next two days in the Puerto Rican *barrio* getting acquainted. He was drawn to the country ways and devout Catholic spirit of these new arrivals, and he immediately applied to the cardinal of New York, Francis Spellman, for a post in one of the parishes where Puerto Ricans were settling. The sudden and surprising change of direction was characteristic.

During the next four years, Illich pressed the American Church to recognize and make room for these newcomers. Father Joseph Fitzpatrick, a professor of sociology at Fordham, was associated with

Illich in this campaign. In an interview which I recorded with Fitzpatrick in 1988, he recalled how Illich's parishioners viewed their young curate:

> He was profoundly revered. He became an outstanding figure. The people in the parish just loved him, and the thing that they always remarked was the devotion with which he said his Mass. They were most impressed at the evidence of great devotion at his Mass. And, secondly, he was very much involved in their lives in a way in which I would say very few priests were involved in their lives at that particular time.[4]

Illich's work with Puerto Ricans in New York culminated in 1956 with a huge outdoor fiesta on the Fordham campus. Thirty thousand people gathered to celebrate the feast day of San Juan, the patron saint of Puerto Rico, in what amounted to a coming-out party for the local Puerto Rican community. That same year Illich was appointed vice-rector of the Catholic University in Puerto Rico, and shortly afterwards Cardinal Spellman named him a monsignor, the youngest in his diocese to be so honoured. In Puerto Rico Illich had his first contact with the institution of mass compulsory schooling conceived as a universal and indispensable precondition for what was then simply called development. His position at the university automatically made him a member of the board that governed the island's school system, and the more he learned about this system, the more curious and the more disconcerted he became. Two things particularly struck him: the surprisingly church-like character of the institution of schooling, and the strange discrepancy between the claims made for schooling and its actual results. Schooling is said to generate social equality, but Illich soon recognized that it actually produces the opposite effect, concentrating privilege in the hands of those whose background has equipped them to jump through its many hoops and putting the poor at a new disadvantage. He began the intensive analysis that would result in the publication in 1971 of *Deschooling Society*.

Illich remained in Puerto Rico until 1960, when his first brush with the hierarchy of his Church forced him to leave the island. This, in his words, was what happened:

The two Irish Catholic bishops . . . had gotten themselves into politics by threatening excommunication for anybody who voted for a political party which didn't proscribe the sale of condoms in drugstores. And this was a month before the nomination [for only the second time] of a Catholic, John Kennedy, as the presidential candidate of the Democratic Party. It was not that I wanted to support Kennedy. But I felt that it was highly unsound to allow the religious issue to creep back into American politics, just because Puerto Rico was the only place where two American bishops had an absolute Catholic majority as their subjects. . . . So I had to do something, [and] . . . I attracted to myself the full odium of exploding that situation. I knew that I was sacrificing any possibility of doing anything publicly in Puerto Rico for many years . . .[5]

Illich, from the beginning of his priesthood, had distinguished two forms of the Church, which he called the Church as *she* and the Church as *it*. To the first, the Church as the repository of tradition and the living embodiment of Christian community, he was, and always remained, deeply committed. The Church, in this sense, he said, is "that surprise in the net, the pearl . . . the mystery, the kingdom among us."[6] But to the second, the Church as a self-serving, worldly power, he was, and remained, a thorn.

Illich's next venture was the founding in 1961 of the Center for Intercultural Formation (CIF) in the Mexican city of Cuernavaca. (This organization was later renamed and became more widely known as the Center for Intercultural Documentation, or CIDOC.) In Puerto Rico Illich had established a summer institute which, in his words, "combine[d] the very intensive study of spoken Spanish with field experience and with the academic study of Puerto Rican poetry, history, songs and social reality."[7] It tended to attract younger priests who wanted to take the church to the people rather than bringing the people to the church. "Properly conducted language learning," Illich said, "is one of the few occasions in which an adult can go through a deep experience of poverty, of weakness, and of dependence on the good will of another."[8] The same idea animated CIF, and it was this emphasis on a sensitive and quizzical humility *vis-à-vis* other languages and cultures that increasingly brought CIF, and later CIDOC, into conflict with the spirit of the times.

The year that CIF was founded was the same year in which President Kennedy unveiled his "Alliance for Progress," an ambitious development-assistance scheme for Latin America. It was the year in which Pope John XXIII called on the North American Church to send 10 per cent of its clerical strength to Latin America as missionaries, and the year in which the Peace Corps was founded. The idea of "development" as a coherent and transmissible cure for "underdevelopment" had been around since Harry Truman put the idea into play in his 1949 Inaugural Address, but it was about to undergo an intensification. The "development decade" was beginning, and Illich set up his Center with the explicit purpose of subverting it. He ridiculed the Peace Corps, called the Alliance for Progress an "alliance for the progress of the middle classes," and sowed doubt in the minds of the missionaries who came to him to learn Spanish.

Illich saw "development" as "a war on subsistence" that would replace a tolerable absence of goods and services by a much more painful condition which he named "modernized poverty." Development, he argued, opens a vista onto "an earthly paradise of never-ending consumption,"[9] but ends up generating needs that cannot be met and demands for services that can never be delivered. At the same time, the glamour that attaches to development dulls the dignity of subsistence and disables the pursuit of self-sufficiency. He made these arguments in the midst of the shattering, almost unimaginable transformation through which he lived. At the beginning of the 1950s, when he began his work as a parish priest, only a small minority of the world's people lived in cities, and much of the great rural majority could still get by with few packaged commodities or professional services. By the time of his death, 80 per cent lived in cities, the majority of them in shadow economies but all keenly aware of their unmet needs and marginal position. Looking back on the sheer catastrophic scale of this reversal, it is hard to believe that the promotion of development was its primary cause or that any critique was likely to have stemmed this tide, but one can still admire the cogency and prescience of Illich's arguments. Calling for "counter-research on fundamental alternatives to current prepackaged solutions," he tried to point poor countries towards paths that

lay beyond the horizon of "huge institutions producing costly services."[10] And he predicted that if these countries continued to see the
world through the monocultural lens of development and to define
progress in terms of schools, hospitals, and highways, the result
would be chronic underdevelopment, grotesque social polarization,
and more acute misery for the millions who would inevitably be
excluded. Forty years later, with the foggy enthusiasms of the development decade long ago dispelled, I can leave it to the reader to judge
whether Illich was right.

Much of Illich's effort during the 1960s was directed at convincing his Church to disentangle itself from initiatives like the Alliance
for Progress and to recognize that "it is blasphemous to use the
Gospel to prop up any social or political system."[11] Mission, he said,
demands searching self-criticism, and a disposition to listen and lose
oneself. It requires an ability to bracket and relativize one's own culture in order to hear what the Gospel says when it speaks in the voice
of another culture. This was not generally the attitude of an
American Church that confused its faith with its culture and took
almost entirely for granted both its power and the good intentions
that justified its exercise of this power. Illich celebrated genuine missionary poverty wherever he encountered it, but in its absence he saw
his vocation as being to provoke and to satirize the complacent
worldliness of the Church. "I always found," he told me, "that if I had
to intervene in public controversies, then the one type of planned violence in which I could engage was to destroy lies through laughter."[12]

"A critical attitude," Illich said, "is one of the ways in which
Christian love for the Church can develop;"[13] and his criticisms of
the Church were fundamental. In an article called "The Vanishing
Clergyman," first drafted in 1959 but not published until 1967, he
indicted the very idea of a professional clergy.[14] The Church, he
said, had become a bureaucratic dinosaur, and its clergy "folkloric
phantoms." He proposed that ordained laymen, not professional
placeholders, should preside at Christian celebrations, and that the
current "tottering," "priest-ridden" "giant" should give way to something much closer to the early Church, in which like-minded
communities celebrated "living and intimate liturgies." He also advo-

cated what he called, in another essay of this period, a powerless Church.[15] And here he aimed not just at the easy target, the Church hierarchy which tries to justify its existence by providing services to the poor, but also at a much more charismatic figure of the time: "the rebel priest who wants to use his collar as an attractive banner in agitation."[16] The proper vocation of the Church, he said, is not to instruct the world, guide its political and social orientation, or provide it with services. All these activities inevitably require the exercise of power and inevitably generate ideological division. The cross, for Illich, stands for the renunciation of power. It foreshadows a unity which is manifest in the world but never belongs to it, a unity always out of the reach of merely instrumental human purposes. The Church exists to discern and celebrate this mystery, rather than to accomplish some social or political end. "What the church contributes through evangelization [that is, preaching the Gospel] is like the laughter in the joke," Illich said. "Two hear the same story — but one gets the point."[17]

Illich's attitude to the Church was typified by his withdrawal from the Second Vatican Council, which sat in Rome between 1962 and 1965. He told me the story at length in 1988:

During the Second Vatican Council I worked with a man named Suenens, then the cardinal of Malines-Bruxelles. The Pope had asked him to be the president of a group of four cardinals who moderated the Council. Much earlier, Suenens had known me pretty well through a variety of circumstances, and he asked me to come to Rome as one of the direct advisors of this committee. We met every day during the second and third sessions. One morning, I asked him if we could have a cup of coffee together up at Quattro Fontane, where he was staying at a little Belgian college. I said to him, "I'm leaving now. Yesterday you proved to me that this Council is incapable of facing the issues which count, while trying hard to remain traditional."

The day before, in the aula of St. Peter's, the bishops had accepted the fact that the document which would come out on the Church and the world would say that the Church could not as yet condemn governments for keeping atomic bombs, that is, for keeping tools of genocide . . . for the moment.

It was a wise decision, *world*-wise.

And I gave Suenens a little caricature which somebody had drawn up for me. In that cartoon you see five popes, with their characteristic noses, one behind the other, all pointing with one finger at one of two objects standing there — an already slightly flaccid penis with a condom filled with semen hanging on it, and an atomic rocket, ready for takeoff. In the balloon was written, "*It's* against nature!" I am proud to have been and to be associated with, and to be loyal to, an agency, a *worldly* agency, which still has the courage to say, even today, "It's against nature!" [The problem is] the finger might be pointing at the wrong object.[18]

Illich's stance towards the Vatican Council was, in his words, "a question of witness,"[19] a question of "taking the moral stance which corresponds to the vocation implied by the Gospel."[20]

Illich at all times stressed his faithfulness and his devotion to the Church, just as he does in his story about his withdrawal from the Second Vatican Council. When presenting his essay "The Vanishing Clergyman" in *Celebration of Awareness*, for example, Illich adds an introduction in which he argues that he is advancing his proposal to deprofessionalize the Church in order to preserve fundamentals like "the value of freely chosen celibacy, the episcopal structure of the church, [and] the permanence of priestly ordination."[21] But his words were not taken in the spirit in which he hoped to be understood. In Mexico, he became the *bête noire* of the ultra-conservative elements in the Church — an Opus Dei paper called *Gente* described him as "a strange, devious, slippery personage, crawling with indefinable nationalities."[22] He also incurred the hostility of the political right by his horrified and outspoken opposition to the official torture that was widely practised in Brazil after a military junta seized power in 1964, and subsequently in other Latin American countries, often with the connivance of the United States. More than once, Illich was physically attacked.[23] And, in the summer of 1968, he was summoned to Rome by the Sacred Congregation for the Doctrine of the Faith — the modern descendant of the Inquisition — commonly known as the Holy Office. He had become, the document drawn up against him claimed, "an object of curiosity, bewilderment and scandal to the Church," and he was to come and answer questions about both his political and doctrinal views.

Illich presented himself at the Vatican and was shown to a subterranean room where his judge awaited him. The interview began with a command that he keep the entire proceeding secret under threat of excommunication. Illich refused. The head of the congregation, Cardinal Seper of Yugoslavia, was consulted, and eventually Illich was allowed to leave with a written copy of the accusations against him.[24]

This text took the form of a questionnaire, divided into four categories: "Dangerous Doctrinal Opinions," "Erroneous Ideas Against the Church," "Bizarre Conceptions Concerning the Clergy," and "Subversive Interpretations Concerning the Liturgy and Ecclesiastical Discipline." The questions, as Illich said later, were of the "When did you stop beating your wife?" variety; to have answered at all would have required him to accept numerous unacceptable premises. "What would you answer," he was asked, "to those who say that you are petulant, adventurous, imprudent, fanatical . . . hypnotizing, [and] a rebel to all authority . . . ?" The rest of the eighty-five questions solicited everything from his views on the doctrine of limbo to his relations with the Mexican poet and essayist Octavio Paz to his supposed role in the recent kidnapping of the archbishop of Guatemala. In some of the questions Illich recognized information from CIA documents which had been leaked to him earlier. In others the hand of right-wing Catholic organizations in Mexico was visible.

That evening Illich wrote to Cardinal Seper that he would not answer the questions. He preferred, he said, to remain silent, taking as his motto "If a man asks you to lend him your coat, then give him your shirt as well."[25] To defend himself would only amplify the scandal his enemies were trying to create and deepen the embarrassment of the Church he loved. He delivered his letter to Cardinal Seper in person the following morning. Seper received him courteously and then dismissed him with the words "Get going, get going and never come back."[26] "It wasn't until I was walking down the stairs," Illich said later, "that it struck me that he was quoting the Inquisitor's last words to the Prisoner in Dostoevsky's story of the Grand

Inquisitor."[27] In this story in Dostoevsky's novel *The Brothers Karamazov*, Jesus returns to Seville at the time of the Inquisition. The Grand Inquisitor has him imprisoned and then explains to him that the Church, out of compassion for weak and suffering humanity, has been forced to embrace the worldly power that Jesus rejected.

Illich returned to CIDOC, which by the late 1960s had grown into what probably can be best described as a free university, hosting seminars which attracted reform-minded thinkers from around the world. And it was CIDOC that became the target of Rome's next move. In January of 1969 the Holy Office placed the Center under a formal ban which forbade any priest, monk, or nun from going there. Illich decided that he had had enough. No charge that he could actually answer had been made against him. And yet he and his institute had been made "the focal point for still another tragic round of disruptive and uncreative uproar within the church."[28] And so he wrote to his archbishop, Terence Cooke of New York:

> These proceeding[s] have cast over me the shadow of a "notorious churchman," and this interferes with my ministry, my work as an educator and my personal decision to live as a Christian . . . I now want to inform you of my irrevocable decision to resign entirely from Church service, to suspend the exercise of priestly functions, and to renounce totally all titles, offices, benefits and privileges which are due to me as a cleric.[29]

A priest, in Illich's entirely traditional view, must be a symbol of unity, an *alter Christus*;[30] and it was clear to him that the intrigues of his enemies had made it impossible for him to be such a symbol. He had always believed that the priestly office should be kept apart from the world of politics. When he had gone to Puerto Rico and assumed the political duties of a university administrator, he had gone to the length of buying a little hut in a remote fishing village so that he could say Mass for people quite unconnected with the world of the university. "I didn't want to get mixed up," he said, "in a conflict between the priestly office of making the other-worldly unity and brotherhood of the liturgy real and my personal stance as a politician."[31] Now the wide publicity that had been given to his troubles with Rome, and the polarization that his proposals had produced within the Church, made any such solution impossible. He never renounced his priesthood as such, and the Church never removed him from its rolls. In fact, when he began to teach at the University of Kassel in Germany more than ten years later, his first paycheque was made out to "Rev. Monsignor Ivan Illich," which is how the bursar's office had found him listed in the *Annuario Pontificio*, the official listing of prelates in the Catholic Church.[32] He simply stopped performing any of the official acts of a priest and gradually passed beyond the horizon of official ecclesiastical concern.

During the next few years Illich would enjoy extraordinary popularity as a writer and lecturer. His books sold out, his essays led the *New York Review of Books* and the *Saturday Review*, and his lectures were mobbed. When he addressed a Toronto teach-in on development, of which I was one of the organizers, the 600-seat auditorium that we had rented would not hold everyone who wanted to hear him and we had to turn people away. This was his moment, and he seized it. When I went to hear him speak in Vancouver just after his book *Medical Nemesis* was published in 1976, he indicated during his talk that he thought he was in Seattle, which probably gives a measure of just how many lectures he was delivering at this time.

Between 1971 and 1976 Illich produced four popular titles in quick succession: *Deschooling Society*, *Tools for Conviviality* (1973), *Energy and Equity* (1974), and *Medical Nemesis*. The first of these, *Deschooling Society*, completed the thinking that he had been doing since he was first confronted with the paradoxes of schooling in Puerto Rico in the 1950s. Universal compulsory schooling, he wrote, produces effects that are precisely opposite to those that its proponents say they intend. It is an item of faith amongst educators, for example, that schooling increases social equality by serving as a ladder of opportunity. Illich, on the other hand, called schooling a system for producing dropouts. He argued that the school, by definition, is a graded hierarchy which focuses aspiration on its highest rungs but sloughs off the majority lower down, and this is especially true in poorer countries which cannot possibly afford to keep all their younger citizens under expensive pedagogical treatment for twelve or sixteen years. This means not only that the majority cannot succeed, but worse, that those who fail are led to blame themselves. As soon as schooling is held out as the gateway to opportunity, those who were formerly merely poor begin to suffer the added disadvantage of being dropouts, whose inferiority is a product of their underschooling.

Illich identified many other perverse effects of schooling. He noted, for example, that it generates numerous institutional imperatives that actually frustrate learning, that it endlessly divides and subdivides knowledge into arbitrary sequences and packages, and that it fosters the illusion that worthwhile learning depends on teaching. He also raised the question of how so counterproductive an institution could exercise the monopoly it does over the dissemination and acquisition of knowledge. Why are the failures of schooling always met by a call for more schooling rather than less? Why do people remain blind, or indifferent, to the obvious contrast between the institution's stated purpose and its actual result? Illich's answer was to define schooling as a ritual, and to define a ritual as a procedure that generates a myth powerful enough to conceal its own contradictions. But this was a ritual, according to him, of an unprecedented kind. All peoples have had their rain dances and their initiation rites, but never a ritual that claimed universal validity, a procedure presenting itself as the exclusive path to an inevitable destination for everyone, everywhere. Schooling had become, Illich claimed, a worldwide religion, and, as such, testified to its descent from the first institution to claim that its services and ministrations were the sole gateway to salvation: the Roman Catholic Church. "I am reminded of the late Middle Ages," he wrote in *Deschooling Society*, "when the demand for services outgrew a lifetime, and 'Purgatory' was created to purify souls under the Pope's control before they could enter universal peace."[33] The Church Universal, according to Illich, was the template for the service society. It was the Church that first gave its clerisy legal jurisdiction over souls and made the faithful dependent on clerical services. It was the Church that made learning a consequence of authoritative teaching, that made standing in the faith a result of correct answers to catechisms and inquisitions, and that made salvation a question of compulsory attendance at various rituals.

Illich described *Deschooling Society* and his other writings of the 1970s as pamphlets.[34] That word may make them sound somewhat slighter than they are, but it is accurate insofar as their purpose was to influence contemporary political discussion. In *Deschooling Society*, for example, he called for the disestablishment of the educational monopoly, and he used the term *disestablishment* in exactly the same sense in which it had earlier been applied to religion. Virtually everyone now accepts that no social privilege, opportunity, or entitlement should attach to membership in a particular religion. "The State shall make no law with respect to the establishment of religion" is how the First Amendment to the United States Constitution puts it. Illich suggested that the same formula be applied to education: "There shall be no ritual obligatory for all," he wrote.[35] It is important to note in this connection that although *Deschooling Society* exposed and satirized many of the follies of contemporary school systems, it did not indict schools as such. In fact, Illich recognized that in certain circumstances a school could be a rational and practicable way of organizing learning. Where he wanted to rally opposition was to schooling as a "radical monopoly," that is, as the *only* way to gain employment and social standing. This political purpose sharpened but also circumscribed his rhetoric. So, while *Deschooling Society* recognizes the deep affiliation between the school and the Church, it does not develop this idea in any sustained way. There are many explosive sentences, dense with implications — he writes, for example, that "pedagogical hubris" consists in the "belief that man can do what God cannot, namely, manipulate others for their own salvation"[36] — but they remain asides in a discourse whose main purpose was hortatory and polemical. The link between the Church's attempt to administer salvation and the overreaching of modern institutions remained, for the most part, an implicit idea in Illich's published work of that time; only in a few later writings, and now here, is it spelled out in any detail.

The idea that Illich urgently wanted to establish in his books of the 1970s was that many contemporary institutions had reached, and were rapidly surpassing, a threshold at which they would turn malignant and counterproductive. Beyond a certain size and intensity, he argued in *Tools for Conviviality*, institutions begin to generate as many problems as they promise to solve. The volume of cars strangles mobil-ity, reading difficulties increase along with educational expenditures, and medicine creates as many illnesses as it cures. But even worse, he said, is that institutional and technical overgrowth colonizes and over-shadows people's most fundamental abilities: to speak one's own word, to be surprised, to die one's own death. One of the examples he gives in *Tools for Conviviality* is the way that language is overtaxed and voided of sense when it is co-opted for institutional purposes. In the corporation, with its endless iteration and reiteration of missions, visions, ethics, and values, but also in journalism, politics, and the pro-fessions, words are shaped to instrumental ends, until, finally, there is hardly a word left that does not automatically insert the speaker in some preformed discourse or invoke some overbearing expertise. Illich wanted to defend what was left of people's self-determination, to restore face-to-face conversation in words not predefined by profes-sional counsellors, and to make *the expansion of freedom*, rather than the growth of services, the criterion of social progress.

One of the ideas to which Illich returned again and again during this time was the contradiction between unregulated technological advance and social equality. In *Energy and Equity*, he took the oppor-tunity afforded by the so-called "energy crisis" of the early 1970s to examine this contradiction with respect to energy use generally and with particular attention to transportation. Until this time, rising energy use per capita had generally been taken as almost synony-mous with social advance. Even in the face of crisis, most discussion continued to focus on how industrial society's energy addiction could be sustained, rather than how it could be overcome. Illich suggested that beyond a certain threshold there is actually an inverse relation-ship between energy use and social justice.

> Beyond a critical speed no one can save time without forcing another to
> lose it. The man who claims a seat in a faster vehicle insists that his time
> is worth more than that of the passenger in a slower one . . . motorized
> vehicles create remoteness which they alone can shrink. They create dis-
> tances for all but shrink them for only a few. A new . . . road through the
> wilderness brings the city within view, but not within reach of most

Brazilian subsistence farmers. The new expressway expands Chicago, but it sucks those who are well-wheeled away from a downtown that decays into a ghetto.[37]

According to Illich, unchecked acceleration disables the majority in many ways: by imposing a pace that makes time scarcer for everyone, by inflicting side effects like congestion and exhaust even on those who cycle or walk, and by dramatically changing the configuration of social space. The expressway on which strangers hurtle by cannot be crossed. "Ambulances take clinics beyond the few miles a sick child can be carried. The doctor will no longer come to the house because vehicles have made the hospital into the right place to be sick."[38] In response to this degradation of social space, Illich pleaded for what he called "counterfoil research," that is, a form of lay research, not committed in advance to expert systems, that would identify the thresholds at which mobility for all turns into high speed for the few. Within these limits, he argued, motorized vehicles could provide benefits for everyone. "To expand life beyond the radius of tradition without scattering it to the winds of acceleration is a goal that any poor country could achieve within a few years," he wrote, "but it is a goal that will be reached only by those who reject . . . an ideology of indefinite energy consumption."[39]

Limits, and the danger of ignoring them, were Illich's theme again in *Medical Nemesis*. The book begins with the dramatic claim that "the medical establishment has become a major threat to health,"[40] and goes on to explore the various ways in which medical hegemony disables its patients by undoing their courage and their capacity to heal, to suffer, and to die. Illich describes this expropriation of health as *iatrogenesis*, an old medical term for harms or conditions originating with the doctor. The word is commonly used today to refer to such, by now well-publicized, medical snafus as getting the wrong drug or the wrong operation, but Illich gives it a much wider reference. He speaks first of clinical iatrogenesis, in which he groups the harms directly due to medical treatment: people made sick by their medicine, their therapy, or their diagnosis; and people made dependent by illusions about the doctor's effectiveness. Next he treats social iatrogenesis — the medicalization of society:

Social iatrogenesis is at work when health care is turned into a standard-ized item, a staple; when all suffering is "hospitalized" and homes become inhospitable to birth, sickness, and death; when the language in which people could experience their bodies is turned into bureaucratic gobbledegook; or when suffering, mourning and healing outside the patient role are labelled a form of deviance.[41]

And, finally, Illich looks at cultural iatrogenesis, which "sets in when the medical enterprise saps the will of people to suffer their reality."[42] Here he argues that unrestrained medical treatment deprives suffer-ing and death of their meaning and undermines the cultural traditions that once allowed people to face them with dignity. The book concludes with a plea for "political counter-measures" to con-tain and limit medical hegemony. Otherwise, he says, life will eventually become so medicalized as to amount to "compulsory sur-vival in a planned and engineered hell."[43]

Like Illich's other writings of the early 1970s, *Medical Nemesis* expresses a mood of urgency that is at once hopeful and foreboding. Rereading these books today, I find them still fresh, still cogent, and still remarkably pertinent; but there is no doubt that they were very precisely aimed at their historical moment, and it is necessary to recall that moment to appreciate fully how generously and whole-heartedly Illich responded to the exigencies of his time. This is not easy today. Many layers of nostalgic legend now encrust the period from the early 1960s to the mid-1970s, and potted, highlight-reel his-tories have often made it appear as little more than the golden adolescence of the baby boom, when a demographic earthquake briefly dressed up as a political revolution, and dissent became a new frontier of consumerism.[44] But, whatever else it was, this was also a period of what Illich called "ethical awakening,"[45] when at least a potential majority recognized that the Western project of remaking the world had reached a crisis, and that a moment of decision was at hand. Illich's "call to institutional revolution" — the subtitle of his *Celebration of Awareness* — spoke to this moment and outlined the marriage of playfulness, austerity, and sense of scale that he felt would be necessary to counteract the prevailing technomania and institutional hubris. He believed that the clerisies that he dubbed "disabling professions" were rapidly gaining the power to set the very terms of existence, and he hoped to inform and galvanize the resistance that was then stirring in various popular reform movements.[46] "The mood of 1971," he wrote in *Deschooling Society*, "is propitious for a major change of direction in search of a hopeful future."[47]

Illich's hopes were not realized. This is not to say that his critiques were without influence — both institutions and professions steadily lost much of their high modern lustre during the 1970s — or that everything worked out exactly as he anticipated, but only that "the natural boundaries of human endeavour" were never "estimated, recognized and translated into politically determined limits," as he had urged.[48] We live today with the consequences of that failure. Illich tried to promote a politics which could challenge and contain runaway technology. (He always preferred the old English word *tools* to the Latinate *technology* but he used the word in the same comprehensive sense in which Martin Heidegger spoke of technology or Jacques Ellul of *la technique*.) In common with other writers of an ecological bent, he wanted to overcome the Marxian reflex that centres politics on the ownership of the means of production, and to put technology itself in question. "The issue at hand," he wrote in *Tools for Conviviality*,

> is not the juridical ownership of tools, but rather the discovery of the characteristic of some tools which makes it impossible for anybody to "own" them. The concept of ownership cannot be applied to a tool that cannot be controlled . . . Certain tools are destructive no matter who owns them . . . [and] must inevitably increase regimentation, dependence, exploitation, or impotence, and rob not only the rich but also the poor of conviviality . . .[49]

The consequences of ignoring the destructiveness of tools — "no matter who owns them" — can be seen in high relief in current Canadian discussions of health care. The health-care juggernaut now consumes, on average, 42 per cent of provincial budgets. At the current rate of growth in spending, it will consume all provincial revenues by 2030.[50] At the same time, there appears to be a wide-spread impression that this system has suffered cutbacks and is inadequate to surging demand. Even more striking from the point of view of *Medical Nemesis* is the fact that what Illich called cultural iatrogenesis has become chronic, as people obsessively pursue med-ically defined images of health and increasingly believe that it is themselves they are seeing in the distorting mirror of medical mon-itoring, screening, and risk assessment. And yet, political discussion focuses almost entirely on the questions of whether health-care services are "delivered" by public or private actors and whether they arrive punctually and equitably. The character and consequences of the services themselves remain marginal considerations, and the question of *what is good, fitting, and sufficient* cannot even be posed in political terms. There could be no clearer example of how far we have passed beyond the threshold at which Illich tried to restrain progress.

In 1976, in consultation with his staff, Illich closed CIDOC. There were many reasons — physical attacks on the place, a changing Mexican economy, the fact that Illich felt it had accomplished all it could[51] — but one of them was Illich's feeling that "the campaigning period" in his life was coming to an end. Practised repetition of his arguments had begun to make him feel, he said, "like a jukebox."[52] Now he wanted to conduct a deeper search for the submerged assumptions that had made the institutions he had tried to change so intractable. He spent time in India and Southeast Asia, and for a time even entertained the idea that he might be able to get a purchase on these assumptions by stepping outside his civilization altogether and learning to speak and write in an Oriental language. The project proved unrealistic, even for a man fluent in all the major Western European languages, and he eventually realized that the furthest he was going to be able to get from what modern persons take for granted was the Middle Ages. As a student, he had been particularly fond of the authors of the twelfth century — Aelred of Rievaulx and Hugh of St. Victor were particular favourites — and this fondness led him to centre his historical studies on that period.

Illich began to teach at German universities, first at the universities of Kassel and Marburg, later in Oldenburg and Bremen. (He
also had various lectureships in the United States: for many years at
the Pennsylvania State University, and also at Pitzer College in
Claremont, California, and the McCormick Theological Seminary
in Chicago.) He taught and studied history with a double motive.
First, he wanted to undertake an archaeology of modern "certainties,"
those ideas and feelings that seem too obvious and too "natural" ever
to be put into question; and he had come to see the twelfth century
as one of the great seedtimes of these certainties. As he demonstrates
in the following pages, contemporary ideas of conscience, citizenship, technology, text, individuality, and marriage all began to emerge
in that era. But, at the same time, the twelfth-century world
remained utterly foreign to a modern sensibility, and this suited his
second purpose: to bring the strangeness and novelty of today's world
into dramatic relief for himself and his students.

> I tried to get people to understand how immensely distant is the mental
> world in which the twelfth-century authors moved. I did this in order to
> pull the students away from their typewriters, and their felt-tipped pens,
> and the telephone which they have to grab — to give them the sense of
> a trip between two space times. And then I tried to keep them there for
> a while, making them aware what strangers they are and how little they
> can use their own concepts, their own modern German or English or
> French words to translate these Latin texts. I prepared them to re-enter
> the modern world with a crucial question about it and, at the time of re-
> entry, to become aware, for a moment, what a different universe they
> are entering when they resume the certainties of the world in which
> they feel at home.[53]

The past, for Illich, always cuts two ways. It bears on the present and,
at the same time, stands apart from it as a treasure and a resort whose
worth lies in its being beyond our reach. So Illich searched for origins
but also recognized that the past possesses a dignity and a difference
which always make it something more than a mere prologue or ideological resource. He rejected the idea that "the past is a primitive

form of the present": "I believe in honoring the dead by research that is public, disciplined, documented and critical," he wrote in the final pages of his book *Gender*, "[but] I will not reconstruct the past with . . . concepts mined in utopia."[54]

Through his historical studies, Illich was able to extend and deepen the analysis he had presented in his earlier books. One of the first certainties he began to analyze was scarcity, the founding assumption of modern economics. Nothing is more certain for moderns than the idea that unlimited demand pursuing limited or scarce resources is the primordial condition of economic life, but through the work of the economic historian Karl Polanyi, Illich learned to question this assumption.[55] In *Trade and Markets in the Early Empires*, which Illich read when he was completing *Medical Nemesis*, Polanyi shows that cultures, throughout history, have in fact carefully limited economic competition and set strict limits to exchange relationships. And they have done so, Polanyi says, with the conscious intention of keeping social life free of the envy and rivalry that arise when goods are perceived as scarce. Subsistence was embedded in social life, and it was only disembedded, Polanyi argues, after a prolonged and painful struggle to liberate markets from social control, a struggle which sets the modern West apart from all other cultures and civilizations. Our situation today, in which "the economy" contains and rules society, is a profound reversal, therefore, of the historical norm.

Illich applied Polanyi's insight to his analysis of development as "a war on subsistence" in the five essays that comprise his book *Shadow Work* (1981). By the late 1970s it was already clear that the high hopes of "the development decade" had not been realized, and its promoters were beginning to put a new emphasis on "self-help." The informal sector became the new focus of development efforts, as economists turned their attention to the underground economy, architects studied shantytowns, and statisticians calculated the value of unpaid work. Illich discerned in this new phase of development a more insidious and more intimate form of colonization. He wanted to shelter what remained of culture from the shadow of scarcity, and this led him to draw a distinction between what he called "the vernacular domain" and "the shadow economy."[56] Both lie outside the market, but they are of radically different kinds. A shadow economy is the complement of a formal economy, comprising all the activities, from shopping to driving to work, which are unpaid but necessary to the maintenance of that economy. The vernacular comprises those activities which lie outside the ambit of economics and which remain "totally refractory to any analysis utilizing concepts developed in economics."[57] Until Illich revived it in *Shadow Work*, the word *vernacular* had been used mainly for untaught and untrained forms of language or architecture. Illich sought to imbue the word with the broader sense of the Latin *vernaculum*, which referred to "whatever was homebred, homespun, homegrown [or] homemade."

> We need a simple straightforward word to designate the activities of people when they are not motivated by thoughts of exchange, a word that denotes autonomous, non-market-related actions through which people satisfy everyday needs — the actions which by their own nature escape bureaucratic control . . . [and] that we want to defend from measurement or manipulation . . . The term must be broad enough to fit the preparation of food and the shaping of language, childbirth and recreation, without implying either a privatized activity . . . a hobby or an irrational and primitive procedure. Such an adjective is not at hand. But "vernacular" might serve.[58]

In breathing new life into this old word, Illich sought to forestall the confusion that occurs when the vernacular is reconstructed as a shadow economy and brought under professional tutelage and thus denatured and deprived of its defining quality. This confusion occurs whenever loving or dutiful attention is redefined as "caregiving," whenever common speech is invaded by self-important professional lingos, or whenever economic value is imputed to actions undertaken for their own sake. By clearly distinguishing the vernacular from the domain of scarcity, Illich hoped to prevent those who are excluded from the economy, or who exclude themselves, from falling under its shadow.

Illich went further in his delineation of the vernacular in his next book, *Gender*, published a year after *Shadow Work*. Here he also took

an uncommon word, up until then used mainly as a grammatical category, and helped to give it the wide currency that is taken for
granted today.[59] In every premodern society, Illich showed, a shifting
but always demanding line divides the world of men from the world
of women, with each gender possessing its own customs, its own
tools, its own ways of speaking. The same location may be women's
space at one moment, men's at the next; here the men may sow the
grain, there the women; societies may be patriarchal or matriarchal,
hierarchical or egalitarian; but there will always be these two complementary spheres, opposing, supporting, and defining one another.
And so long as society is understood as comprising this fundamental
duality, many of the most characteristic features of the modern world
are held at bay. There can be no uniform space, no single standard of
value, no unit of labour fit for all tasks. There can be no common
denominator by which society can be reduced to a self-interested
association of economic individuals competing for scarce resources.
Vernacular gender, for Illich, is part of a world in which things still fit
each other and everything is proportioned to everything else — a
world, he once said, where "a community, like a body, cannot outgrow
its size"[60] because it would then throw everything else out of balance
as well. Only when gender's hold is broken can people be made interchangeable, space uniform, and the circulation of commodities an
unimpeded global flow.

Illich later described *Gender* as a watershed in his career, the
moment when he turned away from what he called "an aggressive critique of the degrading ceremonies . . . of development" and began to
devote himself to historical research on the history of perception.[61] He
wanted to understand how a world could come to be in which every
form of human subsisting is measured and circumscribed within a
monetarized economy, and he saw the budding women's movement as
the scene of the last great act in this drama. Women, in Illich's view,
performed the bulk of what he called "shadow work," work necessary
to the economy but not yet monetarized: housework, child-rearing,
shopping, and so on. Because of this, he believed that feminist scholars were ideally placed to expose the shadow economy in which
women were imprisoned as the inevitable complement of a commodity-

intensive mode of production. "I was strongly convinced," he said later, "that out of . . . the women's studies movement, would come . . . a *radical* questioning of the categories of economics, of sociology, and of anthropology."[62] But the movement in which Illich invested such hope instead opted decisively to pursue equal status within the existing mode of production and left the shadow work to servants, other low-paid workers, and the women willing to bear the opprobrium of being labelled semi-traitorous "stay-at-home moms."

Gender was not generally well-received. Illich tried to make clear that he intended his book as a work of history, not political prescription, but the polemical and even scathing language in which he formulated some of his pronouncements may have led readers to doubt this claim. However, even if his tone had been more tactful, I am not sure how widely he would have been taken at his word. It is true that he was now writing as an historian and not as a pamphleteer, but he was still writing elegiacally about what he called "the sad loss of gender,"[63] he was still doing so at a time when most were inclined to see this loss as a liberation, and he was still making the provocative claim that the feminist pursuit of equality would produce new privileges for a minority of women and new disadvantages for the majority.[64] No wonder, then, that most of the reviews were hostile. He was called a reactionary and accused of romanticism and nostalgia. In Berkeley, where Illich made *Gender* the basis of a series of lectures at the University of California in 1982, seven feminist professors arranged a symposium where they offered rebuttals. Their papers were collected in a special issue of a journal called *Feminist Issues*.[65] One even claimed to find in *Gender* "all the salient features of modern propaganda, as exemplified in classics of the genre like *Mein Kampf*." There were a number of misrepresentations of the book. He was accused of being a closet sociobiologist, for whom biology is destiny, when he had in fact been quite clear that he regarded gender as entirely a matter of culture. He was also portrayed as a man of the past, when he was actually trying to address the contemporary theme of limits to growth. These misunderstandings were influential, and, along with dismissive reviews in more mainstream journals,[66] they created a strong impression that the author was a romantic Luddite

more at home in the twelfth century than the twentieth, who ought
now to fade away like other ghosts from the 1960s.

Gender is a brilliant hodgepodge of a book, and this too may have
contributed to its poor reception. Its footnotes, which comprise 125
numbered and titled bibliographic essays, are as extensive as the main
text, and some of its readers may have felt like Stephen Leacock's dis-
appointed lover who "rode madly off in all directions." Illich was a
man who relished surprise and discovery, and his books were works in
progress, rather than expressions of a finished position or preformed
scheme. The feminist critics of *Gender* were distressed by the impression that they were being addressed *ex cathedra* — an impression that
was no doubt aggravated by Illich's habit of condensing his thought
into pithy, carefully wrought formulas.[67] But when I recently revisited
that book, what impressed me was Illich's enthusiasm, his eagerness
to share his latest discoveries, the sense of a report from a moving
front. Illich left no *summa*, nor even a summary, but a record of explo-
ration. And this tireless curiosity, along with the trans-disciplinary
breadth of his inquiries,[68] made him a thinker who was sometimes
more interested in advancing the frontier at which he was working
than in spelling out the underlying assumptions on which the work
was founded.

Gender was the last of Illich's works to make its initial appearance
with a major trade publisher.[69] I doubt that this was due exclusively to
the hostility the book inspired, but it is the case that all of his subsequent works were first published by small or academic presses, and all
had much smaller sales than formerly. Illich gradually faded out of the
ranks of fashionable authors. He remained an honoured godfather to
those who recognized the upheavals of the 1960s and 1970s as something more than just pixie dust and political quixotism and who
continued to seek alternatives, but he no longer attracted the same
interest from the more prestigious universities, the mainstream media,
or the major book reviews. This moderation of his celebrity was, in
many ways, a blessing for Illich and the circle of friends with whom he
collaborated. He had already foresworn the life of an intellectual dancing bear who could be summoned to sing his old songs on cue; now a
less hurried pace allowed him time to receive those who came to talk

with him, and time to create, with friends, the convivial atmosphere in which he liked to conduct his studies.[70]

During the 1980s Illich's interests developed in several directions. Together with Barbara Duden, he studied the history of the body.[71] He moved away from the language of "values," which he had used in earlier writings, and began to speak simply of the good. The good, as he came to understand it, is what is uniquely and incomparably appropriate in a given setting. It observes a certain scale, displays a certain proportion. It fits, and the senses can recognize this fit, just as they can recognize what is out of tune. Values, on the other hand, are a universal coin without a proper place or an inherent limit. They rank and compare all things according to their utility or their relative scarcity. The value of prayer can be measured by its calming effect on brainwaves; the recreational amenity provided by a forest can be compared to the monetary worth of its biomass; death can be administered to a failing patient when the cost of further treatment would exceed the quality of life it would yield. Values undermine the sense of due proportion and substitute an economic calculus. What is good is what is always good; a value prevails only when it outranks a competing value. With this distinction in view, Illich pursued the history of the senses and studied the ways in which the senses had once been attuned to the good, and the ways in which this attunement had been lost.

In *H₂O and the Waters of Forgetfulness* (1985), Illich reflected on what he called "the historicity of 'stuff.'"[72] The "stuff" in question was water, and Illich's reflections were prompted by an invitation from The Dallas Institute of Humanities and Culture to comment on the city's plan to engineer an artificial midtown lake. He spoke of the way in which the imagination "sings reality," giving a different shape and substance to things in different epochs,[73] and he traced the history of how water had been imagined, from the classical age when the waters of Lethe carried the memories of the dead to the pool of Mnemosyne, right up to Dallas's plan to wash away care with a "public display of recycled toilet flush."[74] His point was that industrial treatment, beyond a certain intensity, deprives water of the metaphorical resonance it has always possessed and turns it into the technically managed scarce resource that he terms "H_2O." It can still serve as a cleaning solvent or add a beguiling sparkle to Dallas's downtown, but it can no longer mirror the water of dreams.

During the 1980s Illich also became more and more aware of the transformation in people's self-perception that was taking place in the shadow of new information technologies. "The book," he wrote, "has ceased to be the root metaphor of the age; the screen has taken its place."[75] He saw the evidence all around him. People were spending more and more time in virtual, or non-local spaces. Words were losing their depth and becoming plastic elements in a communications code. Knowledge was increasingly being conveyed diagrammatically — through pictures, icons, and graphs. And text was being cut loose from its moorage on the page and set adrift on the vast sea of information — landing not just in the ghostly entrails of the computer, but in the genetic text of which many people now assume themselves to be the dictation, and in the myriad other codes — identifiers, bar codes, entry codes, passwords, and so on — that now record and manage people's comings and goings. Illich became convinced that he was witnessing an historical rupture that went deeper than even his direst predictions in *Tools for Conviviality* and *Medical Nemesis*. His response was to investigate comparable watersheds in the past, in an attempt not just to shed light on the contemporary transformation but also to gain distance from it.

The first fruit of this inquiry was *ABC: The Alphabetization of the Western Mind* (1988), co-written with Barry Sanders. It ranges over various epochs in the history of literacy, from the very beginnings of writing to the invention of the binary code that underwrites globalization. *In the Vineyard of the Text* (1992) focuses in detail on one of these epochs, the early twelfth century, when a series of refinements of the written page transformed what Illich calls "monkish" reading into bookish reading, a term he borrows from George Steiner.[76] In form the book is a commentary on the *Didascalicon* of Hugh of St. Victor, a twelfth-century abbot and author who stood, according to Illich, at the very cusp of this transformation, straddling two eras. Monkish reading, or *lectio divina*, was a laborious ingestion and mastication of the written word. Doctors of late classical times sometimes recommended reading as a form of exercise, and many accounts agree that the readers of the early monastic period buzzed and mumbled as they ruminated on Scripture. Hugh, in the image from which Illich draws his title, speaks of a book as a vineyard in which he walks tasting the words as he goes. Then came a whole series of linked changes in the way books were presented. Words were separated, something which had occasionally happened as early as the eighth century as an aid, one source says, to "block-headed Scottish monks" who had difficulty learning Latin, but which now became a regular practice; chapters were distinguished by titles and subtitles; quotations were marked; paragraphs, marginal glosses, tables of contents, and alphabetic indices were added. Taken together, these changes amounted to a revolution in reading. Books became scholarly tools that could be consulted for reference. The reader was no longer physically incorporated into the order of the book but could impose his own order on it. This improvement in accessibility produced what Illich calls "the visible text," and its repercussions spread far beyond the ranks of those who actually read. Even non-readers were touched by the metaphorical resonance of the redesigned book and began to think of their world in book-like terms. "Writing devils" appeared in churches, recording sins for the final reckoning.[77] The literate clergy imposed the idea of conscience as an inner inscription which could be read back to the priest in the new institution of confession. Written deeds replaced oaths. Nature, self, and society all became legible in a new way, and science, in its first modern stirrings, began to decipher the book of nature. Illich refers to this symbolic fallout of the redesigned page as "lay literacy" and urges it as a guide to the way in which people today are recasting self-perception in the image of the computer.

In the Vineyard of the Text is one of Illich's most accomplished works, both rich and original. Hugh of St. Victor was a man to whom Illich felt deeply connected, often referring to him as a friend, and he writes about him in a sweet and lyrical vein. The book also makes a distinctive contribution to the study of literacy, connecting effects often associated with Gutenberg's invention of moveable types with changes in the layout of the manuscript book that occurred three centuries earlier.[78] And yet, Illich's essay received few reviews, and for years I have looked in vain for references to it in other books to which his argument is germane. One would not expect a commentary on a twelfth-century text to be sold in airports, but it is shocking that Illich's book should be so neglected by other scholars.

What this indicates, I think, is that the academy and the wide public Illich had addressed in the 1970s had somehow lost the thread of his intellectual career — perhaps because he was seen as a man whose time had passed, perhaps because his later writings didn't quite conform to the established image that people had of him. Whatever was the case, the extent of the confusion surrounding Illich's public persona was made clear by the wildly varying claims made in the scores of obituaries that appeared in major newspapers throughout the world following his death. The patronizing *New York Times* memorial ("Priest Turned Philosopher Whose Views Drew Baby Boomers in 70's"[79]) seemed to assume that he had died at the moment when he disappeared from the pages of American newspapers. The *Times* of London resorted to legend, describing him as a holy man who had lived "most of his later life . . . in a mud hut . . . just outside Mexico city" and portrayed his intellectual powers as so formidable that he had acquired a fluent knowledge of Greek in a single day from a hotel gardener.[80] In one place he was a "renowned sociologist," in another "a culture critic," and in yet another a "provocative religious radical." The Chilean paper *El Mostrador* believed him to have been "a pioneer of liberation theology,"[81] although Illich in fact believed that the Church had no place in politics of any stripe. There were exceptions to this general tenor, of course, but my general impression was that the world had lost not only a brilliant intellectual but also a fabulous rumour.

I hope that the present book will dispel some of this confusion about Illich and help to reveal both the unity and originality of his life and thought. The revelation is not that Illich was a Christian — he made no secret of his faith, even if his critics sometimes overlooked the extent to which it oriented his outlook — nor is it his claim that the peculiar dynamism of Western civilization is rooted in its Judaeo-Christian inheritance — this is a familiar and uncontroversial argument. What is original with Illich is the idea that the modern West, as defined by its characteristic attempt to manipulate others for their own salvation, is a *perversion* of Christian faith. Some, like René Girard, have seen modernity as a working out of the implications of the Gospel.[82] Others, like Hans Blumenberg, have taken the view that modernity is an attempt to break out of the Christian framework.[83] But Illich is alone, I think, in seeing the modern West as a betrayal of Christian faith.

I believe that this idea continuously grew and took shape in Illich's thought throughout a lifetime's effort to discern how the world he lived in came to be so utterly unlike any world that had ever been. From his earliest studies of schooling he had noticed the Church-like character of the school and called for its disestablishment. By the time *Gender* appeared, the medieval Church's move to establish administrative control over the lives of the faithful had become an important subtext. But it was not until November 1987, when Illich spoke from the pulpit of the Fourth Presbyterian Church in Chicago, that he finally gave the idea a concise and explicit form:

> I want to explore with you a phenomenon that I consider constitutive of the West, of that West which has shaped me, body and soul, flesh and blood. This central reality of the West is marvelously expressed in the old Latin phrase: *Corruptio optimi quae est pessima* — the historical progression in which God's Incarnation is turned topsy-turvy, inside out. I want to speak of the mysterious darkness that envelops our world, the demonic night paradoxically resulting from the world's equally mysterious vocation to glory. My subject is a mystery of faith, a mystery whose depth of evil could not have come to be without the greatness of the truth revealed to us.[84]

This is the thesis that is elaborated in this book. To understand it one has to see first of all why "the greatness of the truth revealed to us" was, for that very reason, uniquely liable to corruption.

The New Testament, in Illich's view, relates the appearance of something radically and explosively new in the world. Often he illustrated this novelty, as he does in these pages, by the parable of the

Samaritan. The story is told in the Gospel of Luke: "And behold, a certain lawyer stood up," the King James Version says, and asked, "Who is my neighbour?" Jesus responded with the tale of a man assaulted by thieves and left "half-dead" in a ditch. Two religious officials come along, but both "pass by on the other side." Then comes a foreigner, a Samaritan, the first to pass who does not belong to the same community as the man in the ditch. And it is he, "moved with compassion," who befriends the wounded man.[85]

What is new here, according to Illich, is the untrammelled freedom with which the Samaritan acts. Modern people are unlikely to notice it, he says, because centuries of preaching have inured them to the idea that this parable exemplifies a rule concerning how one should behave; but Jesus' auditors would have seen in the story a shocking violation of ethical decency. They would have felt that the priest and the Levite had behaved entirely properly in passing the wounded man by, perhaps because he appeared to be dead and was therefore ritually impure, or perhaps because the two religious officials were on their way to the Temple to fulfill much more urgent duties. And they would have felt that he should have been of even less interest to the Samaritan, whose obligations would have extended only to his own people, and not to a foreigner lying beside the road. So what is remarkable about the story is its revolutionary assertion that the neighbour could be anyone, and that who it turns out to be could, as Illich says, "appear arbitrary from everybody else's point of view."[86] No category, whether of law or custom, language or culture, can define in advance who the neighbour might be.

Illich believed that this teaching threatened the very basis of ethics, because, in the world in which Jesus spoke, ethics were defined by the cultural boundary which made them meaningful. Ethics were maxims that expressed an *ethos*, the spirit of a people in a place: they stipulated proper conduct only towards those with whom one shared a recognized bond. But Jesus repeatedly transgressed such boundaries, not just with Samaritans but with all sorts of people whose status ranged from marginal to completely taboo: tax collectors, women of doubtful reputation, the mad, and so on. He broke religious rules, and even questioned the primacy of the family.[87] All this represents, from Illich's point of view, a glorious revelation of the freedom to turn in love towards the other, whoever it may be. What Jesus calls the Kingdom of God stands above and beyond any ethical rule and can disrupt the everyday world in completely unpredictable ways.[88] But Illich also recognizes in this declaration of freedom from limits an extreme volatility. For should this freedom ever itself become the subject of a rule, then the limit-less would invade human life in a truly terrifying way.

It is critically important, therefore, to note a second aspect of the story of the Samaritan: the nature of the appeal that the injured man makes. The relationship that comes into existence between the Samaritan and the beaten-up Jew is a voluntary and bodily tie. It does not fulfill a duty; it answers a call. The Samaritan, Jesus says, is "moved by compassion." He undergoes a conversion, an inward turning around which begins in his guts and ends in a unique and entirely personal relationship. The Samaritan's action, according to Illich, "prolongs the Incarnation" and would not be possible without the Incarnation; that is, it is a *revealed* possibility and not one that innately belongs to human beings. The Samaritan can dare to enter the no man's land that lies between cultures and separates him from the wounded one only because he is enacting God's love, the love revealed in Jesus. He does not abolish the distinction between them; he overcomes it by what Christians call grace, the action of the Holy Spirit.

What is revealed in the New Testament, according to Illich, is a summons beyond all cultural or religious containment. "[F]aith in the incarnate word sacrificed on the cross," he says, "is not a religion and cannot be analyzed within the concepts of religious science."[89] The definition of religion is a complicated matter, and beyond my scope here, but what this means, I think, is that religion is always conducted within the spell of the sacred, that terrible but also protective power which the community must propitiate, obey, and shield from any polluting contact with the profane. What the Samaritan does is to step fearlessly outside what his culture has sanctified in order to create a new relationship and, potentially, a new community. He does not seek God within a sacred circle but finds him lying by the road in a ditch. His possibilities cannot be predicted or circumscribed. He lives, in the apostle Paul's words, "not under the law, but under grace." "We are released from the Law," Paul wrote to the Christians at Rome, "having died to what was binding us, and so we are in a new service, that of the spirit, and not in the old service of a written code."[90]

The Incarnation is the visible and carnal presence of God in the world, and it changes the world, Illich says, in a decisive and irreversible way. Once the Word has "become flesh" and "dwelt among us,"[91] a new choice is set before people. God had already said, through the mouth of Moses, "I have set before you life and death, blessing and cursing: therefore choose life . . ."[92] But now this choice has been made present in a surprisingly intimate and personal way. The Incarnation opens what Illich calls the "expanded horizon" for love within which the Samaritan acts. It allows, in the words of the theologian James Alison, "the untelling of the human story" and holds out the possibility of its retelling or re-creation.[93] But once this horizon is open, a new possibility of denial, or turning away, is also revealed. "If I had not come and spoken to them," Jesus says in the Gospel of John, "they would not have sin; but now they have no excuse for their sin . . . If I had not done among them the works which no one else did, they would not have sin; but now they have seen and hated both me and my Father."[94] Sin, in this new context, no longer means just a violation of the law, but something more — a coldness or indifference to what has been revealed and made possible. "Sin," Illich says, "is refusing to honour that relationship which came into existence between the Samaritan and the Jew, which comes into existence through the exercise of freedom, and which constitutes an 'ought' because I feel called by you, called to you, called to this tie between human beings, or between beings and God . . . It is not in any sense offensive of a law. It is always an offence against a person. It's an infidelity."[95] Sin, on this account, is not simply an evil, or a moral fault. It is a failing against the Spirit, possible only for those who have heard and ignored what they have heard, and visible only in the light of that freedom that Paul says is identical with "the forgiveness of sin."[96]

Sin is an alarming word, and to the ears of many contemporaries it suggests only repressive moralism and a dark condemnation of everything modern psychological hygiene considers healthy and natural. But what people today understand by sin is very often not what the New Testament means by this word at all. They are thinking of the terrors that were produced when the medieval Church "criminalized" sin. For the first Christians, Illich says, "to believe in sin [was] to celebrate, as a gift beyond understanding, the fact that one is being forgiven." The mood in which they lived together was not guilt, or anxiety, but contrition — "a deep sorrow about my capacity to betray the relationships which I, as a Samaritan, have established, and, at the same, a deep confidence in the forgiveness and mercy of the other."

For the first time in history, a community was composed, not of those born to it, but of those who created it "by the equal contribution of each of their spirits." The early Christians made this community by sharing the simple communion meal through which they remembered their Lord, and by a mouth-to-mouth kiss through which they shared their spirits in a *conspiratio* or breathing together. This community possessed an unusual "bodily depth," Illich says, both because of the physicality with which Christians celebrated and because they believed that by eating and drinking the body of Christ they became "living members of his mystical body."[97] But at the same time, Christians recognized that the bodily community they were establishing with the kiss of peace was an other-worldly reality — it was not, as the New Testament says again and again, "of this world."

Charity for these first Christians was an individual vocation, a personal call. They did not yet think of the other-worldly body of which they were members as a social corporation. But this began to change after the conversion of the Emperor Constantine in the early fourth century. A disposition towards faith, hope, and charity became an established religion, bishops were endowed with the powers of magistrates, and the Church began to consolidate its social position by creating charitable institutions. This is the beginning of Illich's story of the corruption of the best which becomes the worst. The Church had taken the first steps towards becoming a social machine capable of producing mercy on demand. And this horrifies Illich, not because he thinks human beings can get along without institutions but because of *what* is being institutionalized. Once the Church becomes a social corporation, it commits itself to using power to "ensure the social presence of something which, by its very nature, cannot be anything else but the free choice of individuals who have accepted the invitation to see in everybody — whom they choose — the face of Christ."

According to Illich, the first generations of Christians were aware that the coming of Christ had created the possibility of a new kind of evil, which they embodied in the sinister New Testament figure of the Anti-Christ. The passage Illich cites, from the Second Letter to the Thessalonians, warns Christians of the deceptions of this "lost One" who has "enthrone[d] himself in God's sanctuary," and it goes on to speak of a new "mystery of evil" at work in the infant Church.[98] Illich discerns in this passage a dawning awareness that the Incarnation casts a shadow and that once there is "Christianity" there will also inevitably be counterfeits that claim its name. He goes on to say — and this, for him, is the important point — that this awareness that the best can become the worst, and that the Church, as the repository of the best, is uniquely capable of this mysterious inversion, soon lost its intensity and moved to the margins of Christian life. Today, the idea of the Anti-Christ is almost entirely associated with Protestant fundamentalism and that strain of anti–Roman Catholic bigotry which associates the Roman Church with the figure of the "whore of Babylon" in the Book of Revelation. To respectable Christians it is an embarrassment, and Illich himself acknowledges the trepidation he feels in reviving this "monstrous" term. He takes this chance, I think, in order to make a crucial point: by abandoning this goad to self-criticism and self-awareness, on which it should have centred its faith, the Church disowned its own shadow.

Illich was often read and criticized as a romantic or a utopian. On what else could his withering criticism of institutions be founded, if not a naive faith in natural goodness and spontaneous order? But I think his true position can be seen in his attitude to the Church, because it is in their capacity as surrogate churches that Illich criticizes other institutions. He did not criticize institutionalization as such, nor did he believe that people were angels who could live without institutional routine. He criticized the Church and its descendants for their lack of self-awareness — their inability to recognize the crucial difference between charity and its institutional counterfeits. But, about institutionalization as such, he was a realist; and, as he says here, he regarded the institutionalization of charity, if not as an inevitable process, then at least as an entirely and understandably human one.

> [M]y hypothesis [is] that the corruption of the best is the worst. And it is part of this hypothesis that the Church's attempt to give this worldly power, social visibility, and permanence to the performance of orthodoxy, right faith, and to the performance of Christian charity, is not un-Christian. As I understand the Gospels, with many others, it is part of the *kenosis*,[99] the humiliation, the condescension of God in becoming man and founding or generating the mystical body which the Church understands itself to be, that this mystical body would itself be something ambiguous. It would be, on the one hand, a source of continued Christian life, through which individuals acting alone and together would be able to live the life of faith and charity, and, on the other hand, a source of the perversion of this life through institutionalization, which makes charity worldly and true faith obligatory.[100]

The Church, Illich says, is an unavoidably ambiguous creature, but this ambiguity could have been recognized and brought into awareness. Instead the opposite occurred. The Church became less and less capable of discerning in the image of Anti-Christ its own tendency to substitute power for faith, and more and more bent on a comprehensive regulation of Christian life. And what began in the Church was gradually built into the unconscious foundations — the certainties, as Illich says — of the modern world.

How this happened is the story this book tells. Illich begins, after he has made an initial profession of his faith, by showing the volatility of the Christian revelation. The perspective revealed in the Gospel, Illich says, "implies a certain foolishness in worldly terms." Christ's life and death represent the supreme refusal to play the ancient game of outbidding power with power. In the words I quoted earlier from James Alison, they "untell" the human story and open the possibility of a retelling. But this retelling must remain provisional and subject to constant revision because its roots lie outside the world. It does not mandate a new religion in the sense of a new establishment that promises to fortify the truth and make it reliable, secure, and effective. Religion cannot be surpassed by creating a new religion, but only by the willingness to live in perpetual but peaceful tension with the inextinguishable desire for security that religion — even "Christian" religion — represents. The Incarnation, the German theologian Klaus Baier once said to me, is "a flickering."[101] It occurs at the moment when the Samaritan turns to the man in the ditch, not continuously; and it is limited to what occurs, that is, it cannot be reproduced outside this unique moment. In fact, Jesus tells the story of the Samaritan in order to frustrate the request of that "certain lawyer" for a permanent airtight definition of "the neighbour," and this is a common occurrence in the Gospel: opponents often try to entangle Jesus in his own words or entrap him in some blunt formula, only to have him parry and dance out of their grasp with a story, a joke, or an answering question.

It is this very delicacy and poise that make the Gospel so liable to corruption and that make this corruption, when it occurs, the worst. Over time, Illich says, Christian notions and practices undergo what he variously calls a flipping, a perversion, or a turning inside out. Freedom becomes legislated duty; "supreme folly" mutates into "brutal earnestness." The possibility of making a new community out of unrelated people who share their breath turns into the social contract on which the modern state is founded. The belief that Jesus is "the image of God" undermines the Jewish proscription of images and makes way for the flood of imagery in which the contemporary world is drowning. And "the heightened awareness of evil" made possible through the idea of sin leads, once sin has been "criminalized," to the fearful isolation of the conscience-stricken individual. Examples could be multiplied, and Illich develops many more below, but what I want to draw attention to here is Illich's notion that it is precisely the glorious refinement of these ideas that constitutes their instability.

I believe that what Illich says in the following pages completes and clarifies what he was trying to do in his earlier writings. Illich put forward, in a number of his books, the idea that the priest is "the precursor of the modern service professional" and the Church the source of the idea that there are "needs common to all human beings that can be satisfied only through service from professional agents."[102] What becomes clearer here, I think, is the enormity of the loss that occurs when care is mass-produced. Sin, for example, is hidden, because all failures become systemic rather than personal. Surprise "is taken out of the face of the other," because one always knows the other, in advance of any actual encounter, as a set of needs which the appropriate professional stands ready to meet. But the capacity for surprise, in Illich's view, is the essence of faith. The Incarnation, he says, "is a surprise, remains a surprise, and could not exist as anything else." It is a pure gift, beyond expectation or understanding, and only faith allows trust in what exceeds comprehension.

> Faith . . . founds certainty on the word of someone whom I trust and makes this knowledge . . . more fundamental than anything I can know by reason. This, of course, is a possibility only when I believe that God's word can reach me. It makes sense only if the One whom I trust is God. But it also rubs off on my relationship to other people. It makes me aim at facing people with a willingness to take them for what they reveal about themselves — to take them, therefore, *at their word* — and not for what I know about them.[103]

Taking others at their word becomes impossible when knowledge gained through diagnosis, sociological categorization, or imputed needs precedes their ever uttering this word. Faith is eclipsed by prediction, hope by planning, and charity by studied knowledge of the other's needs. And, in this way, "the glorious side of the encounter between the Samaritan and the Jew" is obscured.

A friend of Illich's, Kostas Chatzikyriakou, tells the story of taking a friend to hear Illich lecture on medicine. Afterwards, his companion turned to him, puzzled, and asked, "What does he want — let people die?" It's a resonant question, and a common response to Illich's seemingly implacable radicalism about medicine, schools, or what have you. The obvious answer is, yes, he did want people to be able to meet their own deaths as something other than the inevitable termination of treatment. But on another level, I think Illich is badly misunderstood when one tries to discover what he wanted by simply subtracting the modern institutions he criticized and then trying to imagine the incommodious condition that would result. What Illich wanted to do was to uncover and encourage the abilities, intuitions, and encounters that are smothered by the blanket of professional care.

A story from his life may make this attitude clearer. Illich was not a fundamentalist about medicine or anything else. When a hernia made it difficult for him to sit or walk, he submitted to surgery; when an infected tooth bothered him, he had it extracted. He knew a good deal about natural pharmaceuticals. But when a bump that others feared might be cancer appeared on the side of his face in the late 1970s, he decided to leave it alone. He was influenced in this decision by a Pakistani friend, a hakim in the Unani tradition, called Said Mohammed, who told him that this bump belonged to his person and having it removed would throw him out of balance.[104] He had also been told, years before, by his mother's brother, an astrologer, that he would experience trouble, possibly connected with his jaw, and that he should take no action against it. And, perhaps most important, he had his own intuition, as he sometimes told me, that this was a cross that he should not try to avoid bearing.

When this bump grew more prominent, Illich consulted a surgeon friend in Chicago, who advised him that the tumor, though not unequivocally malignant, was dangerous and ought to be removed. Illich persisted in his original decision and sought no medical treatment. (Once, when he was travelling by plane from State College, Pennsylvania, to Toronto in 1989, an oncologist, by chance seated next to him, began to palpate the tumour without Illich's permission. It was as if, we joked afterwards, Illich had come within the doctor's jurisdiction merely by appearing in public with an untreated condition.) Illich lived with this disfiguration for some twenty years. The swelling, which eventually comprised a series of small tumours, grew to the size of a grapefruit, impinging on his jaw and interfering with his hearing, his sleep, and his concentration. The pain was considerable, and, though no one can know how much another suffers, it was clear to his friends that it was often agonizing. He controlled it as best he could with acupuncture, yoga, and a remarkable self-discipline. He also smoked raw opium, which he had to obtain illegally but which he found more effective than the bottled opium he could have had prescribed. On one occasion, when he was passing through customs in London, his opium was discovered in his luggage, but he was able to convince the customs agent to treat it as an analgesic rather than an illegal substance.[105]

Illich's decision to leave his lump untreated was not, I want to stress, a throw of the dice. Cancers can metastasize as a result of surgery — and it is possible that his uncle's clairvoyant prognosis had been a warning against this eventuality — but I do not think any weighing-up of risks entered into Illich's thinking. Indeed, he believed that the ever-growing emphasis on risk calculation in medicine constitutes the ultimate disembodiment, because it invites people to think of themselves not as unique persons but as members of an abstract class for which probabilities can be calculated. Illich simply accepted his affliction as his share in Christ's suffering; and occasionally he quoted, as he does here, a verse from Paul's Letter to the Colossians in the New Testament: "Now I rejoice in my sufferings for your sake, and in my flesh I complete what is lacking in Christ's afflictions for the sake of his body, the church."[106] Illich lived what he believed: that each person is given a story to tell, and that nothing could be worse than to allow that unique story to be shrunk to a "survival rate" or reduced to an assigned "role." To some it may sound perverse, and I know the chance I take in even telling the story, but he treated even his suffering as a gift, and he made more of it than I could have imagined was possible before I met him. He had written in *Medical Nemesis* that "medical civilization" tries to "abolish the need for an art of suffering" and produces "a progressive flattening out of personal, virtuous performance."[107] In his last two decades he got to cultivate this art and to give such a performance. He did it with good humour, great generosity with his time and counsel, expansive enjoyment of life's pleasures, and a growing sweetness in which whatever was left of a great man's pride seemed simply to burn away. By the end, he had drained his cup to the last drop and one morning laid down and peacefully died. No one who knew him well would have dared to say that he died "of cancer."

Illich's life, to me, has as much to teach as his writings, and he says a good deal in what follows about how he tried to live. But before I come to that, I want to say a few words about how deeply and how sensitively he experienced his changing times. By the later 1970s Illich had recognized that the moment had passed when the radical change of direction he had urged would have been possible. The institutions whose counterproductivity he had exposed might have acquired a more ambiguous taste for many of their clients, their priesthoods might have lost some of their prestige, and the rituals of progress become tarnished, but this would only translate into a protective cynicism, and the accommodation of a countercultural element within "the system." What Illich had sought — the disestablishment of all secular churches and an end to their monopolies — would not occur. He had also begun to realize by the early 1980s that the world was undergoing a surprising change of state with the advent of an age of systems in which people increasingly "occupy a new dimensionless cybernetic space."[108] The industrial era had still seen technology as something shaped and deployed according to human intentions. Systems incorporate their users — they have no outside, no privileged standpoint from which an independent intention could be formulated. Many have hailed the "everything is connected" aspect of the systems perspective, but for Illich it was pure abstraction, the dissolution of all boundaries, "a night," as Hegel says, "in which all cows are black."[109] Its hallmark is disembodiment, the loss of the inhabited and personally experienced body. Let me try to make this clear with a quotation from Maurice Merleau-Ponty, both because it lends support to Illich's view and because it defines this view so poetically:

> In the ideology of cybernetics . . . human creatures are derived from a natural information process, itself conceived on the model of human machines. If this kind of thinking were to extend its reign to man and

history; if, pretending to ignore what we know of them through our own situations, it were to set out to construct man and history on the basis of a few abstract indices . . . then, since man really becomes the *manipulandum* he takes himself to be, we enter into a cultural regimen, where there is neither truth nor falsity concerning man and history, into a sleep, or a nightmare, from which there is no awakening.

 Scientific thinking . . . must return to the soil of the sensible and opened world such as it is in our life and for our body — not for that possible body which we may legitimately think of as an information machine but that the actual body I call mine, this sentinel standing quietly at the command of my words and my acts.[110]

If you should doubt that human creatures are now "derived from information processes" or humanity "constructed on the basis of a few abstract indices," you have only to think of the discourse of popular genetics, in which notional entities called genes "cause" this or that condition, or of risk analysis, in which human beings are asked to identify themselves with statistical figments, or of the myriad other contemporary discourses in which imponderable probabilities are supposed to govern human decisions. This replacement of the dense, concretely situated flesh by an abstract construction was a horror for Illich because, from the perspective of his Incarnational Christianity, it is *as a body* that the truth confronts us, and only through the body that we come to know it.

 Illich, cosmopolitan bird of passage though he was, tried to live in "the soil of the sensible and opened world . . . as it is . . . for our body." He sometimes spoke of himself as an exile, a wanderer whose homes had never been more than tents once his native soil was swallowed in the cataclysm that forced him from his home as a boy; but, even so, wherever he was, a place would appear. He camped at the margins of various universities and, as he says here, "soberly milk[ed] that sacred cow" in order to provide a place where his friends could gather for what were called "living room consultations" when I first began to attend them at State College. These seminars, like any intellectual gathering, could have their prolixities and little vanities, as well their moments of inspiration, but whatever occurred remained grounded in friendship, long walks, leisurely meals, and the generous supply of that "ordinary, but decent wine" that Illich convinced the Internal Revenue Service to regard as a professional expense. In this way he recreated the "collegial procedure" to which the university had become, he said, "almost an enemy." He believed that in a world of fading traditions and disappearing places the practice of personal fidelity that he called friendship could provide the soil in which the search for truth could flourish. Through him, a remarkably diverse group of people formed enduring friendships with one another. And, though he was the focus, inspiration, and example around which they first aligned themselves, the web of hospitality and friendship that he spun will long outlive him.

As I mentioned earlier, when Illich died, his obituaries tended to portray him as a man who had had his day. I believe that what he has to say here belongs very much to current discussion. An often remarked feature of our time is the so-called "return of religion." With the failure of all secular utopias, religion is now often the fault line along which societies divide, both domestically and internationally. But the terms in which this division is discussed often presume a neat cleavage between the religious and the secular, with the secular conceived as a space from which religion has simply been removed and relegated to the realm of private choice. I believe that this is an untenable distinction, but not for the reasons sometimes given by the religious who try to abolish it by claiming that whatever is believed is a religion by definition and therefore the secular is no more than a cover for a materialist or humanist "religion." I think Illich makes a much more convincing evisceration of the myth of the secular when he claims that contemporary Western societies are in no sense post-Christian but rather constitute a perverted form of Christianity. He shows here that a whole constellation of modern notions, most too obvious even to raise a question in most minds, are distortions of Christian originals — from "the citizen" on whose shoulders the state rests to the services which are its *raison d'être*; from the planetary "life" that right-thinking people want to conserve to the technology that threatens it. And he further claims that these notions would have been unthinkable without their Christian originals. They owe their very existence, in other words, to the ancestry which they distort, deny, and conceal.

Illich, with admitted trepidation, calls this view "apocalyptic." His hesitancy is understandable, since this word, as it is now used, tends to evoke fundamentalist fantasies of divine vengeance or the gruesome cataclysms that have become a staple of popular cinema. But Illich uses the word in its literal meaning of "uncovering" or "revelation." For him, the contemporary world reveals an evil that can only be grasped when it is understood as an imposture, or simulation, of the Samaritan's unforeseen and unforeseeable response to the man in the ditch. Evil, traditionally, was an absence, a forgetfulness of the good. Illich points to a new kind of evil that appears only when the good is replaced by measurable values and transmogrified into an institutional output. In this case, the good is not just temporarily forgotten, it is rendered imperceptible; and this reversal, whereby the greatest good opens a door to the extinction of the good, is what Illich calls the mystery of evil. He studied Western history as its revelation, a revelation that he believed to be progressive, that is, more evident today than ever before.

Illich invites us to see in the chirpy contemporary discourses of health, responsibility for life, and lifelong education neither a fulfillment nor a forgetting of Christian faith but its demonic parody. For Christians this has the same profound implications that Illich tried to bring to Cardinal Suenens's attention forty years ago when he presented him with the cartoon of the condom and the bomb. It suggests that they are looking for sin in all the wrong places. But there are implications for modern non-Christians as well. Only faith can discern the full mystery of sin — for faith alone, Illich says, can know the glory that is being corrupted — but all modern persons live among the institutions that Illich believed were designed to give "security, survival ability, and independence from individual persons to the new possibilities that were opened through the Gospel." On them, Illich urged clear-sighted, historically informed awareness of their condition. The moment of collective decision may have passed with the dissolution of society into systems, but individuals retain the freedom to renounce the certainties that imprison them within systems and to find the interstices where friendship and personal action remain possible. Illich called it "courageous, disciplined, self-critical renunciation accomplished in community."[111] And in his last years, he often found people who had also given up the illusion that one can behave ethically in a world without boundaries and who were willing to join him in this stance.[112]

Ivan Illich tried to think and to live his Christian faith in the thick of modern ideas and institutions. He pursued his vocation into the real world of schools and hospitals, risk screening and cybertext, and was often discreet about the source of his inspiration. This was his way of "nakedly following the naked Christ," as he liked to quote from St. Jerome. Of all the names he was given, from philosopher to prophet, the one which sticks — and by which he himself wished to be known — is friend. He shaped his course according to the ones who met and claimed him on his way. All of his writings trace back in some way to a personal occasion, and this one is no different. It was given because I asked. It was his testament to me, and, through me, I hope, to you.

I

The Corruption of the Best Is the Worst

For sweetest things turn sourest by their deeds;
Lilies that fester smell far worse than weeds.

William Shakespeare, Sonnet 94

This page intentionally left blank

I

GOSPEL

.

I believe that the Incarnation makes possible a surprising and entirely new flowering of love and knowledge. For Christians the Biblical God can now be loved in the flesh. Saint John says that he has sat at table with him, that he has put his head on his shoulder, heard him, touched him, smelled him. And he has said that whoever sees him sees the Father, and that whoever loves another loves him in the person of that other. A new dimension of love has opened, but this opening is highly ambiguous because of the way in which it explodes certain universal assumptions about the conditions under which love are possible. Before I was limited by the people into which I was born and the family in which I was raised. Now I can choose whom I will love and where I will love. And this deeply threatens the traditional basis for ethics, which was always an *ethnos*, an historically given "we" which precedes any pronunciation of the word "I."

The opening of this new horizon is also accompanied by a second danger: institutionalization. There is a temptation to try to manage and, eventually, to legislate this new love, to create an institution that will guarantee it, insure it, and protect it by criminalizing its opposite. So, along with this new ability to give freely of oneself has appeared the possibility of exercising an entirely new kind of power, the power of those who organize Christianity and use this vocation to claim their superiority as social institutions. This power is claimed first by the Church and later by the many secular institutions stamped from its mould. Wherever I look for the roots of modernity, I find them in the attempts of the churches to institutionalize, legitimize, and manage Christian vocation.

I speak here, not as a theologian, but as a believer and an historian. For thirty years I have declined to speak as a theologian because, in the Roman Catholic Church's more recent tradition, one thereby claims an institutional authority. I have chosen instead to write as an historian curious about the undeniable historical consequences of Christian belief. And I think I can provide evidence for my claim that when the angel Gabriel suddenly appeared before that Jewish girl in Nazareth and said *"Ave,"* he did something that cannot be neglected by the historian, even though it doesn't fit in the ordinary sense within history or the study of history. I believe that that angel told that woman that from that moment on she was to be the Mother of God, and, presuming her maiden-like yes, that he whose name the Jews never wanted to pronounce was to become a living person, as human as you or I. I, therefore, listen to him, as nobody before this event could have listened to another or looked at another. This is a surprise, remains a surprise, and could not exist as anything else. It constitutes an extraordinary kind of knowledge which in my tradition one calls faith. I do not expect everyone to share this sense of what, by now, for me, is obvious; but I do think, nevertheless, that I can demonstrate that the Incarnation, the enfleshment, of the Biblical, the Koranic, the Christian, Allah, represents a turning point in the history of the world for believer and unbeliever alike. Belief refers to what exceeds history, but it also enters history and changes it forever.

The Old Testament of the Christian Bible, taken as a whole, is prophetic. At its heart are people who speak about what has not yet come to be. Older Biblical scholarship tended to ask how it was that such people arose only amongst that particular tribe, or people whom we today call the Jews. Biblical scholarship of the last forty years has altered the question. The authors who have most impressed and interested me have asked: how is it that the Jewish people came into existence around their prophets? What makes the ancient Jews unique is that they became a social "we," an "I" in the plural, around the message that whatever happens in history or can be seen in nature is a foreshadowing, in the sense that pregnancy foreshadows birth. (I mean pregnancy here in the old sense in which a woman was said to be "expecting" or "in good hope," not the current sense in which the womb has become the mapped and monitored public place in which an embryonic citizen resides.) The prophets of Israel made the astonishing claim that they could step outside the family and tribal context in which tomorrow turns in a circle with yesterday, and instead speak about a tomorrow which will be totally surprising, messianic. It is around the announced Messiah that the historically unique phenomenon of God's people comes into existence, and the Old Testament in this sense is pregnant with the Messiah. "The whole creation," the apostle Paul says, "has been, until this time, groaning in labour pains."[1]

The image of pregnancy should not be read as suggesting that the Incarnation was in any sense necessary, pre-determined or inevitable. It was and remains an outworking of pure, unconstrained freedom, and this is something very difficult for the modern mind to grasp. What happens, with us, is the outcome either of chance or some chain of causal necessity. We have lost the sense that there exists between these extremes a realm of gratuity, or gift, a realm that comes into being in response to a call, rather than a determinative cause. The word gratuity itself reveals the loss of this sense. A gratuity today is something trivial, a tip, and the gratuitous is primarily understood as what is un-necessary, un-called for, and, therefore, beside the point. But, in the Bible, this is the primary form of "causation" — from God's summons to Abraham to Jesus' running into Philip and saying "Follow me." The Gospel exacts from its readers the recognition that what it presents is neither necessity nor chance but a superabundant gift freely given to those who will freely receive it.

This gift becomes fully visible only at the moment of its rejection, the moment which I take to be the point of the Gospel, the Crucifixion. Jesus, as our Saviour but also as our model, is condemned by his own people, led out of the city, and executed as somebody who has blasphemed the community's God. But he is not simply executed. He is hanged on a cross, a way of dying with a powerful significance in the Mediterranean tradition. This meaning becomes clear when we examine descriptions of suicide by hanging in Greek and Roman classical literature. The first such account concerns an Italian queen, who is very angry at her people and wants to leave them, so she hangs herself in the woods to die without touching the earth. In that way, she expects her spirit to remain around to haunt her people rather than being absorbed into the realm of the ancestors. In Greek and Roman tradition to hang someone on a gibbet to die without touching the earth is a way of excluding them not just from "our" people here, but also from our people in the other world, from our dead.

If, therefore, we take as our example this man who says, Let this chalice pass from me, because he so much fears it, it is an example simultaneously of loyalty to his people and of willingness to accept being excluded from them by what he stands for. This, in the supreme form, is the Christian attitude towards this worldly community, an attitude which Christians tried to embody in everyday life. The same willingness to step outside the embrace of the community is evident in the parable of the Samaritan. Jesus tells the story[2] in response to the question of "a certain lawyer," that is, a man versed in the Law of Moses, who asks, "Who is my neighbour?" A man, Jesus says, was going from Jerusalem to Jericho when he was set upon by robbers, stripped, beaten, and left half-dead in a ditch by the road. A priest happens by and then a Levite, men associated with the Temple and the community's approved sacrificial rites, and both pass him by "on the other side." Then comes a Samaritan, a person whom Jesus' listeners would have identified as an enemy, a despised outsider from the northern kingdom of Israel who did not worship at the temple. And this Samaritan turns to the wounded one, picks him up, takes him in his arms, dresses his wounds and brings him to an inn where he pays for his convalescence.

The story is deeply familiar. Dictionaries recognize the good Samaritan as a friend in need. The United States has so-called Samaritan laws, which exempt you from tort actions, if you inadvertently do harm while offering aid. This familiarity disguises the shocking character of the Lord's tale. Perhaps the only way we could recapture it today would be to imagine the Samaritan as a Palestinian ministering to a wounded Jew. He is someone who not only goes outside his ethnic preference for taking care of his own kind, but who commits a kind of treason by caring for his enemy. In so doing, he exercises a freedom of choice, whose radical novelty has often been overlooked. Once, some thirty years ago, I made a survey of sermons dealing with this story of the Samaritan from the early third century into the nineteenth century, and I found out that most preachers who commented on that passage felt that it was about how one *ought* to behave towards one's neighbour, that it proposed a rule of conduct, or an exemplification of ethical duty. I believe that this is, in fact, precisely the opposite of what Jesus wanted to point out. He had not been asked, how should one behave towards one's neighbour, but rather, who is my neighbour? And what he said, as I understand it, was, My neighbour is who I choose, not who I have to choose. There is no way of categorizing who my neighbour ought to be.

This doctrine about the neighbour, which Jesus proposes, is utterly destructive of ordinary decency, of what had, until then, been understood as ethical behaviour. This is what modern preaching has not been willing to insist upon, and why this teaching is as surprising today as it was in the beginning. In antiquity, hospitable behaviour, or full commitment in my action to the other, implies a boundary drawn around those to whom I can behave in this way. The Greeks recognized a duty of hospitality towards *xenoi*, strangers who spoke a Hellenic language, but not towards the babblers in strange tongues whom they called *barbaroi*. Jesus taught the Pharisees that the relationship which he had come to announce to them as most completely human is not one that is expected, required, or owed. It can only be a free creation between two people, and one which cannot happen unless something comes to me through the other, by the other, in his bodily presence. It is not a relationship that exists because we are citizens of the same Athens, and so can feel a duty towards each other, nor because Zeus also throws his mantle over the Corinthians and other Hellenes, but because we have decided. This is what the Master calls behaving as a neighbour.

Several years ago, during my annual lecture series at the University of Bremen, I took the Samaritan as my theme because my students had asked me if I would discuss ethics. What I tried to point out to them was the suggestion in this story that we are creatures that find our perfection only by establishing a relationship, and that this relationship may appear arbitrary from everybody else's point of view, because I do it in response to a call and not a category, in this case the call of the beaten-up Jew in the ditch. This has two implications. The first is that this "ought" is not, and cannot be reduced to a norm. It has a *telos*. It aims at somebody, *some body*; but not according to a rule. It has become almost impossible for people who today deal with ethics or morality to think in terms of relationships rather than rules. The second implication, and a point I'll develop more fully later on, is that with the creation of this new mode of existence, the possibility of its breakage also appears. And this denial, infidelity, turning away, coldness is what the New Testament calls sin, something which can only be recognized by the light of this new glimmer of mutuality.

The stress which the New Testament puts on relationship is also visible in the new account of virtue which appears amongst Christians. In the Platonic and Aristotelian teaching, virtue is something that I can cultivate in myself by the discipline of repeating good actions until they have become a second nature. Hugh of St. Victor, the twelfth century abbot who is one of my great teachers, takes this traditional account of the virtues as his starting point, but says that, for a man of faith, each one of them can flower only as a surprising gift which he receives from God, usually through the intermediary of his interlocutor or the person or persons or community with whom he lives. The flowering of virtues, as evidenced by what Hugh calls the delicacy of their perfume, can come about only as a gift to me and not something which I can do on my own, as in classical tradition. Virtue, in that view is very self-centred, building on my powers. Hugh presents the gifts of the Holy Spirit as gifts which come to me through those with whom I live.

Another of my great teachers, the late Gerhart Ladner, tried to define the new thing that came into the world with Christianity in a book called *The Idea of Reform*. I feel a very special sense of gratitude to Ladner because, to my knowledge, he was one of the first to confront the question of how an historian should treat the appearance in history of something new and unprecedented. Thirty-five years ago,

when the word revolution was in the air and I couldn't help but give
my summer seminars at CIDOC[3] on issues relating to this concept, I
demanded of every student that he read at least a certain part of
Ladner's book before coming to the seminar. As Ladner expounds it,
reformatio came to refer in the early Christian centuries to a way of
behaving and feeling that had never been known before. The classical world had known renewal and rebirth as one phase of the eternal
cycling of the stars and the seasons, but this was nothing like the idea,
which had spread throughout Christendom by the fourth century, of
a conversion that would sweep away the culture in which I was born
and leave me in an entirely new state. A source I know from this
period, for example, relates the story of a family of Irish brothers
whose father had been killed. In the society from which they came a
son had an absolute duty to avenge a father's murder, yet these young
men forgot their revenge and went to live as monks on a barren island
where they did penance for their sins. They were able, suddenly, to
step outside the culture which had formed them and lived in peaceful opposition to it.

The mood, or ground-tone, of this new state was contrition. It
was motivated not by a sense of culpability but rather a deep sorrow
about my capacity to betray the relationships which I, as a Samaritan,
have established, and, at the same time, a deep confidence in the forgiveness and mercy of the other. And this forgiveness was not
conceived as the cancellation of a debt but as an expression of the love
and mutual forbearance in which Christian communities were called
to live. This is difficult to understand today because the very idea of
sin has become both threatening and obscure to contemporary
minds. People now tend to understand sin in the light of its "criminalization" by the Church during the high Middle Ages and
afterwards. As I will later explain in more detail, it was this criminalization which generated the modern idea of conscience as an inward
formation by moral rules or norms. It made possible the isolation and
anguish which drive the modern individual, and it also obscured the
fact that what the New Testament calls sin is not a moral wrong but
a turning away or a falling short. Sin, as the New Testament understands it, is something that is revealed only in the light of its possible

forgiveness. To believe in sin, therefore, is to celebrate, as a gift beyond full understanding, the fact that one is being forgiven. Contrition is a sweet glorification of the new relationship for which the Samaritan stands, a relationship which is free, and therefore vulnerable and fragile, but always capable of healing, just as nature was then conceived as always in the process of healing.

But this new relationship, as I have said, was also subject to institutionalization, and that was what began to happen after the Church achieved official status within the Roman Empire. In the early years of Christianity, it was customary in a Christian household to have an extra mattress, a bit of a candle, and some dry bread in case the Lord Jesus should knock at the door in the form of a stranger without a roof — a form of behaviour that was utterly foreign to any of the cultures of the Roman Empire. You took in your own but not someone lost on the street. Then the Emperor Constantine recognized the Church, and Christian bishops acquired the same position in the imperial administration as magistrates, so that when Augustine [354–430] wrote to a Roman judge about a legal issue, he wrote as a social equal. They also gained the power to establish social corporations. And the first corporations they started were Samaritan corporations which designated certain categories of people as preferred neighbours. For example, the bishops created special houses, financed by the community, that were charged with taking care of people without a home. Such care was no longer the free choice of the householder; it was the task of an institution. It was against this idea that the great Church Father John Chrysostom [347?–407] railed. He was called golden-tongued because of his beautiful rhetoric, and, in one of his sermons, he warned against creating these *xenodocheia*, literally "houses for foreigners." By assigning the duty to behave in this way to an institution, he said, Christians would lose the habit of reserving a bed and having a piece of bread ready in every home, and their households would cease to be Christian homes.

Let me tell you a story I heard from the late Jean Daniélou, when he was already an old man. Daniélou was a Jesuit and a very learned scriptural and patristic scholar, who had lived in China and baptized people there. One of these converts was so happy that he had been accepted into the Church that he promised to make a pilgrimage from Peking to Rome on foot. This was just before the Second World War. And that pilgrim, when he met Daniélou again in Rome, told him the story of his journey. At first, it was quite easy, he said. In China he only had to identify himself as a pilgrim, someone whose walk was oriented to a sacred place, and he was given food, a handout, and a place to sleep. This changed a little bit when he entered the territory of Orthodox Christianity. There they told him to go to the parish house, where a place was free, or to the priest's house. Then he got to Poland, the first Catholic country, and he found that the Polish Catholics generously gave him money to put himself up in a cheap hotel. It is the glorious Christian and Western idea that there should be institutions, preferably not just hotels but special flophouses, available for people who need a place to sleep. In this way the attempt to be open to all who are in need results in a degradation of hospitality and its replacement by caregiving institutions.

A gratuitous and truly free choice had become an ideology and an idealism, and this institutionalization of neighbourliness had an increasingly important place in the late Roman Empire. Jumping ahead another 150 years from Augustine's time, we come to a period when decaying Rome, and other imperial centres, were attracting massive immigration from rural and foreign areas, which made city life dangerous. The Emperors, especially in Byzantium, made decrees expelling those who couldn't prove that they had a home. They gave legitimacy to these decrees by financing institutions which would provide shelter for the homeless. And, if you study the way in which the Church created its economic base in late antiquity, you will see that by taking on this task of creating welfare institutions for the state, the Church was able to establish a legal and moral claim on public funds, and a practically unlimited claim since the task was unlimited.

But as soon as hospitality is transformed into a service, two things have happened at once. First, a completely new way of conceiving the I–Thou relationship has appeared. Nowhere in antique Greece or Rome is there evidence of anything like these new flophouses for foreigners, or shelters for widows and orphans. Christian Europe is unimaginable without its deep concern about building institutions that take care of different types of people in need. So there is no question that modern service society is an attempt to establish and extend Christian hospitality. On the other hand, we have immediately perverted it. The personal freedom to choose who will be my other has been transformed into the use of power and money to provide a service. This not only deprives the idea of the neighbour of the quality of freedom implied in the story of the Samaritan. It also creates an impersonal view of how a good society ought to work. It creates needs, so-called, for service commodities, needs which can never be satisfied — is there enough health yet, enough education? — and therefore a type of suffering completely unknown outside of Western culture with its roots in Christianity.

A modern person finds nothing more irksome, more disgusting than having to leave this pining woman or that suffering man unattended. So, as *homo technologicus*, we create agencies for that purpose. This is what I call the *perversio optimi quae est pessima* [the perversion of the best which is the worst]. I may even be a good Christian and attend to the one who asks, but I still need charitable institutions for those whom I leave unattended. I know that there will never be enough true friends with time on their hands, so let this be done. Create services, and let ethicists discuss how to distribute their limited productivity.

Now, when I speak about this, people tell me, Yes, we see that there's a kind of suffering in modern life that results from unsatisfied needs for service, but why do you say it's a suffering of a new kind, an evil of a new kind? Why do you call it a horror? Because I consider this evil to be the result of an attempt to use power, organization, management, manipulation, and the law to ensure the social presence of something which, by its very nature, cannot be anything else but the free choice of individuals who have accepted the invitation to see in everybody whom they choose the face of Christ. That's the reason why I speak about corruption, or perversion.

To go a step further: The vocation, the ability, the empowerment, the invitation to choose freely outside and beyond the horizon of my *ethnos* what gifts I will give and to whom I will give them is understandable only to one who is willing to be surprised, one who lives within that unimaginable and unpredictable horizon which I call faith. And the perversion of faith is not simply evil. It is something more. It is sin, because sin is the decision to make faith into something that is subject to the power of this world.

I want to stress that we're dealing here with the institutionalization, or normalization, of something which to ordinary human reasoning is absurd. That God could be man can be explained only by love. Logically it's a contradiction. The ability to understand it depends on what my tradition calls faith, but that too is something which contemporary people have trouble grasping. Faith is a mode of knowledge which does not base itself on either my worldly experience or the resources of my intelligence. It founds certainty on the word of someone whom I trust and makes this knowledge which is based on trust more fundamental than anything I can know by reason. This, of course, is a possibility only when I believe that God's word can reach me. It makes sense only if the One whom I trust is God. But it also rubs off on my relationship to other people. It makes me aim at facing people with a willingness to take them for what they reveal about themselves — to take them, therefore, *at their word* — and not for what I know about them. And this is very difficult to do after 100 years of psychoanalysis. The various schools of psychoanalysis assume that they can help you find out about yourself by understanding you more perfectly than you do yourself, and this assumption inevitably colours most of our relationships by now. This is as true of the most sophisticated, most fascinating forms of analysis as it is of more trivial and degraded forms. One of the newnesses which come from him who says, I have come to make all things new, is exactly the willingness, in dealing with the other, to accept him for what he tells me about himself. The contemporary sociological assumption, whether psychoanalytic or Marxist, is that the other's sense of himself is an illusion shaped by ideology, by social condition, by upbringing, and by education. Only by taking the predictability out of the face of the other can I be surprised by him. And this is what I've tried to do. I've tried to encourage people to envision this possibility — even when I couldn't talk to them explicitly about who my model is.

Faith inevitably implies a certain foolishness in worldly terms. The Saviour of Israel died, hung on a cross and ridiculed by everybody entitled to represent Israel. The first representation we have of the Crucifixion was found in the ruins of ancient Rome on the outside wall of what archaeologists assume to have been a brothel. It pictures a crucified man with the head of a donkey and below him a man in an attitude of prayerful devotion. "Anaxamenos adores his God," says the inscription. This image is the first historical indication that the *Crucifixus*, the body on the cross, had a meaning for Christians, and it has remained a mystery whether it was intended as a mockery of Christian belief or as a Christian's affirmation of his understanding of himself as a fool. Either way it exemplifies an understanding of Christianity as a form of foolishness, an understanding that remained alive in the Eastern Church until the late nineteenth century. In the Western Church, if you wanted to step outside of the world and give yourself totally to a life of Christian prayer, you could only do it by becoming a monk. In the Greek Church, you had the choice of becoming either a monk or a fool; but this foolishness had to be entirely gratuitous and not secretly motivated by a desire for perfection.

I mention this because it seems to me that one of the ways of understanding the history of Western Christianity is as a progressive loss of the sense that the freedom for which Christ is our model and our witness is folly. The Western Church, in its earnest effort to institutionalize this freedom, has tended to transform supreme folly first into desirable duty, and then into legislated duty. It is folly to be hospitable in the way the Samaritan is — pure folly if you really think it through. To make of this a duty and then create categories of people towards whom this duty is owing witnesses to a brutal form of earnestness. More than that, this inversion of the extraordinary folly that became possible through the Gospel represents a mystery of evil, and it is to this mystery that I now want to turn.

2

MYSTERIUM

In the first two generations of Christianity, each Christian community had a prophet. We know of it through the Acts of the
Apostles and the letters of the apostle Paul. Both sources insist that
each community needs a prophet to be a good community. Now, the
prophets of Israel were people deeply convinced that God's word was
taking flesh in their mouths, and that around this enfleshment
of God's word, the people of Israel could come into existence. But
once God's word had become flesh in the womb of Mary — the
Middle Ages called her the queen of the prophets because she
brought forth the word in the flesh — there was no longer any need
for the word of God to come through the mouth of a prophet.
Prophets, in the strict sense, no longer fit into the life of Jesus or the
life of the early Church. So what did these prophets have to say to
the Church that the other teachers and preachers mentioned in these
first Christian documents could not say? I think they had to
announce a mystery, which was that the final evil that would bring
the world to an end was already present. This evil was called Anti-
Christ, and the Church was identified as the milieu in which it would
nest. The Church had gone pregnant with an evil which would have
found no nesting place in the Old Testament. Paul in the second
chapter of his second letter to the Thessalonians calls this new reality the *mysterium iniquitatis*, the mystery of evil. He says that
something unbelievably horrible has come into being and begun to

grow with his foundation of communities around the Eastern Mediterranean, something whose full extent won't be grasped until some future moment at which he places *apocalypsis*, meaning the end of time and the world. This something, he insists, is mysterious and belongs to those things which only the initiated Christian can know. To outsiders who do not accept the divinity of the apparent rebel crucified by Pontius Pilate, it remains veiled.

What is impressive about the transition from the early Church to the established Western Church is how thoroughly this mystery disappeared from the Church's teaching and the concern of most of its members. It re-appeared from time to time in the prayers, writings, and sermons of mystics and reformers; but the Roman Church did not centre faith on its existence, and neither did most of the Reformed Churches. Is it not surprising that this belief should have faded, that Church doctrine would not have picked it up, talked about it, and made it central?

The *mysterium iniquitatis* is a *mysterium* because it can be grasped only through the revelation of God in Christ. This must be recognized. But I also believe that the mysterious evil that entered the world with the Incarnation can be investigated historically, and, for this, neither faith nor belief is required but only a certain power of observation. Is it not the case that our world is out of whack with any prior historical epoch? The more I try to examine the present as an historical entity, the more it seems confusing, unbelievable, and incomprehensible. It forces me to accept a set of axioms for which I find no parallels in past societies and displays a puzzling kind of horror, cruelty, and degradation with no precedent in other historical epochs. To give a very superficial example, just because it comes readily to mind, think of the polarization of incomes during the last twenty years all over the world, not only in the United States, but much more violently in the world at large. I recently saw a statement which inspired confidence that the 350 richest people in the world earn as much as the bottom 65 per cent of the world's people. And what worries me most about that is not the disparity as such, but the fact that that 65 per cent can no longer live, as they could thirty years ago, without recourse to money. Then many things were still not monetarized; subsistence still was functioning. Today they can't move without buying a bus ticket. They can't get heat in their kitchen by collecting wood but have to buy electricity. How to explain this extraordinary evil?

I would say that this question can be looked at in an entirely new light if you begin from the assumption I spoke of earlier: that we are not standing in front of an evil of the ordinary kind but of that corruption of the best which occurs when the Gospel is institutionalized, and love is transmogrified into claims for service. The first generations of Christianity recognized that a mysterious type of — how shall I call it? — perversion, inhumanity, denial had become possible. Their idea of the *mysterium iniquitatis*, gives me a key to understand the evil which I face now and for which I can't find a word. I, at least, as a man of faith, should call this evil a mysterious betrayal or perversion of the kind of freedom which the Gospels brought.

What I have stammered here, talking freely and unprepared, I have avoided saying for thirty years. Let me now try and say it in a way that others can hear it: the more you allow yourself to conceive of the evil you see as evil of a new kind, of a mysterious kind, the more intense becomes the temptation — I can't avoid saying it, I cannot go on without saying it — of cursing God's Incarnation.[1]

Let me give another concrete example, because I was thinking of it this morning, of the perversion of love of which I'm speaking. It concerns a man in a Mexican village whose kidneys got ruined, I guess by tequila. The local doctor said, We can only help you by providing you with a new kidney or with kidney dialysis. They took him off, and he died miserably, not so long afterwards, in hospital far from his family. But the need for kidney dialysis or kidney replacement had been injected into the entire village. And why should the poor be excluded from a privilege given to the rich? I sat down with pencil and paper with a man who knows the situation in Mexico, and we worked out that the cost of that poor drunkard's last months was equal to the purchase price of forty-two homes of the kind in which the people who now need kidney dialysis live. Why is it that none of our major churches is able to condemn this ritual, myth-making ritual, as something which a Christian can't engage in as a recipient, as a researcher or as a devoted doctor or nurse? My idea is that it is because people do not see the underbelly of that evil, the way in which it is contrary to freedom in the deep sense, and so they just find it confusing. They don't know what to do, or how to react.

I know I risk being mistaken for a fundamentalist preacher in applying the monstrously churchy term, Anti-Christ, to this new evil. I would have preferred to simply speak about sin, but I was afraid that by using that term I would only heighten the guarantee that I would be misunderstood. Let me now face the extreme difficulty many people will have in understanding what I want to say. This difficulty does not lie in arcane speculations about what person or what power Paul meant to refer to in his letter to the Thessalonians, but in grasping the seemingly ordinary idea of sin. I believe that sin is something which did not exist as a human option, as an individual option, as a day-to-day option before Christ gave us the freedom of seeing in each other persons redeemed to be like him. By opening this new possibility of love, this new way of facing each other, this radical foolishness, as I called it earlier, a new form of betrayal also became possible. Your dignity now depends on me and remains potential so long as I do not bring it into act in our encounter. This denial of your dignity is what sin is. The idea that by not responding to you, when you call upon my fidelity, I thereby personally offend God is fundamental to understanding what Christianity is about. And the mystery that I'm interested in contemplating is a consequence of the perversion of faith throughout history, a perversion that has come to haunt us by the beginning of the twenty-first century and is exactly related to my understanding of sin.

All right, you might say, why not simply say "sin" then and dispense with this fantasy-laden, fundamentalist, Biblical, churchy idea of the Anti-Christ. Perhaps I can, but I must first clear up some of the difficulties associated with the contemporary use of the word sin. As far as I can understand, I live in a world which has lost the sense for good, the Good. We have lost the certainty that the world makes sense because things fit together, that the eye is made to grasp the sunlight, and is not just a biological camera which happens to register this optical effect. We have lost the sense that virtuous behaviour is fitting and appropriate for human beings, and we have lost it in the course of the late seventeenth, eighteenth, and nineteenth centuries with the rise of the concept and the experience of value. Good is absolute: the light and the eye are simply made for each other, and this unquestioned good is deeply experienced. But once I say that the eye has value for me because it allows me to see or to orient myself in the world, I open a new door. Values can be positive but also negative, so the moment I speak, in philosophy, about values, I assume the existence of a zero point, from which values rise or decline in two directions. The replacement of the good by the idea of value begins in philosophy, and is then expressed in an ever-growing economic sphere within which my life becomes a pursuit of values rather than a pursuit of what is good for me, which can only be another person. What else could it be?

Now, in the tradition within which I'm speaking, sin allows a heightened understanding of evil. Evil is the opposite of good — it's not a disvalue or a negative value — and sin is a mysterious aspect of evil, a personal offence of God which is intelligible only in the light of the new freedom exemplified in the parable of the Samaritan. But, if I'm right, the replacement of good and evil by value and disvalue has destroyed the basis on which sin was predicated, because sin cannot be connected to negative values. And this has made it impossible to convey the idea that modern horrors can be fully grasped only by those who understand their sinfulness, their direct contradiction of the new freedom proposed in the Gospel.

Whether I'm right in my interpretation of Paul, I leave to the theologians. I will bow to their judgement as to whether my view is inside or outside the fold of orthodoxy. I am trying to understand what Paul's sentences say to me as a man who is deeply impressed, almost carried off his feet, by contemplating what the need for education, the need for ever-increasing health services, the need for shelter have generated in the modern world. I am guided as an historian by Paul. He tells me something which I must struggle to grasp, and it's not so difficult if you take him seriously and try to learn to see what he wanted to say. I'm not claiming authority in interpreting Paul, but still I suspect that I might be correct.

3

CONTINGENCY, PART I:
A WORLD IN THE
HANDS OF GOD

Christianity brings something new into existence. The Jew could walk, as one old expression says, beneath the nose of God. He could walk in God's sight and be guided by his word, but the Christian made a new claim: that he could encounter God in Christ and Christ in the unknown one who knocked at his door and asked for hospitality. We have talked already about how, in the age of the Church, this idea of the neighbour, this idea of acting out of a love which is a gift, gets corrupted by being defined as something which can be institutionalized, which charitable institutions can do much better than a bunch of individual Christians. Today I want to take up another uniquely Christian notion which I believe provided the door through which technology, in the Western sense, came into existence; and that is the idea of contingency. I will not argue that technology as we know it was in any sense a necessary, or inevitable consequence of this idea. I see this outcome rather as a surprise, a puzzle about which I would like to provoke curiosity.

Hans Blumenberg was one of the master thinkers of our time. He was a German professor, whose particular speciality was the epochal transformation that began to occur in European society around the time of Nicholas of Cusa [1401–1464] and Copernicus [1473–1543]. You can't really study that transformation without taking into your hands his various works, now finally translated and available in English some twenty or thirty years after they first appeared. Blumenberg has a little article on contingency in the big standard German Lutheran encyclopaedia, *Religion in Geschichte und Gegenwart*, which is so pointed and concise that I couldn't possibly improve on it, and so I'm going to closely follow his exposition, using my translation, sometimes quoting word for word, and sometimes expanding and commenting as I go.

Contingency, Blumenberg says, is one of the few concepts that are of specifically Christian origin, even though the word itself is derived from a Latinization of a concept in Aristotelian logic.[1] Contingency expresses the state of being of a world which has been created from nothing, is destined to disappear and is upheld in its existence by one thing, and one thing only: divine will. The idea that the world is contingent at every instant on God's will begins to be evident only in the eleventh century and is not fully fleshed out until towards the end of the thirteenth century. This is an event in the history of philosophy, but I believe that I can show you later on that what philosophers of that age expressed was a transformation in people's feelings. The world comes to be considered as something contingent, something indifferent to its own existence, something which does not bear within itself a reason or right to exist. This is something extraordinary. Other more competent persons may wish to try to compare this idea with Buddhist or Zen or Indian philosophical systems. My knowledge of these systems is too slight to allow me to try, and so I'm going to show that this idea of living in a world which doesn't carry within itself the reason for its own existence, but gets it from an absolutely necessary, personal, ever-creating God belongs to the unique axiomatic certainties of the twelfth, thirteenth, and fourteenth centuries. At this moment, the world's very existence takes on the character of something gratuitous. The world which is around me, the cat over there and the four red roses which bloomed during the night are a gift, something which is a grace. This moment of our being together, which I'm enjoying immensely, is not predetermined by some *karma*, isn't chance, isn't logically necessary, but rather is a pure gift. It's a gift from that Creator who keeps beings in existence, and, by understanding things in this way, we can also see our own activity in sitting here in an entirely new light.

Now let me return to Blumenberg. The coming into existence of the antique cosmos, the cosmos of Aristotle, the cosmos of Plato, he says, was in no way dependent on the act of someone's will. The coming into being and the continuation of the world was simply an expression of its fitness for existence. Contingency played no part. This sense of things began to change with Augustine. Augustine answered the question of why God created the world with the incredible assertion *Quia vult*, because it pleased him, because he willed it, because he wanted it. In Spanish, I would say, *Porque me da ganas*. You can't quite catch the flavour of *ganas* in English, but it refers to a will which comes from pretty deep in the stomach. The world's existence, in this view, is the result at every moment of a sovereign act. One consequence of this strange belief in the sovereignty of will, of One will, of God's will is that it allows Scholasticism to make a distinction between essence and existence, between what things are and that they are — "cat" doesn't yet mean that there's a cat there — a distinction which also indicates the structure of the whole cosmos. It could just as well be that God would not have made us the gift of bringing this or that thing into existence.

According to Blumenberg, the scope of the idea of contingency expanded during the Middle Ages. In Dante [1265–1321], on whom I was fed as a kid, the operation of contingency in his *Paradiso* reaches only to the sphere of the moon, which is still within the Aristotelian scheme of things. For the Christian of the fourteenth or fifteenth centuries, it reaches beyond the moon. God himself is dragged into the realm of contingency. The will of God, Duns Scotus[2] says, is its own cause. This emphasis on the freedom of God which one finds in the Franciscan tradition of Bonaventure,[3] Duns Scotus, and Francis himself, and which is so unsatisfactory to the modern mind, has two sides, and I'm speaking now as one who was strongly tempted by the great Franciscans. Bonaventure, for instance, brought God nearer to me by making him more like me. And absolute resignation before the will of God is something profoundly beautiful. But, it is also true that the emphasis on the supremacy and inscrutability of God's will in

Franciscan philosophy is finally pushed to the point where this will becomes arbitrary. Contingency at this point takes on the meaning which it still has today in English and French: mere chance, or instance. All one can say about what happens is that it happens because it happens.

One already sees this voluntarism, as Blumenberg calls it, in the thought of St. Thomas Aquinas [1225?–1274], but there it still remains poised and balanced, not yet tipping over into arbitrariness. Thomas, as you know, was important to me, both as a counterweight to the Franciscan tradition, and in a biographical sense. One of the great moments of my life, a moment when I was both proud of myself and humbled as never before or afterwards came when Jacques Maritain[4] had a heart attack while teaching at Princeton. I was then a twenty-six-year-old guy working as a parish priest among Puerto Ricans in New York, and I got a call from the Institute for Advanced Studies asking me to take over the seminar Maritain had been conducting on Thomas's *De Esse et Essentia*, his crucial book on the issue we're discussing today.

Thomas makes a distinction between the possible and the necessary, rather than between the possible and the real, and it is the hypothesis of some recent scholarly writing on Thomas that Thomas wouldn't have arrived at this distinction if he had not been under the influence, coming from southern Italy, of Arab thinkers and holy men. The life of these men was marked, as you know, and is still marked by the recitation five times a day of a prayer in which Allah is referred to as the womb of what is and what is necessary: *Bismillahi rahmani rahim*. In this formula *rahim* means "the merciful, the all-good," but the word literally means womb, or more precisely the particular movements of the womb when it is inflamed by love.

Thomas senses the presence of God in everything and even every idea of which he can conceive, and not because this is the law of reality but because this is his goodness and his will. But, for Thomas, this will remains shrouded in the mystery of God, who is, above all, truth, truth beyond any conception, any imagination, truth which we better not even call "truth" because it is so far away from what we ordinarily call truth. And truth is good. And this sense of mystery keeps

Aquinas balanced, and not yet on the slope that leads towards modernity. One has to say, however, that a conception of God's will as arbitrary is latent in Thomas's conception of God as the supreme intellectual, and in this sense he does prepare the way for an understanding of the world outside of contingency.

Blumenberg argues that the beginning of modernity coincides with an attempt to break out of a world-view defined overwhelmingly by contingency. With the late Franciscans like William of Ockham [1285?–1349?] things still are what they are by the will of God; in the thought of René Descartes [1596–1650] each being finds in its own nature, what it is in itself, a reason and a claim, not only to existence, but to being what it is. Things are no longer what they are because they correspond to God's will but because God has laid into what we now call nature the laws by which they evolve. You can see the consequences of this idea in caricature in the genome project which is giving skyscraper-like visibility to a world in which contingency has become chance within genetic codes. For a long time, through the seventeenth, eighteenth, and even into the early nineteenth century, many of Descartes's successors remained true Christian believers who affirmed that God made the world as it is by placing the seed of nature into each thing. But the possibility of understanding things without reference to God had been created, because once God's will has become totally arbitrary it has also become, in a sense, redundant, and the connection between God and the world can be easily cut.

Contingency, in this sense, is a precondition for the modern view that each of us contains and possesses our own *raison d'etre*. But I want to be as clear as I can about this term precondition. I am trying to point to notions which, in my opinion, can only be explained as the fruit of a widely shared understanding of the newness of the Gospel. And I use the word notions, in preference to category, concept, idea or word, in order to try and convey the involvement of feelings, feelings about the self, the other, and the world, as well as a certain conceptual and linguistic shaping. I am trying to put things as prudently as I can, but this is my research hypothesis, and I feel it would be wrong to allow myself to be deflected from it. I believe that this understanding of the newness of the Gospel, the coming of this fool who was crucified, is something which goes on over the centuries. There is no other way, in my opinion, to explain the way in which St. Thomas Aquinas unfolds the notion of contingency in his voluminous, cathedral-like pages except as a digestion and penetration of Gospel truths, truths about the Incarnation, the embodiment, the enfleshment and mutuality of love. And I call the discovery, shaping, and full formulation of this notion a precondition for modernity, not because modernity is founded on the idea of contingency, but because it was only in a society in which people had strongly experienced the world as lying in the hands of God that it would be possible, later on, to take that world out of God's hands.

One way of illustrating this is to look at the change in the meaning of nature between classical and modern times, as the historian Carolyn Merchant has done in an easily understandable book called *The Death of Nature*. One thing was certain in antiquity: nature was alive. There were different and conflicting philosophical interpretations of what nature was; but to all of them was common the certainty that *natura nacitura dicitur*,[5] that nature is a concept, an idea, an experience derived from birth-giving. Therefore, if we say of things that they are "natural," we say they are "born." This idea is deeply affected in the twelfth century by the sense of contingency. The whole of nature lay in God's hands, where it acquired its aliveness through God's constant, creative support. And Merchant quite correctly argues that, with this elevation, and, for me, glorification of classical nature, the condition was created by which, once nature was taken out of the hands of God, it could also lose its most essential quality, which is its aliveness. If, therefore, we look into the rise of natural science, and science altogether, in the seventeenth and eighteenth centuries, we are faced with research on a nature which not only lies outside of the hands of God, but has lost that basic characteristic of aliveness, which it had all through antiquity in our tradition. And once you have to do with a science which studies the working of a nature no longer alive — you can call it mechanical, you can call it necessary or give it any name you want — an issue comes up, which is characteristically modern: How do you explain, how do you speak about life in a nature and among natural things which are not born but are, so to speak, mathematically programmed?

So contingency creates the condition whereby, in the sunset of contingency, nature loses not only its relationship to God, which was given to it in the high Middle Ages in this clear and explicit form, but also another characteristic which had nothing to do with Christianity: its aliveness. Modern science pre-supposes a nature which is not alive. But its precondition was the linking of the aliveness of nature with the constant creative activity of God. So we have to be very careful here because we are speaking about new insights which, for me, are very frequently glorious new discoveries, steps forward in the assimilation of the New Testament, but which also open up new possibilities of perversion and betrayal. A contingent nature at its noon is gloriously alive, but it is also uniquely vulnerable to being purified and cleaned of its aliveness in the sunset of contingency. And I have to see the newness of this concept in order to be fully aware of what is lost in its sunset and, ultimately, in the night which follows. What is dragged into oblivion is not just the Christian interpretation of nature, which I used here as an example. Classical Mediterranean certainties about nature, so deep that they are never discussed, are also enveloped in this night. To say it once more: once the universe is taken out of God's hands, it can be placed into the hands of people, and this couldn't have happened without nature having been put in God's hands in the first place.

4

CONTINGENCY, PART 2:
THE ORIGIN OF TECHNOLOGY

At this point, I want to take up a connected, and, I think, equally pregnant notion, and that is the idea of cause. This is an idea that has not been sufficiently studied by historians, but I believe that in the twelfth century there was change in the meaning of this word which was connected with the way in which the sense and the feel and the thought of contingency then permeated society. Up to this time, when philosophers spoke about *causa* — allow me to stay with the Latin, in order to indicate that I mean the idea of cause as it was then understood — they spoke in the tradition of Aristotle as it was fed to them through that great bureaucrat and saintly semi-martyr Boethius [480?–524?] and later on through Isidore of Seville [560?–636], another great bridgehead in the transmission of the meaning of Latin words to the high Middle Ages. *Causa*, in the Aristotelian scheme, has four subdivisions. There's *causa efficiens*, which refers to the source, or the reason, or the motive for an occurrence. If I move this pencil from here to there, then I'm the efficient cause of the movement. Then, there's a second reason why a thing is what it is, a reason we no longer call a cause, and that's the *causa materialis*, the material cause which refers to the character of the stuff out of which it is made. Next comes the *causa formalis*, the formal cause. It refers to the soul, or genetic plan of a thing — the formal principle that gives a cherry tree its unique and characteristic

wood, leaf, flower, and fruit. And, finally, there's a fourth reason for
being, the *causa finalis*. Things are what they are because they are
ordered to a given end. They have a goal, or proper purpose. *Scientia*,
for the first Christian millennium, consisted in understanding what
things are in the light of this fourfold structure.

Then, in the thirteenth century, something new and strange
appeared in philosophy. I will speak of philosophy first because
philosophers express the mentality, and the cultural certainties, of
their time; but, as you will see in a moment, I am speaking of society
as much as of the ideas of a handful of monks in a few newly founded
university chairs. At the beginning of the thirteenth century, the *causa
efficiens*, the only one of Aristotle's four causes that we still call a
cause, got, so to speak, a stepchild. The category of *causa efficiens*
developed a new sub-category called the *causa instrumentalis*, which
was a cause without intention.

Now, if you ask me how I stumbled on this interesting development, to which no one else, so far as I know, has yet given any
importance, I would have to say that this is because no one else has
had the luck and the burden of studying scholastic philosophy as a
friend of Carl Mitcham's. Carl Mitcham — I can't help but drag him
in here — is a man considerably younger than I who taught at Penn
State at the same time as I did and who has an extraordinarily vast
knowledge of people who have written on what is now called the
philosophy of technology. He's a kind of universal geographer of this
field, who can tell you who's who and where each one stands and
which river of thought runs close by and through which mountains
the river runs, and so forth. When McGrath asked him to write an
article on the philosophy of technology for the final volume of its
revised *Encyclopaedia of Philosophy*, he claimed that technology
hadn't yet made it into the hard core of philosophical thought
because philosophers, and I would add historians as well, have always
dealt with the concept of "tool" as if it were primordial and had
always been around. Mitcham questioned this, and, with him, I
learned to question it too.

Now, I'm the author of a book called *Tools for Conviviality*. When
I wrote that book, I also believed that the idea of a tool as a means

shaped to my arbitrary purpose had always been around. But, if you look more carefully at what happened in the thirteenth century, this is not true. It's true that Aristotle has magnificent pages about the working devices used by smiths or woodworkers or jewellers, but what he speaks about are the *organa*. The word *organon* means both this pencil which I am holding in my hand, and the hand which holds it. My hand without the pencil, and my hand armed with the pencil are both *organa*. There was no way of distinguishing the pencil from my hand. *Instrumentum* had mainly a legal meaning, but not the meaning a legal instrument has today. It could not yet distinguish a tool from its user. Only in the thirteenth century was a *causa instrumentalis* distinguished as a subset of *causa efficiens*. Here lies the beginning of the possibility of putting together in one box, as I did in *Tools for Conviviality*, a car, a school, a scalpel, and an axe and seeing something in common between them. By this time tools or instruments in this new sense were already part of common, everyday speech. This is shown by two books which appeared simultaneously in 1128, *De variis artibus*, in which a pseudonymous monk calling himself Theophilus Presbyter writes on the instruments used by various artisans, and Hugh of St. Victor's *Didascalicon*, in which Hugh writes about the science of mechanics, the first time anyone has ever done so. The Latin word for mechanics derives from the Greek for machine, but Hugh has his character Dindimus give the term a revealing fantasy derivation, claiming that it comes from the word for adulterer, *moichos*. *Moichos* refers to "sowing wild oats," as one might say in English, and the term applies because this new kind of *causa efficiens*, which has no purpose in itself but only obeys the intention with which it is used, has, at first, a wild, not quite legitimate character. Tools are helpers which act partly like God and partly according to the laws of God, and, in this way, constitute a kind of wild oats.

Now, where did this idea, for which I think contingency was a precondition, come from? This question was answered, for me, by the work of a neglected and forgotten historian by the name of Theodor Litt,[1] who some twenty-five years ago wrote a book on the heavenly bodies. I said a few minutes ago that, up to the time of Dante, one could still suppose with Aristotle that beneath the sphere of the moon contingency, in the sense of chance, governs our affairs. Chance ruled the world of animals and plants and impersonally allocated fortune and misfortune. But, then this idea was replaced by a radically new conception of contingency, a conception which saw the entire cosmos as dependent at every instant on a personal, creative source. What Mr. Litt called to my attention were the limitations of the Thomists, like Jacques Maritain and Étienne Gilson who were my teachers. Litt is able to show that when these scholars quote Aquinas on the motions of the heavenly bodies, they truncate his sentences in order to spare their modern students the distraction and embarrassment of recognizing that Thomas takes it as an obvious reality that angels govern the spheres of the planets and are appointed by God to do so.

When I had compiled a list of, perhaps, twenty-five such misleading and slightly ashamed sentences in my teachers, Carl Mitcham and I went back to Thomas Aquinas and re-read his teaching about the heavenly bodies. And what we discovered was a universe of continuous creation, lying continuously in the hands of God, a universe that would disappear if his hands disappeared, and which is necessary only insofar as it depends on his will. To contemplate such a universe was to cultivate a sense of contingency, a sense of having received as a free gift one's own existence and the existence of everything which God has invented and brought forth; and this sense, in my view, saturated social life. In a universe conceived in this way, the question of how God governs the world had to be re-thought. Christian popular culture had already been imbued for six or seven hundred years by neo-Platonist ideas, conceptions and images, which pictured the universe as a spiritual hierarchy governed by a King much greater even then Charlemagne. In this picture the administrators of the great King's rule were angels who took over for him the governance of the different planetary spheres. And angels, as one knows, are pure spirits. They have no *materia*; they're not juicy beings. They are beings of pure fire, an extraordinary fire which is taken from God. So these angels had to be given *media*, intermediaries, means by which they could influence the area of material reality which they were to govern. These were called the heavenly bodies. And in order to allow the immaterial angel to make contact with reality through the spheres, the spheres had to be conceived as a special type of *causa efficiens*, which was totally obedient to the intentional user, who is the angel.

For the moment, I'm pretty much alone among historians of science in pointing to a world conceived in the spirit of contingency as the origin of the modern conception of tools. And I can only hope that this beautiful discovery will stimulate others to pursue the proof or disproof of something which seems obvious to me, but which, scientifically, remains a hypothesis. But if this is true, then there's a deep connection between the appearance of tools and the ways in which popular piety explained the connection between the macro- and the micro-cosmos and the ways in which this connection was expressed in architecture, in poetry, and in the great miniatures of the time. If angels have tools, why shouldn't all professions, all estates — they then spoke of it more that way — have tools or devices? Why shouldn't it then be legitimate to speak about the tools of production? Why shouldn't it be possible to think about objects of daily use as products of human intention and the use of the appropriate tool?

It should be clear by this point that I think that modern technological society stands in the same relation to this discovery of tools, as the death of nature does to the discovery of nature as a continuous and contingent creation. It was in order to make thinkable the mystical experience of God's constant creative activity that people began to reflect on the intermediaries that allowed an almost Byzantine, Western Emperor-God to administer the world. And, as a consequence, the idea arose that God's people participated in this ability to make and to use tools. That was Hugh of St. Victor's brilliant idea. Hugh supposes that God at first placed the soft, furless, clawless, virtually toothless human beings he had created in a paradisical garden where these would not be disadvantages; but, because they sinned and took the apple from the forbidden tree, nature changed and became inhospitable to them. So, in order to give them a chance to survive in this new milieu, for which they weren't created, but in which they now had to live as a punishment for sin, God gave them a consolation, a *remedium* for the consequences of sin, which he calls the mechanical arts of which I spoke a moment ago. Just as God's angels use tools, so men have learned how to be weavers and smiths, carpenters and cobblers in order to protect themselves against the cold and to be able to walk on this world, full of thorns. In imitating God's use of instruments, they don't create but only make things which are a necessary remedy in their fallen condition.

This is Hugh's refined, glorious, and original account of how and why people became tool users. He wrote it, as I have said, at the beginning of the twelfth century, which was a period of extraordinary technological change. I won't go into detail here, but iron production expanded enormously, and the power of water was used for the first time, not only to turn mills, but to drive the hammers that broke up ore, and the claws that prepared wool to be spun and woven in the proto-industries of men like St. Francis's father in Perugia. Technological development was intense, but the newly discovered tool still had something black, something not quite respectable about it. The mechanics, as they were called, who knew how to repair mills, were still considered slightly fey, as though they might be in touch with the devil. It was only with the sunset and eventual disappearance of the sense of contingency, when the world fell from the hands of God into the hands of man, and constraints on technological development began to fall away, that the tool could be unreservedly glorified, and the way opened for a fully technological society.

"Okay, Ivan," you'll say, "why in the world should this matter to those who study the philosophy of technology?" I'll tell you right away: Everybody whom I have gotten in touch with, intellectually, through Mitcham, every single one of these people believes that the tool, device, medium, instrument, whatever you call such a free-standing means, is a natural, obvious, inevitable, and timeless concept. I can demonstrate this, in caricature, with a story. Some ten years ago, I was called in by the director of the Bavarian National Museum, who had been put in charge of creating a museum of schools by the Bavarian minister of education. By this time, half of the design was complete and couldn't be changed because of budget limitations. This man who was the director wanted to rethink the second half of the museum because he had understood from my book *Deschooling Society* that education was not something people always needed, nor "tools" something which had always existed. He wanted to put these ideas into question in the second half of the museum, and, as a result, there's a museum in Lower Bavaria where, on one side, educational needs and man-the-tool-user are taken for granted and on the other side these ideas are, in a museum fashion, questioned. But my point here concerns the first half. When you enter this museum, the first thing which faces you is a huge fresco, where you see Mother Neanderthal cooking and Father Neanderthal carving the Venus of Willendorf, that marvellously fatty, oldest sculpture of a woman in European archaeology and, in the process, teaching Little Boy Neanderthal how you use tools.

Now this is the sort of thing I would expect from educators, but from philosophers I expect something more. And Mitcham's insight really makes it necessary to say that tools, devices, society's accent on instrumentality, and its preoccupation with means of production and management are things that have a beginning, which I would set in the course of the thirteenth, fourteenth, and fifteenth centuries. And everything which has a beginning in history might have an end. If it is true that "tool" is an age or epoch-specific concept which is characteristic of a certain period, a period during which the concept of tool, or technology, as one more often says, becomes perhaps the most unquestionable of everyday certainties, then the possibility is opened of doing what I have been trying to do during the last fifteen or twenty years: to claim, or, at least, establish the hypothesis that sometime during the 1980s the technological society which began in the fourteenth century came to an end. Now I recognize that dating epochs involves interpretation and perhaps some fuzziness in assigning beginnings and endings; but, nevertheless, it appears to me that the age of tools has now given way to the age of systems, exemplified in the conception of the earth as an ecosystem, and the human being as an immune system. I was not aware of this watershed, when I wrote many of my earlier books, and I am at fault for having persuaded some very good people who read me seriously that it makes sense to talk about a school system as a social tool, or about the medical establishment as a device. Strangely one of these old students, Max Peschek, a man who came late to the university, never finished, and now ekes out a living as a tango teacher in Bremen, has been conducting a seminar among his friends about the fundamental mistake of Ivan Illich. What Illich did not understand, according to Peschek, and he is certainly right, is that when you become the user of a system, you become part of the system. The distinction between the hand and the thing which it holds, which became fundamental for thinking in the thirteenth century, has disappeared. Thinking about the world, not in terms of causality, but in terms of systems analysis has brought us into a very new era, into which we couldn't have come if we hadn't moved out of the world of tools. And the world of tools, I'll say it once more, could not have taken the shape it did without the adoption throughout society for a few hundred years of the explicit spirit of contingency.

To this point I have not pointed my finger at the Church, which will surprise the friend who once asked me, Ivan, why is it that you always lay such stress on the Catholic Church in the twelfth century? And I said, Because I'm speaking only of Western Europe, and there *is* nothing else. And there is, of course, a Church connection in this case. The concept of *causa instrumentalis* had barely been enunciated, when the great theologians of the late twelfth and early thirteenth centuries began to speak about a new device called a sacrament, another churchy idea with which I'll have to frighten non-Christian listeners.

If, in some way, the ritual presence of the Church in a Europe increasingly structured and influenced by it can be put into one command, one mission, that mission was *omnia benedicere*. There was nothing which shouldn't be blessed, blessed in the sense of praising God for having made it: the newborn baby, the woman who has survived childbirth, the wedding ceremony, the marriage bed. Praise God for its existence. *Benedicere* also meant to put something under the special protection of God, to ask God not only to hold it in his hand, but to put the other hand on top of it. I happen to have been a pupil of a man who wrote a four-volume study on the benedictions of the Middle Ages. You would be amazed at all the things which can be blessed — even compost had a special blessing.

In the thirteenth century, theologians, following, no doubt, an old tradition, found the term *instrumentum* extremely useful for naming

seven among these blessings as so special as to require the separate
category of sacraments. Blessings and sacraments became separated
from each other. Blessings can be pronounced by anyone, whether
householder, priest, or Pope, who is within the Church and wants to
praise God and ask him at this moment to look with particular favour
on something. Sacraments are something else. They are actions
which require an instrument. This instrument is deployed by a
human being and then used by God himself as a device to accomplish, and to accomplish, inevitably, a certain purpose. Take water, say,
"I baptize you in the name of the Father and the Son and the Holy
Ghost," and I will be a member of the Church, even if the one who
baptizes me — this is the extreme case — is a pagan. Correct performance of these seven rites constrains God to use them as
instrumental causes towards the desired end. They thought about the
sacraments as *instrumenta divina*, and this new thinking about sacraments became one of the foci of Church renewal in the thirteenth,
fourteenth, and fifteenth centuries, as well as a major point of discussion in the period of the religious wars following upon the
Reformation.

5

THE CRIMINALIZATION OF SIN

In order to introduce the topic of this talk, I first have to introduce Paolo Prodi, who has been my teacher on this subject. Paolo and I met a good thirty years ago, when he had a scholarship at the Woodrow Wilson Institution in Washington. And there, in conversation with him, I found for the first time someone with whom I could discuss a point to which our common teacher, Gerhart Ladner, had led us. Ladner's preoccupation was the idea of reform — he wrote a book of that name — which he felt could not be understood unless one first grasped the Old Testament idea of an inner turning around, a turning inside out and upside down. This becomes in the New Testament the concept of conversion, and reconversion to the Other, the Friend, who is, of course, God become man, but who is known through the one who faces me at the moment. Ladner insisted on the unprecedented evil which can result from this unprecedented commitment to reform. He believed that a recognition of this evil was essential to the understanding of Western history and, at the very same time, he recognized that such a recognition was possible only for those who accepted the radical newness of the idea of reform as embodied in certain monastic communities which adopted it as a lifelong, theocentric practice of mutual conversion.

With Paolo I had, for the first time, an opportunity of reflecting, with a man several years younger than I, on the way in which the Western, Roman Church attempted to give a juridical shape to the household rules by which monastic communities lived together. This attempt to create a canonical establishment, that's the technical term, out of the way of life of Franciscans or Dominicans, was the only way of preserving a certain spirit in an institutional form, but it produced a deep corruption. It led, as it has always led historically, even in the first generation, to a toning down of the message of the founder and to an abstract formulation of the melody in which he sang the Gospel. We've already talked about this.

Again and again Paolo and I met. He became a fully recognized academic, chairman of history at the University of Bologna, founder of the Institute of Italo-Germanic Historical Studies in Trento, rector of the University of Trento, and president, for many years, of the commission which appoints all humanity professors in Italy. (Unhappily, of the eighty-two items by Paolo Prodi that I was able to discover in the Library of Congress Catalogue, which I can now search on-line from Mexico, only one is available in English.) On the subject which I'm about to broach, I bow to his authority and feel pretty certain that he is right, and I say this having also carefully read his critics and satisfied myself that I am not allowing friendship to outshine my critical intelligence. But I would hardly dare to say what I'm about to say, if he were looking over my shoulder, because I will take liberties which are neither academically legitimate, nor necessarily kind. I'm sure, if he reads it later, he will bear with me.

I want to speak about the twelfth century, a period which I regard as an important historical hinge. Some of the reasons are subjective. There is no other period in which I dare to speak of my personal acquaintance with as large a percentage of the surviving authors. And my acquaintance with these authors has long made me puzzle over their extraordinarily fresh way with language and with concepts. Learned writing at this period was still overwhelmingly in Latin, though vernacular literatures had begun to appear, but it was a Latin unlike the dull, incompetent church and kitchen Latin of the eleventh century. There was a renaissance, but a renaissance unlike that of the fifteenth-century humanists who wanted to get back to classical Latin and modelled their styles on Cicero and Livy. The writers of the twelfth century invented a new Latin style, according to what they had to say, and made it beautiful. How it happened is a mystery, and something of which few students are even aware.

The twelfth century can be interpreted as a turning point. I know that historians choose what they will write their poetry about, and that some other scholar more conversant with the time of Charlemagne might claim the same for the Carolingian renaissance, but I think there really is a turning point there. It is the time, as I've already discussed, when the idea of a tool comes into existence. It's the time in which the idea of text detaches itself from the actual, gooey word-stuff on the page and becomes something more general and immaterial.[1] And, it's the time — to come at last to my theme — when sin is criminalized.

We have already spoken about sin as a new kind of evil that shadowed the Christian possibility of finding God in the face of the other. This new kind of love made possible a new kind of very personal betrayal and demanded a new practice of mutual forgiveness and forbearance amongst those who accepted this Gospel. In the sixth, seventh, and eighth centuries sin became connected with doing penance. And, then, in the twelfth century, the Church found it desirable, for reasons which I'll explore in a moment, to define that intimate betrayal of the friend, or of God as a crime.

I want to look at three issues which touch on this movement of criminalization, or legalization, in the twelfth century: the history of the oath, the history of marriage, and the way in which the institution of confession became a device with which to lay the foundations of the modern state. But I need to ask you first to remember that, in my explorations of how religiosity materializes previously unthought notions and makes them fleshy and impressive, I'm speaking in a Western, and at this date, entirely European context. Even Orthodox Christianity was outside this Western development, at least until the nineteenth century when the Russian czars decided they wanted to have a church as good as that of the Pope.

Remember, also, that what I will say emerges from a continuing conversation with perhaps two dozen people of whom Prodi is one. If I speak about this group as a "we," it is because we recognize that, as intellectuals, we have the common task of trying to understand the cultural density of our time by exploring its formative axioms which have now disappeared. And this can only be done by establishing a certain distance from the present and trying to look at today with twelfth-century eyes. If, for example, I attempt an imaginary conversation with Peter Abelard [1079–1144?], I have to deprive myself of the assumptions that suffuse the words we use today. Such an imaginary conversation can be an extraordinarily effective heuristic device because it forces me to look critically — *cum grano salis*, with a little bit of salt, as the Romans said — at every word which I use in conversation today. This gaze into the present through the eyes of people who had faith can reveal what remains hidden to those who probe the past with the abstract instruments of contemporary social science.

And one final prefatory remark for those who may think I am less an historian than a novelist who happens to know Latin very well, and has read huge amounts of secondary literature about the twelfth century as well as the primary sources: I admit that I strongly believe in something which is usually called tradition. There is a physical and bodily tie with earlier generations, which makes the type of history I am doing something more than just dredging up memories. And, by placing myself in the tradition of twelfth century thinkers, I become aware of the search for Christian perfection, for the flowering of the gifts of the Holy Spirit, that animated these men. They cultivated a charity which couldn't have been financed through taxes, a charity which expressed a love more free than would have been possible without Christ's example. They felt they had been invited to love God in the flesh, as the son of Mary, and this faith was the ground of the concepts and the certainties with which they lived.

I have to begin my exposition by pointing out certain technological changes that were occurring in Europe at the time because they underlie the turn in Christian religiosity which took place in the twelfth century. The horse collar was invented, and this immensely increased the pulling power of horses and allowed them to replace oxen, which were much slower, in ploughing the deep, wet soils of Europe. This increase in speed, range, and efficiency meant that fields could be located much further from home and that the cultivators could live together in villages and still reach their fields. This consolidation led to the establishment of parishes, centred on the parish church. Christian rural life ceased to be a dispersed style of life in tiny hamlets and became community-centred. In common speech the parish came to mean the community, and I believe in English law the word parish still refers to a secular entity.

Religious practices were an intimate part of this new sense of locality. There were, for example, special devotions based on relics: we have the right arm of such and such a martyr, and we will concede to you a fragment of it if you establish a village which is friendly but far enough away not to interfere with us. Days devoted to the cult of a certain saint became market days. Religiosity, word fields, and fundamental concepts interweave and intertwine, and this interweaving of religion and society gives the European peasant or villager his special character, which distinguishes him from the farmer of the New World. It was in this milieu, that the Church developed practices intended to support and stabilize the Christian practice of neighbourliness, practices which would then survive into a world without villages in which they no longer had the same application.

It was in this new world of parishes that we see a striking change in the nature of oaths. And here I am closely following the argument in a glorious lecture of Paolo Prodi's. By the thirteenth century oath-taking had become fundamental to European culture, in a way it had never been before. In the twelfth century, for example, the Church defined the formation of the basic cell of society, namely, the family, as a mutual contract made by two free people who choose each other and confirm their choice by an oath sworn before God. The oath makes the marriage a sacrament, so called, which places it under God's seal and protection. To see how very surprising it is that the oath could become a Christian entity, a Christian practice — I'm speaking now as a pupil of Prodi's, may he forgive me — you have to recall that there is, in the New Testament, nothing more absolutely forbidden than oath-taking. Let me quote the verses from the Sermon on the Mount as they are found in Matthew, Chapter 5, in the Jerusalem translation: "You have heard how it was said to our ancestors, 'You must not break your oath, but must fulfill your oaths to the Lord.' But, I say this to you, do not swear at all, either by

heaven, since that is God's throne; or by earth, since that is his foot-
stool . . . Do not swear by your own head either, since you cannot turn
a single hair white or black. All you need to say is 'Yes' if you mean
yes, 'No' if you mean no. Anything more than this comes from the
Evil One." This is again one of those rule-breaking innovations of
the New Testament. The importance of oath-taking was as certain
and as fundamental as the existence of a threshold over which I can
bring a guest, or the local boundaries which establish the nature of
virtue in a particular place. It was, if you like, one of the fundamentals of feeling human, an anthropological constant. All cultures seem
to possess this possibility of giving special weight to a statement, to
an utterance, by making it clear that I'm taking my own flesh and
blood into my mouth when I say it. Women, characteristically, take
their hair into their hands when they take an oath; a man may
take his balls or a piece of his soil into his hands. The Norseman
holds on to his ship. By oath-taking, I incarnate my own statement.

So the total proscription of oath-taking in the New Testament is
something radically new, and what I would like to understand is why
and in which context does Jesus proscribe oath-taking? He does so
in the context of the covenant between God and his people. The
covenant of the Old Testament consisted in God taking an oath
to Abraham. It is his prerogative to take an oath and, thereby, establish Abraham and his descendants as his people. People do not swear
before God. Only God incarnates himself in the word of the
prophets and in his people. The New Testament continues this
covenant and excludes the oath. Instead of joining people through
an oath, the New Testament proposes to unite them in the Holy
Spirit. This is historical fact, not theology or preaching, and it was
understood in a very physical way. The high point of Christian ritual and ceremony still consists in a communal meal of bread and
wine, a *symposium*, but in the first centuries of Christianity there was
also *conspiratio*, that is a breathing into each others' mouths. That's
what Christians did. They came together to eat and to kiss, to kiss
on the mouth. In this way they shared the Holy Spirit and became
members of a community in flesh, blood, and spirit; and so long as
this ritual remained the basic way of constituting the community,

there was no sense of *conjuratio*, that is of establishing community by swearing to each other. It is, therefore, very surprising to find that oaths only became part of Roman law under one of the early Christian Emperors, Theodosius, whose Codex first recognized oaths as a legal instrument.

Prodi examines how this could happen, how people could tire under the enormous burden imposed on the ordinary word of having to be always truthful, and how this could lead them to make an institution of their mutual engagement by calling on God to witness their oaths. This re-introduction of oaths reaches an epochal point in the twelfth century at the height of feudalism, which was based on *conjuratio*, or oath-taking. It was then that the relation of love in its supreme form, the commitment of a man and a woman to each other forever, on the model of the Gospel, became defined as a juridical act, through which an entity called marriage comes into existence. And for this juridical act, God becomes, so to speak, the necessary instrumentality when he is summoned as a witness. The fealty of citizens in Europe's expanding cities was conceived along the same lines — as a contract sealed by a divinely-witnessed oath. This *conjuratio*, or swearing together, in the face of God, gives the European city the particular quality of sacredness which it takes on between the thirteenth and fifteenth centuries. It reaches a high point when Girolamo Savonarola [1452–1498] chases the Medicis out of Florence and insists on the God-willed basis of city-life in the *conjuratio* of the citizens.

It is surprising to me that medieval historians have not really noticed this. When they speak about a contractual society coming into existence during the twelfth, thirteenth, and fourteenth centuries in Europe, and then becoming a model for the modern state in the late Renaissance and on into the nineteenth century with the establishment of the nation state, they locate the origins of this society in the *conjuratio*, the swearing-together of burghers and artisans which allowed them to regulate their trades and commerce under the protection of a feudal lord. I think the emergence of this type of society can be discerned even earlier, and I would point particularly to the Fourth Lateran Council (1215), where marriage was defined in this new way.

Someone who *has* noticed the novelty of this type of marriage is the anthropologist Jack Goody. Goody travelled the world like a butterfly collector, gathering the many forms of marriage, and he wrote marvellous stuff about how it is done from place to place: if the marriage is arranged by the parents or the uncles, if consent is required and so on. Then, when Goody returned to England as an older man, he realized that Western thinking about marriage is unique. It had never existed before and could not be found anywhere else. Never had it happened that Joan would bring Johnny home and say to her father, "Johnny's the man I'm going to marry." Getting Joan and John married had been an affair among patriarchs, or an affair of families or go-betweens. The idea that marriage is a free, individual act modelled on that freedom in the spirit which we have received through the parable of the Samaritan was unthinkable. So Goody went to some friends, who were medievalists, and asked them to help him to write a book on medieval marriage. The resulting book² was an extraordinary breakthrough, but it was also full of mistakes, and this allowed most medievalists to dismiss the book. What does Jack Goody know of the Middle Ages? they said. Their anger and their prejudice prevented them from reading him carefully.

Within the perspective of the Gospel, adultery had taken on a new and unprecedented standing. In the old story of Susanna and the elders in the book of Daniel, Susanna would have been legally stoned had she been found guilty of tempting the two old men who observed her nakedness as she bathed in the pond in her garden, but no Jew would have imputed sin to her in the modern sense. In the teaching of Jesus even the most secret of imagined adulteries is seen as an infidelity which is offensive not only to your wife but also to God, to Christ, in whom we are united in the flesh through his act of love. Then, in the twelfth century, this sinful infidelity became a crime. The marriage oath legalizes love, and sin becomes a juridical category. Christ came to free us from the law, but Christianity allowed the legal mentality to be brought into the very heart of love.

My point here is not to impute fault to the theologians and church lawyers who reconceived the union of a man and a woman as a Christian marriage in the twelfth and thirteenth centuries. What I'm trying to emphasize is what Jack Goody noticed: the sheer novelty of the idea that a man and a woman can contract with each other in the matter of their intimate access to one another, which is precisely what the Lateran Council talked about. The idea that households are founded by the free choice of one man and one woman marks a major epoch in the formation of the individual. It is the first attempt to give women the same status as men and to attribute to them the same legal and physiological capacities. Marriage is torn out of the family and community nexus in which it was formerly embedded and put into the hands of individuals. And this is the foundation of the idea that social entities come into existence by mutual contract.

I also want to draw attention to the fact that, in the new legislation about marriage, for the first time in history — and there are good historians who have studied this — the woman's consent to the desire and will of her future husband is just as important as his will in relation to her. In Rome, when one spoke about *consensus*, it meant that the father had asked the son, "Are you willing to shack up with Flavia?" In the case of the woman, the idea of having the father or the family or the uncles seek her consent begins to appear only in the late ninth and early tenth centuries. There is, for example, at that date, a record of an aristocratic woman from Brittany, who appeals to the Pope for relief from her husband's abuse and says that she had always resisted the idea that she should become this man's wife. To the best of my knowledge, the first clear statement by a woman that she is a wife by virtue of her consent is made by Héloïse, in one of her letters to Abelard. She was by then already a nun, but she wrote to him that she was and would always remain his wife because she had freely consented to their liaison. If I had the skill I would write a novel about Abelard and, and in it there would be a scene in the Paris tavern where Abelard played his songs. Sitting there, by chance, would be the old monk Gratian, from Bologna, who first codified church law; and he would watch as Héloïse, having escaped her uncle's house through a window, entered the tavern and explained to Abelard her revolutionary conception of marriage. It would be from this overheard conversation in a Paris tavern, according to my conceit, that the great lawyer and jurist would take the idea that marriage is created by the free consent of a man and a woman.

But, to return to my main theme, Prodi has promised me that if I can wait another seven years, he will present me with the finished manuscript of a book in which he will argue that this extraordinary criminalization of sin holds the key to understanding Western political concepts for the next 500 years. In the meantime, I can only look at chapters, but these already show how this could happen. Part of his explanation concerns the struggles over the power of investiture which took place in the tenth and eleventh centuries. Investiture is the power to name, or invest, a bishop, and the Pope and the Emperor each claimed that he was uniquely competent to do this. This period was also an epoch in the history of law during which it came to be understood that the Emperor and the Pope had separate and distinct jurisdictions, within which each was solely capable of making laws. Two courts, two juridical spheres, began to separate. And this happened just at the moment I spoke of earlier, when parishes came into existence and Europe was transformed from a landscape of hamlets into a landscape of steeples, on which clocks would soon appear. As these steeples were erected, the Church, through the Popes of the time, began to take a new approach to what today would be called pastoral care. By 1215 we find in the pronouncements of that same Fourth Council of the Lateran of which I spoke a moment ago, a sentence which has, several times in my life, been important to me. It reads this way: every Christian, be they man or woman, will go once a year to their pastor and confess their sins or otherwise face the penalty of going to hell in a state of grievous sin. This codified a dramatic departure from the prevailing practice, up to this time, of public confession and public penance. Another new law made it an extraordinary misbehaviour for the priest to speak about what he heard in confession. It is remarkable to me as someone who is interested in the university and its procedures that the implications of these new laws have never become a major issue in historical studies. One significant feature of this sentence is that it distinguishes women from men, rather than simply addressing every Christian, and this gives women a new recognition in law. It also establishes the pastor as somebody who, in secret, judges or takes a juridical position in front of each Christian male or female. This makes the forgiveness of sin, in an entirely new way, a juridical act — a juridical act organized on a model or hierarchy which reaches down from the steeple into the hearts of the people, and therefore creates a court structure far beyond what any emperor could ever have even thought of creating. This becomes even clearer when you consider the idea which also emerges at this time of reserved sins, that is sins too grave for the local magistrate to deal with which had to be sent on to the higher magistrate, the bishop.

So a juridical state structure was created, and sin was made into something that could be dealt with along the lines of criminal justice. But because in confession one accuses oneself, this also involved a new concept of the *forum internum*, the inner court. If you look up the word forum in a history of law, as I did this morning, it will tell you that during this period the *forum ecclesiasticum*, the bishop or Pope's court, and the *forum civile*, the emperor's or lord's court, get separated from each other. But much more significant is the fact that people begin to be taught what a court is by being told that they have to accuse themselves with true sorrow for having offended God and with a true desire for amendment. To create this sense of a *forum internum*, or conscience, is an enormous cultural achievement, though something of which I was not aware until Prodi pushed my nose into it.

As you know, I have written a book called *In the Vineyard of the Text* in which I argued that the development of conscience is linked to the new prevalence of writing around this same time. Conscience was conceived as an inner writing, or record, and this idea was reinforced by the appearance in churches of statues of writing devils who note people's sins, and by the image of the Last Judgement as the reading of a book in which all sins are recorded. Prodi has made me more hesitant about attributing all this to the appearance of a new kind of text. For him the primary implication of the idea of a *forum internum* is that the law now governs what is good and bad, not what is legal and illegal. Church law became a norm, whose violation led to condemnation in hell — a fantastic achievement and, I would argue, one of the most interesting forms of perversion of that act of liberation from the law for which the gospel stands.

I do not want to be understood here as speaking against confession. I practise it. I am only trying to indicate a crucial moment in the transformation of the impiety which I commit by betraying love, which is the meaning of sin, into a crime which can be judged in a juridical fashion within an institution. Anyone who understands what I'm saying as taking sides in current discussion about the practice of confession in the several churches which have retained it has missed the import of my argument. In fact, I consider the wise use of the confessional over the last 500 years as, by far, the most benign model of soul counselling, pastoral care, and the creation of an inner space for deep conversation, centring on my feeling of sinfulness. It is incomparably better than anything else which I've seen so far in my service, and I include my experience with modern psychology.

Something else that's interesting about this requirement of annual confession is the way in which it was circumvented by the faithful. The Council had conceded that people might not want to confess to their own priest, and had therefore allowed confession to some other priest, with permission. Christians in massive numbers used this provision to avoid confessing to the pastor who lived among them. The foundation of the so-called mendicant orders, the Franciscans and the Dominicans, provided two enormous pools of friars, with the power of hearing confessions anywhere where they came to preach, and they became the principal confessors.

Now, to return to that pregnant sentence produced by the Fourth Lateran Council, it enjoins the duty of confession on women just as much as on men. As I've said, this is the first important statement of the legal equality of women with men. This equality is also reflected in the Council's new definition of marriage as a contract which is entered freely and knowingly by a man and a woman, rather than being dictated by their families or their milieu, and which constitutes a legal reality with standing in heaven. This definition is simultaneously a statement about individuality, about the coming into existence of conscience, and about the equal legal standing of man and woman.

I once had a chance to discuss this point with Michel Foucault, who was then working on his *History of Sexuality*; and I suggested that, with the establishment of this legal equivalence between man and woman, in which each is put into the same box of individual with a conscience, the possibility of sex really came into existence. Until this time, gender had divided men and women into incommensurable categories. Men's customs were different from women's customs. Infidelities could only be judged within the context of the two genders, which together formed the people. The marriage contract put them on the same level, and, as a result, the sin of adultery became the same kind of crime for either a man or a woman without distinction.

The Fourth Lateran Council of 1215 belongs to the high Middle Ages, and is one of this period's most grandiose occasions, but it is my contention that it is also a key to understanding what happened in the early modern period, during what is called the counter-Reformation. This period begins with the Council of Trent, which sat for thirty years trying to adapt Catholic doctrine and practice to the new situation created by the appearance of competing churches, as well as by the appearance of an entirely new view of ecclesiastical power. For the first time, the bishops who were delegates to that Council, met as representatives of the Church rather than of Christianity, as had been the case ever since the early Church councils of antiquity. They sat there not only as believers but as magistrates. And they discussed the affairs of a church in which the frontier between its rules and its doctrine had begun to crumble. There was no longer a clear distinction between the personal feeling of being sinful, which goes beyond the feeling of being guilty, and the feeling of guilt resulting from disobedience to Church rules. The internal forum had come into existence, and people began to feel bound by the laws of the Church. This makes it difficult to tease apart the legal and the dogmatic pronouncements of that council, as its great historian Hubert Jedin has shown.

At the Council of Trent, which sat at Trento in northern Italy during the generation after Luther, the Roman Catholic Church presented itself as a *societas perfecta*, as a law-based church, whose laws were obligatory for its members in conscience. This self-understanding was reflected in the legal and philosophical thinking of the time, which had begun to portray the state in the same terms, that is as a perfect society whose citizens internalize the laws and constitution of the state as the demands of conscience. In other words, through the criminalization of sin, the basis was created for a new way of feeling citizenship as a command of my conscience. The Church laid the groundwork by abolishing, or, at least diminishing and making permeable the frontier between what is true and what is commanded; and, on this ground, the state was later able to claim an allegiance founded on conscience.

I believe there is a parallel between the argument I am making here, and the one I made earlier about the way in which the spirit of contingency led to the death of nature. In that case I asserted that the doctrine of contingency, in which the world was conceived as lying in God's hands, would later allow the world to be taken out of God's hands, and that, in consequence, nature would lose not only the intensity which came from its being a product of continuous creation, but also its very aliveness, its being a living womb, which had never before been doubted. And I said that you cannot really understand modern science and technology unless you can see them as a perversion of the spirit of contingency. So now I would argue that, if we want to understand the idea of *patria* of the seventeenth, eighteenth, and nineteenth centuries, the idea of fatherland, the idea of mother tongue, to which I owe sacred loyalty, the idea of *pro patria mori*, that I can die for my fatherland, the idea of citizenship as something to which my conscience obligates me, then we have to understand the appearance of the internal forum in the Middle Ages.

I also want to say briefly in conclusion — I will take up the point at greater length in our next session — that the criminalization of sin opened Christians to new fears, a point on which I have learned a lot by reading a French historian called Jean Delumeau who has made it his task to study the transformation of fear between the twelfth and the nineteenth centuries in a never-ending series of fat volumes. Through the Incarnation, as I have said, a new kind of betrayal becomes possible. The Christian is called to be faithful not to the gods, or to the city's rules, but to a face, a person; and, consequently, the darkness he allows to enter him by breaking faith acquires a completely new taste. This is the experience of sinfulness. It is an experience of confusion in front of the infinitely good, but it always holds the possibility of sweet tears, which express sorrow and trust in forgiveness. This dimension of very personal, very intimate failure is changed through criminalization, and through the way in which forgiveness becomes a matter of legal remission. Once the sinner is obligated to seek legal remission of a crime, his sorrow and his hope in God's mercy becomes a secondary issue. This legalization of love opens the individual to new fears. Darkness takes new shapes: the fear of demons, the fear of witches, the fear of magic. And the depth of these fears is also expressed in the new hope in science as the way of banishing this darkness. In my index cards I give this subject matter the heading "UFOs, Unidentified Flying Objects," an anachronism obviously, and I think the phenomena that I group under this heading are almost an inevitable result of the criminalization of sin. These fears are easily exploited by politicians, and Delumeau contends that this is one of the main ways in which the power of the state is consolidated. I will return to this subject.

6

FEAR

I have spoken to you more than once about what happens to the idea of virtue when it is suffused by the light of the new freedom which allows the Samaritan to step outside his own milieu and pick up that half-dead Jew in the ditch. Perhaps today we would call that Samaritan an intolerable and violent Palestinian since the point of Jesus' story was that the one who helped was a foreigner, and even an enemy, to the man in the ditch. In the classical world, virtues were inculcated by the willed and intended repetition of good acts until a habit of acting in a good way was created. In the Christian context, virtue acquired a new meaning. As a Christian, I know that the practice of virtue requires help. In an ultimate sense it requires God's help or grace, but any reasonable reader of the Gospel will understand that that help comes to me through the other who faces me. This is how, concretely, I encounter the Lord. It's a very intimate thing I say to you, and I'm really embarrassed to say it in front of these microphones you have put on my desk here in Ocotepec. Nevertheless, I dare it. I don't risk it; I dare it. I dare to allow people to listen to how I speak to a friend.

Now the virtues. For forty years, I've again and again read the great thinkers of the twelfth century on this subject. They offer a beautiful psychological analysis of how the virtues can flower if one receives special graces. And one of the virtues which can flower into a gift of the Holy Spirit is called fear! I try to stand in a tradition in which fear of the right kind is not only a form of virtuous behaviour, slowly developed by regular practice, but is also something which can be elevated to the status of a gift from the Holy Spirit. There's a gift of fear. So, before we rejoin our conversation about the criminalization of sin and the way in which it generates anxieties, depressions, worries, fears, discomforts, and feelings of helplessness in a dark and imprecise world, let's not forget that there are two ways of speaking about fear.

Now, how can fear be the flowering of a virtue? My good old masters explain it by distinguishing two kinds of fear; *timor filialis*, the fear of the child, and *timor servilis*. When I say *timor filialis*, I stretch out my fingers, like a son who says, "Let nothing come between me and you. I fear that I might be the cause of allowing something to interfere between us, father." I remember a friend who almost dropped when I first said this to him. For him fathers were to be feared but only with *timor servilis*, the fear of the servant. When I explain this servile fear to kids, I put one shoulder forward and both hands before my face in a posture that says: "Don't hit me." There's an extraordinary wisdom in cultivating *timor filialis*, the fear that I might do anything or might allow anything to happen, which would put an obstacle in the road on which we have slowly advanced in learning to know each other, love each other, and bear each other; and, at the same time in recognizing that *timor servilis* is also legitimate. Your patience with me would cease to be a gift if I weren't afraid that I really deserve a kick, that I really deserve your turning away from me, because you are tired of dealing with me.

Servile fear, the slave's fear of being hit, and of deserving it — let's just assume that for the moment — is highly rational. I deserve to be kicked if I behave in a certain way. Many people whom I know, people who are only a little bit younger than I, think that they never deserve to be hit. I know parents who are terribly afraid that their hand may slip and that they may hit their kid. And I know professors of psychology and supreme court judges who will tell me that, should they do so, these parents would be committing a crime. Many have renounced the idea that the development of servile fear can be something good, that you deserve a kick, or the anger and condemnation of your *vis-à-vis*, if you behave in a certain way. But, the moment you give up servile fear, you endorse the consequences of your own improper, or uncharitable actions. If I come to believe that only a remote institution can deal out a type of correction, which is not merely Socratic, but which touches and pains me, then I've already denied my vulnerability in front of you as a person whom I want to love and who wants to love me. The father's duty to correct his son can be accepted — I'm not saying as legitimate — but as good only by a child who has learned to fear his father's hand. I'm not speaking here for wife beating, or for English prep school caning. The institutionalization of punishment produces the horrors which we then have to somehow limit and bring under social control through laws, proscriptions, and entitlements to protection. But I am suggesting that young people with children not be afraid to make themselves feared as parents as a basis for their children's filial love.

Servile fear and filial fear are interdependent on a very deep level. I need to know that my offence was personal, my ingratitude was personal, the disappointment which I produced was personal, and ought not to be eliminated by running to confession or to a psychologist or psychiatrist. Only if I have a *vis-à-vis* who insists, "Son, you offend me," can I live in constant watchfulness not to let anything come between me and the other who passes by. Such watchfulness requires this foundation of fear and trembling. (I'm foreshortening here, and I know I cannot avoid being misunderstood and even giving scandal to some people who are listening.) If I had to choose a sentence from the Old Testament for my blazon, it would be *Timeo dominum transeuntem*: I fear the Lord is passing me by. I fear that the moment will pass me by, and this extra way in which I can be since the Incarnation will be lost. This is the precise opposite of the fear that I will do something which deserves my exclusion from your friendship. Now, what I have just said needs to be in some way understood before we can really address the way in which the criminalization of sin gave new shapes to fear — the fear of hell, for example, or other diabolical fantasies of the fourteenth century.

I have already begun to tell you about some of the terrors which appeared during this process of criminalization. Each person's heart becomes an open forum, the heart is incorporated in a new way into society, and the modern citizen appears. The idea of hell becomes more prominent and the fear of hell increases. The devil takes on his strange embodiment, which goes hand in hand with human disembodiment, the disembodiment of man. These are what I call UFOs, and they express the fear of the void when you move from the orderly pattern of the heavens to the cold net of geometry underlying Descartes. Fear of witches is another example.

These phenomena lie along one corridor of my memory palace. There with increasing interest, I have stored references to hell in one room and, in another, references to the devil's appearances. Behind other doors are angels which govern the spheres, guardian angels, and seraphs. There is this extraordinary friend of mine, Gabriel, and there are also the devils, because they are fallen angels. But the door I really want to enter now is marked guilt.

During that century to which I'm a witness — the twelfth century — you see the appearance of a new kind of self. The "I" which is always the singular of a "we" begins to disappear, and there appears a new "I" protected by that strange wall of privacy which runs a few inches from my nose. This is the self I need in order to live in modern society, and that I have to abandon if I want to understand the "I" of people for whom "I" is the singular of "we," and not the "we," the plural of "I." It came into being when the Church imposed a juridical order on self conception, and established an interior forum, and this began a new epoch of fear — I say "fear," but I want to speak of dark powers and presences as well.

Let me try to explain what I'm getting at in the following way, though it might not work out: you certainly have read the Gospel accounts of the temptations of Jesus and probably know some of the various, magnificent literary attempts to understand and interpret the scene in poetry, in novels, and in essays. The devil came and took Jesus out into the desert. The Gospels call this devil the Satan, which means the tempter. And what the tempter invites him to do, ultimately, is to worship power, the powers, the powers of this world. Jesus replies to the tempter, "You shall worship only God, not power"; and, with these words, the New Testament creates the cosmic atmos-

phere in which the Samaritan can dare to step outside his culture, and
the guardian spirits that watch his "we." He can claim that even
though, as a Samaritan, his "I" is the singular of a "we," he can tran-
scend this limitation and reach out to the Jew. In a certain way, he is
superior to the most powerful demons, watchdogs, dragons, horrors,
and menaces which, in the world before Jesus, guarded the "we."

The Moslem is very close to the Christian in this respect. When
the Moslem five times a day commends himself in that lonely but
always communal prayer towards Mecca — for me, a most attractive
practice — he also shapes his soul to understand what I'm saying: that
the believer is free of the terror which guards the "we's" unity. The
believer prays in the name of Allah, the all-merciful — the words literally mean loving origin and womb — and locates the origin of his
"I" in that relationship. Because God has assumed his people in a
bridal relationship, which is the same in Mohammed or in Jeremiah,
I can stand here in his name and say, I'm not afraid of the world. I'm
only afraid of creating obstacles, and I only fear what I deserve, even
though I know that he will forgive me, and I won't get the stick. My
inner sphere, atmosphere, and horizon is not one of dread but one of
union with the Lord of the universe, who became a man to make me
divine. As the Church Fathers said, the other side of the mystery of
ensarcosis, God becoming flesh, is the mystery of *apotheosis*, man
becoming divinized. He doesn't have to be afraid of dark powers,
unless he freely submits to them. And that he does through betrayal,
through what we call "sin." In the clarity of faith, one can see sin as the
betrayal of a love of which I was made capable, but which goes beyond
anything I could expect within history. Sin is a willed step back into
the fear of cosmic powers, only the sinner falls back into a world of
powers which oppress him, without the culturally shaped defence
which beliefs, rituals and traditions provided for each historical "we."
The sinner, as distinct from the evil man of the past, or of other cultures, is a man who falls into the hands of the powers of this world
without going back to a "we" which he has transcended by accepting
the possibility of reaching beyond his own limits.

It is in this way that I interpret metaphysically — ontologically, if
you want — the source of modern fears: the new darkness, the new

loneliness, the new sense of being abandoned, the new types of despair and lostness, the nightmare which is no longer that horse which Robert Graves beautifully brings forth from old traditions. I speak for a tradition that has encouraged cultivation of the fear that I might step in the wrong way and, in that way, put a shadow upon our relationship, cloud it, interrupt it, perhaps even break it — it depends on me. Only if you understand this, is it possible to recognize the cultivation of fear of the stick as something rational and appropriate in view of my weakness, my mortality, my vulnerability, my egocentricity. And only if you understand this double cultivation of fear, is it also possible to grasp the evolution of fear in Western societies after the Church redefined sin as a legal rather than a personal offence and left the sinner prey to an entirely new kind of interiorized guilt.

It is possible that in our time fear has changed its quality again. We have gone from a revelation of the unspeakable, un-understandable capacity of industrial man to generate horrors, as foreshadowed in Kafka, and magnificently shaped in the poetry of Paul Celan, to the age of Prozac. And I'm speaking here not only of that one drug but the direction in which it wants to go, with chemistry of a technical, psycho-manipulative kind. We're now living in an age in which it might be fruitful to envisage new types of darkness. Imagine the degree of impotence of the person who has slipped into conceiving himself as an immune system. Imagine the new kind of death experienced by those who control themselves by chemicals, or by psycho-dietetic obsessions. Or imagine daring swallowed up by risk. How can one even name the unease that I earlier called "darkness." It's not the blues, or *les gouffres*, "abysses," as one can say in French. These are the spaces in which one has no hold which have opened up beyond the watershed which I think we have crossed within the last twenty years, and for which we are intellectually unprepared. Now it is not the devil but DOS[1] that sits on my belly.

Whatever had a beginning will have an end, and the fears which have prevailed during the 800 years of what I have called the epoch of technology may now be giving way to new forms of disorientation. Where dark clouds on the horizon once held the Horsemen of the Apocalypse, threatening but not quite graspable, something very new has appeared. And what makes it so new is that this contemporary loss of freedom is fundamentally related to the perversion of the Gospel promise of an unprecedented freedom.

Do you remember the occasion on which we were together in Oslo at a conference organized by Nils Christie[2] on the expansion of prisons? It was a crazy situation with numerous heads of prison systems all exposing how their systems generate more crime and act as an unstoppable leak in the state budget, and then explaining how it couldn't be otherwise and why they still felt responsible for keeping their positions as chief commanders of correction in Russia or in Texas — it makes no difference. They wanted to know what impression this had made on me. And I said to them, I see you as the organizers of a ritual which creates a myth. The ritual in which we participate by paying taxes, or calling the police makes people aware that others are less free than they are. Why is this effective? Because one of the deepest horrors of modern man is to recognize to which degree that inner fear, to which he doesn't know how to relate, makes a sham out of his freedom.

One of the reasons the two of us got involved in the project of doing these conversations was to explore the question of what it is necessary to renounce in order to live in the present world. I'm not talking about the renunciation preached by the deep ecologists, or by New Age teachers of enjoyment whereby I can have more fun or a lovelier life. I'm speaking of a type of renunciation which has been, from the beginning, the logical precondition for the practice of love.

I think I would start a little bit too high if I began now to speak about Jesus' absolute request that, if you came from solid, middle-of-the-road, practicable Judaism into his little sect, you renounced the freedom to separate from your wife. You renounced an opportunity which the Jew had. You renounced the need to belong to the "we" in order to find your "I." The place outside of Jerusalem, Golgotha, where the cross was put up, became the symbol of this renunciation. As in the Temptation, he renounced changing the world through power. Christians who imitate him soon discover that little practices of renunciation, of what I won't do, even though it's legitimate, are a necessary habit I have to form in order to practise freedom.

What a beautiful, innocent world it was when people could still practise this renunciation by not eating chicken soup on Friday. I still remember that world. It made no sense in Europe during the Second World War when meat was rationed anyway, and I forgot about it. But when I came to New York, I found that people really were concerned about not eating meat on Friday.³ And, during the six weeks of Lent, they would give up something which was hard for them in order to learn how to give up other things. I remember my boss on the first days of the first Lent which I spent in the United States. We sat down for breakfast, and he was as grouchy as anything. And I asked him twice, Sir, did I do something wrong? No! Did I offend you? No! Do you feel badly? Yes, it's Lent and I've given up smoking my cigar. Well, punishing me was a funny way of going about his renunciation, but I love to think of it because it reminds me of the things which, in the modern world, we can give up — not because we want a more beautiful life, but because we want to become aware of how much we are attached to the world as it is and how much we can get along without it. These unnecessary things have now multiplied to such an extent that you can't easily give a social shape to them. Some people will give up writing letters on a computer — not because it's bad, and not because they don't like to have to answer letters at the speed of e-mail. Others will give up the services of physicians or, as somebody whom I know has done, guaranteeing that each of his children will get a college degree.

The certainty that you can do without is one of the most efficacious ways of convincing yourself, no matter where you stand on the intellectual or emotional ladder, that you are free. Self-imposed limits provide a basis and a preparation for discussion of what we can renounce as a group of friends or a neighbourhood. I have seen it, and I can witness to it. For many people who suffer from great fears and a sense of impotence and depersonalization, renunciation provides a very simple way back to a self which stands above the constraints of the world.

And such renunciation is especially necessary in the world in which we live. Tyranny of old was exercised over people who still knew how to subsist. They could lose their means of subsistence, and be enslaved, but they could not be made needy. With the beginning of capitalist production in the spinning and weaving shops of the Florence of the Medicis, a new type of human being was being engendered: needy man, who has to organize a society, the principal function of which is to satisfy human needs. And needs are much more cruel than tyrants.

7

THE GOSPEL AND THE GAZE

During the first four years of the 1990s, I focused my reading and my teaching on the history of the senses. In doing so, I took advantage of the fool's freedom which my renunciation of any permanent teaching position has given me. When I'm invited as a guest professor, I can really choose to teach what I want to teach, and not be restricted to a subject or method imposed on me by my hosts. So how did I come to the decision that it would be an important thing to dedicate a significant fraction of my time to this subject in the final years of my life? Why did I want to try to understand hearing, seeing, smelling, touching, walking, feeling by looking at them from the past?

I wanted to do this because I somehow had to explain how the senses can be satisfied in subsistence cultures where there is practically no money in circulation and few marketed commodities. I wanted to understand how doctors, working in the Galenic tradition, made people feel well without healing their diseases. Today, if I say to a doctor, "Give me something to make me feel well," he'll say, "First, let's figure out which diseases we have to remove." But I want to say, "Never mind what you call the disease. Let me live. Let me feel well."

I realized that, in order to understand the past in its reality, I had to get into body history. This has been a major project of various friends of mine, particularly Barbara Duden,[1] who has studied the perception of the female body in past centuries. It's clear that when people in the past spoke, for example, about getting into balance, they were speaking about something that they perceived in quite different terms than the modern person who monitors himself in the light of medical constructs. So, in order to zero in on that "something," which people experienced as a sensual feature of everyday life, I focused on the history of the gaze.

The activity of the eyes has been understood very differently at different times. It was understood in one way by Euclid, in another way in Alexandria in late antiquity, in another way in the European Middle Ages, and in yet another in the modern scientific view. And I have suspected for a long time that, when people looked at each other or at the world it was not just their understanding of what was going on that varied, but also their experience. In Latin, for example, the *pupilla*, from which we take our word for the pupil of the eye, meant that little image of myself that I find reflected in your eye when I look at you, and this way of understanding the gaze was also a way of experiencing it.

My grasp of classical Greek is too weak for independent research, but I finally ran into a book on the history of the gaze by Gérard Simon[2] which confirmed my suspicions. Simon made me understand that none of the classical theorists of optics, like Euclid, dealt with the effects of light, as a modern optician would. They dealt with the activity of seeing. When we think of a mirror today, it's as a device which reflects rays from a source of light. But up until roughly the year 1000, the mirror was considered a very mysterious, dangerous device which broke the ocular ray of the one looking at it. This ocular ray was considered to be the active projection of the viewer, the way in which his sight grasped the things of the world. When the great opticians of antiquity observed the way in which a stick inserted into water appears broken, they understood that the visual ray emanating from the eyes had been broken by the surface of the water, not that the light reaching my eyes had been broken. When they spoke about the kind of line I see when a bird flies by — let's say a swallow that passes very close — they spoke about the distraction of my visual ray.

Simon was someone I felt I could trust without doing the research myself. He established to my satisfaction that up to the year 1000 there was a science of *opsis*, the Greek word for seeing, but not of optics as we now take that term. *Opsis* dealt with what we do with our visual rays. It surprised me that Simon could assert this with such clarity because, among the strange volumes I've discovered in my sniffing and searching through libraries is an extraordinary dictionary dealing entirely with Greek quotations about light. Hardly anyone seems to have purchased it — it was published in 500 volumes, and 300 were left at the publisher — but what is remarkable, in the light of Simon's assertion, is the fact that this dictionary's author never seems to notice that seeing among the Greeks is not conceived along modern lines at all but rather is explicitly described as an erection out of the *pupilla,* as loving as other erections are. When I look at you, I caress you with my eyes. If I look at your face, let's say, my ray proceeds to its surface where the sun brings out your colour. My ray and your colour are then mixed and brought back to me by my withdrawing the ray into the liquid, glassy, inner part of the eye, where the image is understood.

All right, Ivan, you may say, this is highly interesting antiquarian knowledge you're parading here. But what does this have to do with the thing which we are discussing? We set out to discuss my opinion, which I think rather plausible, that, with the New Testament, some very new forms of perception — not only of conception but also perception — came into the world. I believe that these forms have had a definitive influence on our Western manner of living, shaping our way of dealing with each other, and our way of thinking about what is good and desirable. I also believe that this influence has been mediated by the Christian Church, which bases its authority on its claim to speak in the name of the New Testament. The Church, according to me, attempted to safeguard the newness of the Gospel by institutionalizing it, and in this way the newness got corrupted. This was the thesis we set out to explore. So why the visual ray?

The heart of the New Testament message is that the infinite, the good, the wise, the powerful — that One whose name the Jews wouldn't pronounce, that Allah, and now let me finally say God — that that God not only became words in the mouths of his prophets but also became flesh in the womb of a little girl. The flesh which John the Evangelist remembers, with tears in his eyes, that he touched, when he lay his cheek on the shoulder of Jesus, as he presided at the Last Supper, is the flesh of the God-Man. Because of this, human flesh gains a new dignity. Human beings become worthy of a new respect, not as social entities but as uniquely enfleshed persons.

I know further from statements in the New Testament that Christians have always believed that the Church itself is a body, which comes into existence by Christians feeding on the sacrament, and by the water of baptism which signifies their immersion in this new body. In the liturgy of the mass, they shared this body by eating it, and they shared its spirit by the mouth-to-mouth kiss which was also part of the early Christian celebration of the Lord's Supper. What came to be in that celebration was a body, and not a body in the abstract sense in which one speaks of the body of Shakespeare's writings or the body of a building, but a body of true flesh and blood.

Later on I will develop the idea that modern people mostly live in what I call the iatrogenic body, which is produced by medical diagnosis. For 300 years we have been losing the sense of body that people once felt. And this loss has been aggravated, or so my strange reading has led me to think, by the discourses of jurists, philosophers, and theologians who construe the body only abstractly when they speak about the organs of the state, the body of the people, or the body of the state. I remember how scandalized a friend was when the French ambassador came to bring me an invitation from M. Giscard D'Estaing to participate in a certain meeting. The letter said, "*Les organs de la présidence désirent se mettre en contact avec monsieur.*" *Honi soit qui mal y pense.*[3] There were no bad thoughts in the mind of the diplomatic secretary who wrote that. It shows you how much she has lost any sense for what "body" was.

In my quest for a clearer understanding of what "body" once was, the history of the gaze proved particularly propitious because of the way in which seeing was once felt to be an act of bodily intercourse with the object of my gaze. This study also provided me with a way of reflecting on the disembodiment which seems to me characteristic of more modern times. Now, if I speak about this disembodiment as an historical progression, which proceeds over a period of 2,000 years, I realize that an historian working on that scale is as much a poet or a novelist. And, like a novelist working out chapters as he turns his psychological intuition into a book, I have to define epochs within this progression. So the first chapter in my study deals with the age of *opsis*, the age of the erectile *pupilla*. The next epoch is well-described by Johannes Kepler [1571–1630], who speaks about light as a postal courier, as a rider, as an imperial messenger, each light ray bringing the news of the world into my eyes. And now we are in a third epoch, which I have to struggle to find words for. In this new world I am constantly faced by images, TV images, computer images, advertising images, graphic representations of quantities, and so forth. And I would argue that during the last fifteen years seeing has become something different than the reception of images along the lines of Kepler's model of postal riders bringing light into my interior. It has become rather a form of participation in virtual worlds, where one actually steps into moving images, and virtuality becomes the real form of objectivity. These are the steps in the disembodiment of the gaze.

So long as the gaze was considered to be a willed action, it was seen as subject to moral decision, and as capable of being trained as speaking or hearing. *Opsis*, according to Euclid, is not just an intellectual study but also underpins appropriate moral behaviour. One learns doubt in the face of appearances. Is the object of my gaze a reflection, a mirror image, or am I really touching it? Do I reach my destination, the eyes of the other, or am I being distracted by the watery substance of the intervening air between us, which deflects my visual ray from what I want to search for in order to love it? The age of *opsis* was the age of the moral gaze. Optics were the basis for the appropriate moral use of the eyes, as searching, touching bodily parts.

If you open any old book of asceticism, any book which teaches you how to meditate, or how to live in the presence of God — the kind of books that were being patronized forty years ago and are now being rediscovered as full of a psychological sophistication which goes beyond what Sufi and Zen masters can bring us — if you open such books, the *custodia oculorum*, the guarding of the eye, is always a major chapter. It will tell you how the eye must be guarded from seeing the wrong things, from seeing not interior vision, but what the Greeks called *phantasticon*, which refers to dreams, apparitions, follies created by my wishes. There was a strong belief in the existence of a set of inner senses, which were a source of real experience — and in Mexican villages, I can assure you, they still are — and this belief led, among ascetics, to a very careful attempt to train young people to guard their eyes. In the second millennium this mainly involved guarding them from what might come in. In first millennium, it was mostly about preventing the eyes from rushing on something which is out there, touching it, and bringing it home. Today it is very difficult to speak about the guarding of the eyes, or to understand appropriate seeing as part of virtue.

Modern people have trouble grasping how there can be good or bad uses of the eyes. Perhaps we retain a few traces — as a boy I can remember being taught to keep my eyes to myself and refrain from the kind of indecent looks that might be elicited by a lady's cleavage — but this bourgeois code was essentially repressive. What the ancient Greeks and, even more, the Greek Christian Fathers had in mind was something different. When they spoke of the *custodia oculorum*, they referred to the constant awareness that I can train my eyes, as I can train my hands, to repeat the right look onto the right object which I have chosen as a model, and which I want to interiorize. Like hospitality or any other virtue, the good gaze develops through practice. Frequent repetition makes it part of my stance, my inner habit, for which the Greeks have the wonderful word *hexis*. Greek verbs possess not only active and passive voices but also an intermediate voice which refers to accustomed or habitual states. So, as well as speaking about walking, or, if one is a dog, being walked, it can also signify something like "the way I'm used to walking." One, therefore, has the possibility of developing a *hexis*, a habit, a virtue, of properly using these two glorious things — *lumina*, stars, they were called — in my skull.

One possible way of indicating the existence of a good gaze is by reference to its opposite, "the evil eye." In all premodern societies, the evil eye is feared. The anthropologist George Foster has written a beautiful article about the evil eye as a dark crystallization of envy.[4]

Nothing is more fearful to most peoples than envy, and one of the
major steps in the emergence of modernity was the disappearance of
the fear of envy. Dread of the evil eye ceases to be a medical problem
somewhere around the middle of the nineteenth century in the countries which have now become rich. In our Western medicine, from
the time of the very first Arab-influenced medical schools, envy was
considered a bad disease. Very few diseases had names, but envy, like
the plague, was one of them. Physicians diagnosed it by a yellowing
of the eyes, which they could see, by paleness of the cheeks, and especially by paleness of the behind. It has been argued that what replaced
the disease of envy was concern for social justice which became
both the antidote to envy and its vicarious practice. But the reason I
bring up the evil eye here is just to illustrate how powerful and how
physical a force the gaze once was.

I felt that by speaking about this issue of the history of the gaze I
could bring contemporary students to understand what I mean when
I speak of the new accent placed on the body through belief in God's
incarnation. The Incarnation invites me to seek the face of God in
the face of everybody whom I encounter. And it makes me believe
that, even though you and I will be ashes pretty soon, there is something in our bodily encounter, which is outside of this world in which
we now are. Our bodiliness takes on a metaphysical quality, which it
makes more than just an accident of the moment.

I wanted to talk to a contemporary audience about two things:
first about this mysterious new glory, thickness, phenomenological
density which the body takes on under the influence of Christianity,
under the influence of the Gospel, under the influence of the belief
that he who knocks at the door, asking for hospitality will be treated
by me as Christ, not *as if* he were, but as Christ; and second about
how the secularization of this faith produces the extraordinary contemporary disembodiment, which is one of the most frightening
experiences which anyone who has lived for the last twenty years
with open eyes must have had.

Here I was helped by another French author, Alain Besançon,
who claims, in a very well written, somewhat difficult book, that what
distinguishes the Western gaze from all other historically known

forms of gaze is its uneasiness with images.[5] The history of the Western gaze, as something which it is my task to form and regulate, is deeply shaped by an attitude for which I have coined the term iconoscepsis, or scepticism in front of the image. There are well established Greek terms for iconoclasm, the breaking up or destroying of images, and *iconodulia*, devotion to images, so it seems a reasonable step to invent a third term for that wariness, doubt, and questioning before images which has been characteristic of our Western culture since the time of the pre-Socratics.

Besançon convinced me — I was doubtful at first — that philosophy itself came into existence as a hesitancy before the gods of pre-classical Greece. In pre-literate Greece, there had been an overlap between gods and the images by which they were represented. Then, in the couple of centuries before Socrates, in the newly literate Greek society, an attempt was made to shift the accent which had previously fallen on images on to concepts. It is love of which you want to speak in philosophy, not Aphrodite; water, not Neptune; war or struggle and not Mars. It is the centre, it is the light, it is life, not the sun.

A shift takes place from concrete images to words and concepts, and a relationship with these concepts becomes possible. Consequently, God — the God, the ultimate God, the invisible God — becomes something which is thinkable, even though it's not imaginable. I am still not completely sure of this, but it seems as if this is one of the beginnings of *skepsis*, of hesitancy in front of pictured thinking, thinking in images. It allows a distinction to be made between gods and the statues which represent them, or between the emperor and his representation. People recognize that the statue is not the god, or not the emperor, and yet still deserves the incense or other honours due to the original. Images were, in this sense, unproblematic in classical antiquity, and reflection on what images, in essence, are and what they do is largely absent from classical philosophy.

Christianity, at its origin, enters a world in which the image has been rejected, overcome, and transcended by philosophers, and so is not considered a major problem. It enters it, at first, as a sect of

Judaism, a crucial point because the Jews maintained an extraordinarily radical attitude towards images. "Thou shalt not make unto thee any graven image or any likeness of any thing that is in heaven above, or that is in the earth beneath, or that is in the water under the earth."[6] Images could distract people from adoration of the living God. This strict prohibition of image making in the Jewish tradition presented a major difficulty to the disciples and early followers of Jesus. They felt that they had seen the Son of God, that Jesus was not just the ultimate prophet, who had once again incarnated God in words, but that he was God in the flesh. And, as such, they said, he was the image of the Father.

So the Christians began, during the first few centuries, to represent in frescos, and mosaics, not only scenes from the New Testament, not just faces and figures from the Bible, but images of Jesus as *pantocrator*, the Lord and Master of all things. In those first centuries he was never pictured as the Crucified, but as the Redeeming King standing in front of the glorious, golden sign of the cross. They represented the one whom they worshipped, in clear contradiction of the Jewish mandate to make no image or likeness.

By the fifth century, the Byzantine churches of the Mediterranean were filled with overwhelming mosaics, all of them figurative, all of them representing images of persons, however stylized and over-dimensioned they may have been. It is surprising, in retrospect, that during these 400 years of Christian expansion, first as a network of communities and then as a more or less established church, no one much noticed the parallel between Christian imagery and pagan statuary. The pagan statues of gods were simply declared to be false gods. The statues of emperors were denied religious worship. But the rejection, and sometimes breaking up of these images, did not stimulate any questioning of Christian images until the fifth century.

In the fifth century, the icon, *ikonos*, the image, for the first time, became explicitly problematic. And I cannot but connect the eruption of this concern with icons to the radical novelty of Christianity's conception of the flesh and to the challenge it presented to traditional ways of thinking about the body. Icon was a term of wide reference, which could be used not just for the bust of the emperor or the stamp of a signet ring but also for the *phantasticon*, the inner image which my inner eye sees, or for the nonsensual geometric image of which Platonists and neo-Platonists spoke. No general theory tied these various usages together. The first iconology, the first systematic reflection on the icon, we owe to the Greek Church Fathers. They needed such a theory to explain the sentence of Paul's in his Letter to the Colossians which says that Christ Jesus is the image of the invisible God. What does that mean? they had to ask themselves. "He's the likeness and the splendour of the Father's glory," says Paul. How can a human being be the image of the Invisible? And yet they knew by faith that Christ, as God in the flesh, was a substantive image. And so they returned to Genesis, the first book of Moses, and of the Bible, where it says that God created man according to his image and his likeness. Reflecting on the nature and import of images became almost a sport in the monasteries of Anatolia, in what is today Turkey. This turn towards a philosophy of images took place shortly after Ptolemy wrote his Optics, a work in which the image is of as little concern as it was in the Optics of Euclid before him. Ptolemy continued to study the gaze and the impact of certain devices on it. It was the outgoing and returning visual ray that concerned him; and, if he spoke of images, it was only as the internal representation of the external scene.

The tension between the Old Testament proscription of images and the New Testament account of Christ as the image of the Father came to an explosive head in the year 726. It was fifty years before the birth of Charlemagne, a time already well into the Middle Ages, when expanding Islam had become a major threat to the continued existence of Byzantium. Leo III was then the Emperor of Byzantium, already called Constantinople, or the Town of the Emperor, and he had won a battle in which he had stopped the iconoclastic, image-destroying Moslems. A revival of the Jewish command had come out of Arabia with a vengeance and had swept away the images from the churches with the progress of the Islamic armies from Egypt through Asia Minor into Greece. Right after his victory over these notoriously iconoclastic Moslems, the Emperor went to the bronze main gate of his palace and removed the image of Christ that was above it and replaced it with a simple symbol: a cross. With this ceremony, he started a fierce debate that raged for several generations. Its issue was, can Christians bow and pray before an image? For the first time the question of iconoscepsis, which caused the Greeks to doubt the desirability of speaking of love only in terms of the beautiful deity, became an occasion of civil war. The icon bowers, the iconodules, held that the cult of images was a legitimate form of piety, and that this form of devotion was a liturgy that had been customary since the beginnings of the Church.

A true and pretty bloody war began about the gaze. And, in the midst of that war, a man who has not so far been discovered by the historians of *opsis* makes his appearance: John of Damascus [675–749], a very articulate defender of the Christian devotion to images, but also the first great analyst of what the difference is between gazing at an image and gazing at the flesh in front of you. It was his doctrine which prevailed at the Church council, called by the emperor, at which an assembly of prelates, bishops of the Eastern and Western churches came to the conclusion that the cult of images is legitimate. At the close of that council, the icon of Christ was again placed above the bronze door and remained there until, half a millennium later, the Moslems took it down.

How was the issue resolved? John of Damascus expressed the consensus of the great majority of the Council Fathers, with his doctrine that an icon is a threshold. It is a threshold at which the artist prayerfully leaves some inkling of the glory which he has seen behind that threshold. In John's language it is a *typos* of the *prototypos*, which is in heaven. The icon is a window into eternity where the risen Christ and his mother, also assumed bodily into heaven, are already in the glory of the angels. The prayerful person, who bows before the wall of icons which separates the people from the mysterious altar, uses the beauty created by the artist in prayerful painting, in order to step devoutly through the *typos* to the *prototypos*. So although he bows before an image, it is an image which reflects the real flesh of those who have already been incorporated in the body of Christ. By engaging in this devout and pious expression of respect, John explains, the worshipper not only touches, with his eyes, what is beyond the

threshold represented by the icon, but he also brings back the min-
gling of his gaze with the flesh of the resurrected. And by bringing
back the flesh of the resurrected he participates in the construction of
the Church as a true fleshy body here on earth.

This way of dealing with the icon, not as a picture, but as a
threshold, had been kept alive in the various liturgies of the Eastern
Church: Russian, Greek, Syriac, and so on. I once had the chance to
read a report of some Soviet art historians, who had found a particularly beautiful and precious icon in a poor woman's hut. They wanted
to expropriate it for their art museum and tried to justify this to her
by asking her to imagine how thousands of people would see this
beauty in the museum. The woman answered, An icon is not to be
seen but to be prayed with, it has nothing to do with a museum.

This highly sophisticated view of the image as a gateway, not for
information, but for a bodily reach into the beyond, never became the
principal way of looking at holy pictures in the Christian West. In
fact, at precisely the same moment, a very different type of artistic
activity began in the West: the so-called *evangelium pauperum*, the
Gospel of the non-readers. While the Gospel was read from the pulpit of the tiny churches of the time by the priest or deacon, a scroll
with the Gospel scenes painted on it unrolled from the front of the
pulpit. Quite a number of them have been preserved. So the Second
Council of Nicaea, which established, for the whole Christian
Church, the doctrine of the legitimacy of icons, was taken by the
Western Church as a justification for the making of teaching devices
designed to make preaching more palatable and more long-lasting by
illustrating the sermon.

Now, before I go on with this rough account of the evolution of
the picture as a teaching or information device, I want to return for a
moment to the history of optics and, more precisely, to the point at
which the optics of Euclid and Ptolemy were revolutionized. This
feat is usually ascribed to another Greek, like the first two a citizen of
Alexandria, city of light, who was charged by the sultan with the task
of stemming the floods of the Nile because he was a very well-known
mathematician and engineer. After he had carefully considered the
problem, he realized that it couldn't be done, so rather than return to

the sultan and risk losing his head, he moved out into the desert to study sunlight. He knew that an eclipse was coming, and, because an eclipse can't be looked at directly, he shut himself in an Egyptian tomb where he could observe it as it shone through a pin-hole on to the back wall of that tomb. Then, he noticed that the after-image of the partially-eclipsed sun remained in his eyes even when he closed his lids. This led him to turn classical optics upside down: instead of the eye reaching out to the world, he concluded, things must be brought into the eye by light. Al-Haytham was the man's name — he was called Alhazen in the Latin West — and his treatise on optics was the first to advance the idea that the visual cone has its base in the eye and its apex on the object, rather than the other way round. As this work became known, it had a considerable influence on Western philosophy. If, for example, you read Thomas Aquinas, who was not yet under the influence of the new theory that vision is an effect of light, he still conceives the action of the intelligence as a going out of my spirit. The intelligence abstracts general or universal properties from its objects by reaching out to them and bringing these abstractions back. Less than a century later, Late Scholasticism held precisely the opposite theory as its standard explanation: an object radiates a tiny image of itself, the so-called *species*. The multiplication of these appearances, the *multiplicatio speciorum* makes knowledge possible. Man is therefore under the impression of the world, and no longer conducts a virtuous and self-initiated intercourse with it.

Now, to return to John of Damascus, it was through his beautiful, and, to me, convincing doctrine that the image was legitimized. And this legitimization was the cover under which, in the West, the picture became a teaching device, an edifying *aide-memoire* for Gospel scenery, which could be used to prop up the sermon. In the West, after the thirteenth century, pictures are painted as representations of scenes, and not as thresholds foreshadowing the glory behind them. The basis had been laid on which our world of objectivity is built.

We are, therefore, here again, at a point where an enormous, extraordinary belief — namely, belief in the flesh already in eternity, and accessible to the gaze of faith which reaches from darkness into eternal light — led to the acceptance of the cult of images. This decision, as I understand it, was thoroughly in line with the Christian spirit, in the way it links the visible and the invisible worlds. But it also laid the foundation for the world which now surrounds us, the world of iconomania. And this is what I call the *perversio optimi*, the perversion of the best, in which a first, perfectly innocent step leads eventually to the digitalized, interactive TV screens, and on to ever newer and stranger developments in a long, drawn-out martyrdom of the image. The doctrine of the Second Nicene Council helped to undermine the Jewish, and later Moslem, prohibition of images, which was founded on the idea that images can turn us away from the real, and portraits excuse us from facing the person portrayed, until, finally, the person seems to remember the portrait. And, in this way, Nicaea made possible the victorious march of the image in increasingly secularized forms over the centuries.

As part of this history a marriage takes place between the legitimized image and the modern optical theory which begins with Al-Haytham. In classical antiquity, the gaze was considered to be a psychic proboscis, a hand. Looks were called *psycho podia*, the hands and feet of the soul's out-reaching. The Council of Nicaea explained the icon as a way of leading the gaze through a shadow of glory into a union with the reality beyond, which it then brings back. The icon was not yet a place *in* which to see things but *through* which to see them. The image of which we speak today is something very different. The modern theory turns the visual ray around and speaks not of *psycho podia*, reaching out from the eye, but of postal riders bringing in the image, or of *species* which are received and recognized within the eye. Beginning in the fifteenth century in Florence, and later on in the Netherlands, painters began to conceive the gaze as an image-generating and image-recognizing activity. A new skill was developed: to paint the image beyond the window in such a way that it would be a facsimile, a likeness, of what I would see if I turned around and looked through a real window onto that scene. Through the art of perspective, an attempt was made to represent reality as it is and to allow the viewer to contemplate it at length and in detail. This idea of an optical facsimile was made possible by the modern optical theory. You cannot use a facsimile as a substitute for reality when the gaze is out-reaching. The possibility of making painting representational is deeply tied to the transition from seeing as a virtuous activity to seeing as a passive, or at least partially passive reception and digestion of images borne into the eye by light.

At the beginning of the sixteenth century, Leonardo da Vinci dissected the bodies of hanged men, whom he purchased from the executioner, in order to draw the innards. And he instructed his pupils to draw everything they saw. Nature, he told them, cannot be seen until it has first been drawn. In the belly of a hanged man, the eye at first perceives only a bloody mess. Only by drawing it again and again can it gradually be seen and understood. Leonardo's teaching foreshadows the thinking of the seventeenth century, when this idea of objectivity will be much more fully developed, and reality will be ever more closely identified with its objective representation. To stay with the example of anatomy, the body is increasingly shown in the way in which it appears to a draftsman working from the rules of monocular, fixed-standpoint perspectival representation. An accompanying text will discuss features of the image marked with an "A," a "B," or a "C." Modern science basically began with the interpretation of designs. In many areas of Europe, you couldn't get a degree at the university, much less become a state employee, if you didn't pass an exam in drawing, because reports home, reports to your chief, reports to the king had to be illustrated to be credible. But this was still an illustration which placed the designer in the picture, even if invisibly, through the rules of perspective.

Then, in the early nineteenth century, a new way of conceiving images appears. The image comes to represent what is really out there, and not just what the anatomist or the draftsman sees. In scientific treatises, the demand for perspectival representation, for perspectival objectivity is abandoned, and objects are represented as measured, or as mapped, or as seen in an architectural drawing in which the gaze is assumed always to be perpendicular to the object represented. The draftsman creates a virtual space, into which he places things as they are, and not as they are seen by him. And the viewer is asked to look at an object — a cut through a brain, a baby, a muscle — in a space into which he never could reach. Jonathon Crary has made this very clear.[7] He points to optical devices like the stereoscope as precursors of the virtual, non-local spaces that are so ubiquitous today. In the stereoscope two photographs taken through two lenses several inches apart were viewed next to one another in a small dark box. The device enhanced the plasticity of the scene or object pictured; and one of its first uses was to advertise the wares of Parisian brothels to passers by.

This was at first no more than a curiosity, but what impresses me so much is the speed with which, during the second part of my life of seventy years, virtual spaces, images and other objects presented in virtual spaces, have spread. There are quite a few serious thinkers now who claim that, among the most profound changes of the last twenty-five years is the ubiquity of virtual spaces from which we are asked to derive our knowledge. Perhaps it's now becoming clearer why I spoke at such length about icons. The icon was conceived as a threshold to a super-reality into which only faith could lead. The virtual space asks you to look into a nowhere in which nobody could live.

The icon, I would argue, cultivates my ability to see the misery of a slum, or to be present on a bus, or during a walk through the streets of New York. It allows me to shed, through my gaze, some light from the beyond on those whom I touch. Experiences in the virtual realm, on the other hand, lead me to see what is virtual and disembodied about others. They become clothes hangers so to speak for the abstract "programming" which I bring to my encounter with them. This is why I am so passionate about making my students reflect on the ideas I've been discussing. Antique optics is concerned with preparing a virtuous way of seeing and making you aware of the pitfalls into which your visual ray can fall. I think that a contemporary optics ought to do the same — to make me aware of what happens when I establish the habit of consorting with the seductive non-entities that are constantly being conjured up all around me and of how this preponderance of the virtual affects my everyday intercourse with others. And this is especially critical because many of the younger people with whom I have had to do during the last seven or eight years really believe that they have a binocular camcorder in their skulls, and can only conceive the training of the gaze in terms of technical improvements in their rate of digital digestion.

8

HEALTH

My young friend Juanito, a baker's son from a northern Mexican city, came here to show me his doctoral thesis and was very proud to point out his dedication, which stated that the work did not contain a single sentence which could not have been copied from one of my books, articles, or lectures. I was delighted. Then he asked, "*Maestro, y que tu haces ahora?*" And I said, "*Me ocupo de salud.*"[1] Ah, he said, very interesting, you have returned to theology. I had meant health, but this misunderstanding is possible in Spanish, where the same word *salud* means both "health" and "salvation." The context decides if I'm speaking of one or the other.

To this tiny interview, I owe my slowly ripened decision to make it known that I am not acting as a Catholic theologian. This is an institutional and juridically determined function within the Roman Church. And through lucky circumstances, nobody can tell me that I am a theologian. I am no theologian. I don't want to act as such.

However I know also that I could not have analyzed medicine without bringing into this analysis my passionate attempt to understand a little bit of the Gospels, as well as my knowledge of the Church Fathers, and the great minds among the monks and churchmen who contributed to the 1,500 years of Western Latin culture. I'm sorry that my Greek isn't good enough to give me direct access to Christianity's Eastern tradition.

So I began to reflect on Juanito's question. At the time, three things puzzled me deeply: the prolongation of life, the killing of pain, and the diagnosis of diseases. And in each case I was deeply surprised to discover that the words we use today could not have been used or understood by those who were called physicians in even the relatively recent past. It would have made no sense, for example, that there should be people around who prolong life, either by selecting only the probably long-lived foetuses for birth, or by fighting life-threatening elements in the environment, or by keeping people on drips to suffer for a few weeks or months more.

I found out that at around the same time that German philologists began to claim that education meant "to lead out into freedom," the Hippocratic Oath was being redefined.[2] Traditionally it had been understood to say that I, as a medical man, will have nothing to do with death, implying, I will neither procure it nor fight against it. Now it became, I will do everything I can to prolong the patient's life. I became aware that throughout history in all cultures there had been people, from witches to masseurs to acupuncturists, who had tried to relieve pain, to make discomfort bearable, and to help and encourage people to face reality; but never had anyone spoken of *killing* pain until the middle of the nineteenth century, when, as I learned from an historical dictionary of Americanisms, various concoctions began to be sold in the United States under the name of painkillers. That's the first reference to the idea that you can kill pain without killing a person. And the term has stuck, although you still can't use it in any other language. At the same time, people began to have diseases, rather than to be sick.

After I wrote *Medical Nemesis* I thought I would find help in understanding how this ghastly world could come about in which most people are convinced that they should do everything possible to prolong their own lives, and those of their relatives, and consequently need Ronald Dworkin's "Philosopher's Brief" and the Supreme Court of the United States to decide if they may be administered death as they are administered life.[3] In the twenty-five years since *Medical Nemesis* was published, the field of medical history has expanded magnificently, and the history of anatomy, the history of physiology, the history of hospitals, and the history of medical care have all thrived, but I'm afraid that no one wants to face the question of what it does to human beings to live in an a-mortal world, a world in which there are no dead around. It was clear to me thirty years ago that if the struggle against death became a competence of the physician, and the physician was therefore put in charge of life "from sperm to worm," as my old friend Bob Mendelsohn[4] used to joke, then execution would inevitably become a medical duty running parallel to the fight against the onset of death. Everyone is now forced to assume responsibility for his own death, which is no more than the cessation of life. How far we are from Girolamo Savonarola telling Fra Domenico,[5] You cannot choose your death but only accept the death which has been destined to you and hope that you are fit to bear it with dignity.

I am frightened by a world in which, as my great Indian teacher Debabar Banerjee[6] says, the number of diseases that everybody can contract is at least two dozen times greater than it was in 1970. The production of disease definitions, the number of conditions that can now be diagnosed and ascribed to us, has multiplied more rapidly than any other form of production I can think of. This is our strange privilege. And what twenty years ago could only be feared as a consequence of increasing demands for care has become a reality. Now every layman must be taught how to offer professional care and counsel to himself and others. The professionalization of the layman and the transformation of professional care into self-care has reached a high point.

At this point I can go no further without mentioning, although I hesitate, the resurrection of the dead. Some will say that this is the belief of Christian fanatics, now set aside by reasonable church people who have understood during the last twenty or thirty years how we can translate the mythologems of late Roman times into modern English. Others will relate the resurrection of the dead to the contemporary literature on near-death experiences, which has shifted death from the realm of the occult into the quasi-scientific realm of unidentified flying objects. Trying to introduce the resurrection of the dead into these kinds of discussion can only be an unwelcome intrusion, but I really can't take up the question of the relations of salvation and health with which I began without bringing it up. And I do have a predecessor, who is, once again, the apostle Paul. It is related in the Acts of the Apostles that Paul gave a speech in the *agora* of Athens which very much appealed to his listeners.[7] The Athenians were a most civilized people, and the *agora*, the public square — I'm speaking now as an adoptive New Yorker — was something like Washington Square at its best moments. People listened with great enthusiasm to Paul's talk about Jesus and his death on the cross. But then he wanted to speak about the resurrection of the dead, and that was too much. That's enough for today, they told him, come again another time and tell us about this.

I can't come another time. I have to speak now. The resurrection is a crazy hope in which I share, but I don't want to discuss it here as a dogma. Rather, I want to raise the question: What kind of body can conceivably be the subject of resurrection? About what kind of body does it make sense to talk this way?

That question leads me straight into a period of medical history which I did not know when I wrote *Medical Nemesis*. When you study medical historians, you are studying people who have written during the last hundred years. In the early twentieth century a bunch of professors in Leipzig had the idea of saying, It's not enough to read medical biographies or investigate the history of hospitals; medicine itself, as an enterprise, is guided by a body of ideas, by some supposed knowledge, and we must study that and make it our theme. Half of these guys became ugly Nazis, and the other half of the older men emigrated to the United States and congregated at Johns Hopkins. This established medical history as an academic subject in the United States and later in England.

Now, when you study medical history, right from the beginning, there is an assumption that sometime around 1650, or perhaps even earlier when William Harvey published his *De Motu Cordis*, on the movements of the heart, in 1628, the medical paradigm shifted. Up until then, physicians were people who had dealt with a body characterized by a balance of cosmic elements which was expressed in the flow of its juices — muck and blood and gall and so on. This so-called humoural paradigm, in which health was a balance of bodily humours, was then succeeded by an organic paradigm, in which bodily organs were the key entities. In this account medical history turns on the scientific paradigms of doctors. The assumption is that while models of the body may have changed, doctors have always diagnosed a disease, made a prognosis, and offered therapies. When I wrote *Medical Nemesis*, I was taken in by this assumption. Ten years later the British medical journal *The Lancet* asked me for my ruminations about *Medical Nemesis* in retrospect.[8] And I said, When I wrote *Medical Nemesis*, I was not aware of how far the iatrogenic power of medicine actually extends. When I spoke of iatrogenesis in that book, I used the term in the way in which everybody in medicine ordinarily uses it — to refer to doctor-generated harms, or the production of disease through too much medicine, the wrong medicine, the wrong combination of medicines, the irresponsibility of the doctor, experimentation by the doctor, mistaken identity in which the wrong person's foot is cut off because he has been assigned the wrong number, and so on — all those horrors which were news then and by now are taken totally for granted. What I had not realized, I said in that article, was the degree to which the very experience of living is changed through modern medicine.

If I had to rewrite that book, if I had to say something today, I certainly wouldn't speak anymore about the medical enterprise being the major threat to health. This is now well-known. I would speak rather about the radical change in the attitude of the university-based and university-trained healer during the course of the eighteenth century. When I look at how doctors behave with patients before this change — and by now, I have five or six good studies which do this — what they do is listen. They listen to a patient's story and then make an anamnesis, which reflects the patient's self-awareness, which usually takes the form of complaints. The patient comes to cry on the doctor's shoulder. And when I analyze what patients tell the doctor, it is about how they feel, how they feel in a sense of which even modern English retains some traces. I cannot any longer say "How do you feel yourself?" but even if I say "How do you feel?" it still suggests "How do you sit in yourself? How is it today? How is that 'who' who you are today?" So the doctor asked the patient about his seat and his stance within himself and in relation to the world around him. This, for me, is a certainty, which I can document in hours of lecture — I can't do it all here — though not yet in a sufficiently beautiful way to make it credible in professional circles. What the doctor treated was what he got through the verbal confession of the patient. It might be, My right eye has given out since I saw that man being hanged, or, I'm blind in my right eye, although sometimes I see, or, I feel that the juices don't run down my left leg anymore since my landlord in a most uncivilized way threw me out of the house. I could tell hundreds of such stories. And the doctor not only hears what the patient says, but he also immediately qualifies what kind of a character the patient is, in the humoural, today we would almost say astrological, sense. So he notes, This sanguine man reports on a blockage of his red flows to the tips of his toes on the left side, and then translates this observation into the much more detailed, specific, and beautiful Latin language of Galenic medicine, which he has learned at university. So the doctor's task is essentially an interpretive, or exegetical, one. He makes an exegesis of what the patient reveals about himself and then reframes it in explicitly medical terms which allows the doctor to see which plants or animal excrements, or whatever it may be, are related to the same issue. In Western post-medieval, medical manuals, plants were classified by the human organs to which they related. In the middle of the classification chart stood a miniature man, and each plant, or assembly of plants, was related to his liver, or his stomach, or whatever the case might be. Doctors listened to stories about experiences of flow and blockage, about the coldness or warmth of these flows, about their biting nastiness, or about the overwhelming sweetness which a certain patient says takes away his good judgement whenever he sees that woman's face; and their science consisted in relating these predicaments to cosmic elements which might help in these circumstances.

Any medical history book will show you how doctors in 1600 or 1700 or 1800 misdiagnosed obvious diabetes. They weren't interested in the object "diabetes." There weren't more than six or seven words for diseases in use, and these named things like the bubonic plague that were regarded as a punishment from God. They referred to social phenomena, and not individuals. Doctors did not fix malfunctioning body parts; they helped people to get back into balance. It was only beginning sporadically in the late seventeenth century, and increasing through the eighteenth and nineteenth centuries, that the doctor's task became something totally different. Doctors began to listen to their patients' stories in order to pick out significant signs, signs which increasingly they could confirm or disprove by palpating organs, as doctors still did in my youth, and eventually by making tests of all kinds. Today this has reached the point where one can say that medicine provides people with bodies. I said earlier that medicine provides people with diseases, which is true, but, above all, it provides them with bodies. Contemporary bodies are the internalized image of the diagnostic tests and visualization techniques used in medicine, and such bodies are introjected through alternative medicine, as much as through established medicine.

I vividly remember when one of the main scholars then writing on body history in the United States came to visit my friends and me. The first thing we must do, he very sweetly trumpeted, so that we can understand each other, is to sit down and go through an internal visualization. He wanted me to apply my inward gaze, as though my eyes were sonar equipment or magnetic resonators. First you must feel your heart, he said, concentrating on the right chamber, and whatever he connected with the right chamber, then the left chamber, and so on. And he believed that he was leading us out of the medical paradigm, when in fact he was leading us ever more deeply into the iatrogenic, doctor-made thing with which most people today run around.

In this village in Mexico where I am speaking I could introduce you to a woman who sells subscriptions to a sort of medical comic book, which helps people who can hardly read to acquire iatrogenic bodies. She's a widow who works as a maid and does this to pick up a little extra money. In the process she helps to disqualify, veil, and repress the sense of themselves that a lot of Mexicans still run around with, and to break the connection between people's feelings and the plants that grow around them.

I will return eventually to the resurrection of the body, but first let me take another step. Thirty years ago, when I lectured in Pakistan, I met a man to whom I feel great gratitude, a physician who is now dead named Hakim Mohammed Said, who was then the head of the Unani Association of Pakistan and the world. I had spoken about the shadow cast by the medical struggle against pain and death and, afterwards, he approached me and said, Mr. Illich, what you are really telling us is that if we allow our techniques to be pressed into this campaign to kill pain and fight death, we will become the most effective importers of the Western Christian ideology. He still understood that a physician has to leave the bedside of someone for whom he can do no more, that there is a moment when the balance can no longer be restored and nature breaks the healing contract. He saw that there is a point beyond which the attempt to kill pain becomes a crime against nature. The physician can soothe, relieve, encourage, but then he must take his leave. His task is not a struggle for this-worldly immortality.

We are faced with a Western cultural history in which at a certain point the medical establishment began to perceive that its task was no longer that of a learned profession, engaged primarily in a work of interpretation and exegesis. Instead it became concerned with the production of a body built from disjointed elements forced together into a system, a body which is no longer conceived as a *microcosmos* having its place in a *macrocosmos* along with plants and minerals, waters and stars. One important epoch in this change was the separation of medicine from philosophy. This coincided with the establishment of universities, which was a sequel to the so-called Gregorian reform, the first effective reform of the clergy initiated by Pope Gregory VII [1020–1085] in the eleventh century. He decreed that clerics with concubines would be deprived of their privileges and their income. At the same time, advances in agriculture were bringing into being villages which provided the first real tenures for curates. Financial security for parish priests, along with the threat of dismissal if they continued to live with a woman, made the idea of clerical celibacy juridically enforceable for the first time. Church law also decreed at this time that priests would not deal with medical matters. So, just at the time that philosophy was separating from theology, medicine became the third, and law the fourth, subject division within the new university; and it remained thus until the time I studied.

Medicine at this time still meant the Galenic tradition, named after the Greek physician and philosopher Galenus [129–200?], who practised in Rome in the second century A.D. It was he who transmitted the riches of Aristotle into the Western tradition; and, if you look into his works, you will find that 90 per cent of his quite voluminous writing is concerned with physics or metaphysics, and only about 10 per cent with what we would call today diagnosis and treatment. But, through the separation of medicine and philosophy, this tradition was eventually eclipsed and the interpretation of the felt body was replaced by the external observation and manipulation of the anatomized body. Philosophy was deprived of the body, and the body was deprived of its cosmic belonging.

Now, to conclude, and to return at last to the question of resurrection, I think there are two important ways in which what happened to "body" in the Western tradition bears on my fool-ish belief in the resurrection of the dead. First, I hope I have established that the bodies of modern persons are ascribed or attributed bodies, constructed from medical observations, even though there always remain beneath this iatrogenic body certain rests, or remainders of true feeling. But the body that is subject to resurrection is the felt body. This is a body which is so much yours and so much that with which, and in which — I'm borrowing these words from the Eucharist — you are facing me that I can't even make theoretical statements about it. The persons to whom salvation was promised, if they would follow the folly of Christ, knew themselves as something deeply experienced and not as something ascribed and attributed. The felt body is mortal. And when your grandmother died, she continued to be around as part of the resurrected body of Christ, or of the assumed body of the Virgin. What an abysmal difference from the diagnosed body.

To understand this, I think you have to follow the practice of those historians who take the past so seriously that they become puzzled by present-day certainties, the certainties with which they live

and which they are forced, *prima facie*, to use as the means for constructing the categories with which they try to study the past. Among
such historians, the central question is the opposite of the one usually
asked. Instead of asking how people could think as crazily as the doctor who thought he could heal a woman who had suffered ten years
from constipation by administering ground corals and cutting her at
the ankle to let blood, they turn the question around and ask how it
is possible for me to believe today that I possess organs that can be
replaced when they go wrong by my buying new ones from people
recently deceased. For anybody who studies history seriously, it is a
major puzzle how we, today, can live with what, to the people of all
previous times and places, would have been considered unfeeling brutality and absolute nonsense.

My concern is, How could such nonsense be historically
prepared? And that question brings me to my second link with
the resurrection, and takes me to my story about Paul. Paul told the
Athenians something they didn't want to hear. Come back another
time, they told him politely. They were delicate people, decent, well-
educated people, and they must have been shocked by his claim.
Faith in the mystery of the resurrection of the body did lead in the
course of Western culture to a new respect for the body, but it also
tended to destroy the myriad body images that had existed in the
world's different cultures, each with its unique body percept. During
the course of Western history these old body cultures have been gradually replaced, or perhaps overshadowed is a better word, by respect
for the resurrected body of Christ. But once that respect disappeared,
a void space was left, into which you could put any construct.

One final point of clarification: It might be objected that my
claim that the opening to modern medicine lies in a perversion of the
Gospel is refuted by the penetration of modern medicine in places
where Christianity never penetrated. This objection mistakes my
claim. I'm not saying that only those who belonged to the old order
can be receptive to the new order. Christianity provided the nest, but
that doesn't mean only Christians will be receptive to what has now
hatched. Indeed, most of my young students in Bremen are not much
different in this respect from [say] the Japanese. I found out recently

that of the 200 people who attend my Friday classes, only seventeen could recognize the expression "on earth as it is in heaven" from the Lord's Prayer — a phrase which is more distinctive in Luther's German translation than it is in King James English. They are in the same boat as the Japanese, or any other people, when confronted with the medical institution which serves as the public relations agency for the ideological, scientific, and financial conglomerate which is interested in iatrogenic bodies. Increasingly physicians are called in to give some credibility to the body which Windows 95 assumes that I have, that is mine. My argument does not deal with the question of why this body is so attractive. I only say that this body is demanded by the enormous institutional ritual of modernity. You need such a body to take the car, jumping kangaroo-like from place to place, without touching the earth, engaging in hours of windshield view, where you are always looking at somewhere where you are not and where reality, insofar as it still exists, is passing you by. You need it to live in a world where knowledge is always the revelation of an educational agency, whether it's the school or the help program built into your coffee maker. All these things assume the kind of body the doctor tells you you have.

9

PROPORTIONALITY

For all worlds before our own, at least all those of which I know anything, it is a certainty that there is a correspondence between what is here and what is beyond. Heaven is mirrored by earth. The baby I saw in a woman's arms yesterday is a cosmos, a microcosmos. When I look at this baby, I see something which appears, at first sight, utterly dysymmetric[1] from what I see when I look up at the stars, and yet they fit at every point. They are both complementary and mutually constitutive, that is, the existence of one implies the other. Each people discerns this complementarity through a specially trained gaze which anthropologists call culture, though I would rather speak of the art of seeing the cosmos, bearing it, suffering it, and enjoying it. The assumption that the world is a net of correspondences is the background, the magma which all circum-Mediterranean cultures presuppose; and, as far as I can understand, this is the same for all Far-Eastern cultures and for the Mexican, Aztec, and Mayan cosmos, of which I know a little bit as well. You cannot enter any of those worlds without the assumption that all existence is the result of a mutually constitutive complementarity between here and there.

When the idea of contingency, of constant creation by the will of the Lord in heaven, made its appearance, it had an ambiguous effect on this cosmic conception of reality. In the hands of Hildegard of Bingen [1098–1179], a nun, contemporary with Hugh of St. Victor, living on the Rhine, the sense of contingency seemed only to heighten her enjoyment of the relations between the microcosmos and the macrocosmos, and she wrote magnificently about the cosmic correspondences between plants and parts of the body, or among stars, colours, and metals. But the sense of contingency, for others, was a step in the direction of monism, because a world in which everything immediately depends on God can be interpreted as a world reducible to a basic homogeneity or oneness, and this deeply undermines traditional cosmology, which is gendered and considers the dualities of male and female, up and down, heaven and earth to be fundamental and irreducible.

Perhaps I can tell you a story which will make clear just how much European thought threatened the worlds in which other peoples lived. It comes from the time of the great outward expansion of Europe, when the first missionaries reached China and Japan. The first to succeed in gaining a hearing in China was Matteo Ricci [1552–1610], an Italian with a well-trained memory who had succeeded in mastering the Chinese language and who was finally admitted, after nearly twenty years in China, to the imperial city of Beijing. Ricci's attempts to attract and convert the Chinese intelligentsia provoked a strong reaction, and letters streamed into the Imperial Court, calling attention to the fact that this was a most dangerous and poisonous man. Ricci was trying to make himself understood in Chinese, so he didn't speak about God — God, or gods, not being a very Chinese idea, seemingly — but instead talked of a master in heaven. This was the idea that scandalized the Chinese, as the marvellous French Sinologist Jacques Gernet has shown in his analysis of these writings.[2] Everyone called the Emperor's attention to the same objection: if we were to admit a master in heaven, the perfect balance between heaven and China, heaven and earth, would be broken. China would cease to be — to be! — this world, the centre of this world, the reason for this world, as heaven was the reason for China. These learned Chinese literati understood that the spirit of contingency, even at the time of its very advanced sunset, was still poisonous and upsetting for China for a metaphysical reason: because China was based on an equal balance, a perfect balance, between up and down, above and below.

The correspondence of heaven and earth was fundamental to all classical thinking. I once, as you know, analyzed this correspondence in relation to what I called "gender," by which I did not intend what that word later came to be used for, the social aspects of sex, but rather a certain way of perceiving duality. In the world from which we come, and in which in certain residual ways we remain, things are what they are because something inevitably corresponds to them. Nothing can be thought, felt, or experienced unless it has this correspondence. Thomas Aquinas, of whom we spoke earlier, says that you can't think about anything — any thing! — without knowing that it corresponds in some way to a will that is good, that is essentially good, that something fits it and it fits something. The idea of objects, concepts, perceptions that don't have a fit might occasionally have dawned on thinkers of the past, but it was not something that could really be lived.

The loss of this sense of fit can be traced from the early years of the seventeenth century on into the eighteenth and early nineteenth centuries. The best way I have found so far of explaining it to my classes at Penn State, the University of Pennsylvania, and the University of Bremen is in terms of the history of music. I invite someone who knows how to play the guitar to the front, and then give that person a monochord. A monochord is an old device which is hardly known today. When my friend Carl Mitcham tried to find me one at Penn State, people asked, What the hell is that? He did find an old professor in the music department who remembered using one as a student, but none could be found, until at last he hunted one up in the physics department, where it was stored for possible later use in the museum. It's an elongated wooden box, about the span of a man's arms, with single string mounted on it. This string can be stopped at any point along its length in order to demonstrate musical relationships. So in my class the person serving as my assistant demonstrated various divisions of the string, halving it to sound an octave and then stopping it at one third of its length. Suddenly, in this class of 150, sometimes 200 people, a number of faces lit up. They could hear the harmony produced by what musicians call the fifth or the quint. If the finger stopping the string was moved by even a

fraction of an inch, it didn't sound the same to those who could perceive it. Arrangement of these perceptibly harmonious sounds
defined music throughout most of its long history.

But music, like human nature, has a glitch. If you repeat the fifth,
that is, if you take the longer part of the string and again divide it in
a ratio of 1:2, you take the first step in what is called the circle of
fifths. If you keep repeating this operation, taking the fifth of the
fifth of the fifth and so on, you will finally return to your original
note, sounded several octaves higher. Except you don't quite arrive at
your starting point. There is a small discrepancy, which the old
Greeks called a *comma*. The circle of fifths doesn't come out quite
right. This has always been a problem, and a point of discussion
among musicians, but it was only around the time of Bach that its
solution became a serious task. They wanted to see if they couldn't
rearrange the circle of fifths in such a way that they made each step
slightly disharmonious — in effect averaging out the *comma* — in
order that the circle of fifths should end where it began. This was
in order to prevent individual instruments, or instruments playing
together, from getting more and more out of tune if they ventured
into keys remote from their starting point. The process was called
tempering the scale, and it turned out to be a very difficult task, only
fully achieved in the nineteenth century, when it became possible to
measure the vibrational frequencies of musical pitches and to use log-
arithms to make the complex calculation of how much to shave off
the tail of one quint and how much from the nose of the other in
order to make the scale come out right while still giving the
untrained ear the impression of being in a harmonic, rather than a
tempered, scale. The key figure was the eminent German physicist
and physiologist Hermann Helmholtz [1821–1894].[3]

From this point on, natural harmonies no longer defined and limited what music could be. Musical tones were no longer known by
their fit. Individual sounds, precisely machined and measured,
became the raw material of music. Music could be passed between
instruments. Orchestras could stay more or less in tune. Diverse
forms of musical expression from all over the world could be com-
pressed into a single system of notation. But in this homogenization,

what was lost was the cosmic dimension in music, its ability to sound the music of the spheres.

I should make clear here that I'm not speaking against Beethoven, and, even less, against Mahler. I'm even delighted, though some people say I should be ashamed of this delight, with Richard Strauss. All I'm saying is that music played on tempered instruments differs radically from all previous music. It requires that I learn not to hear disharmony, even though disharmony is the substance out of which my enjoyable musical experience is being made. And this change in music corresponds to numerous other changes which are occurring around the same time. The tempered, and therefore universally interchangeable, musical scale, in which pure harmony has been replaced by an approximation, relates, for example, to the appearance of the medically produced body of which we spoke yesterday. With tempering, music becomes, in a sense, objective. Local peculiarities are ironed out in the same way that the person's stance, or standpoint, is washed out of the objective body. And, of course, this self-objectification intensifies with contemporary photographic devices that make people think of themselves as something like a camcorder.

Mathematics goes through a similar change a little earlier. The ancient Greek feeling for geometry was comparable to the feeling for music we've been discussing. The analytic geometry pioneered by René Descartes removed the natural background against which the figures of geometry had been studied, and replaced it with a network of coordinates. In philosophy, as I also mentioned earlier, ethics ceases to be the science of the good, which is known by its proportionate relationship to the will, its fit, and is replaced by the science of tempering values. The good is or is not, like a perfect fifth in music. Values can be more or less. They assume a point zero, from which negative as much as positive values can be elaborated. Evaluation of the world becomes fundamental for thinking.

This loss of proportionality points to the historical uniqueness of modernity, its incomparability. The poetic, performative quality of existence was erased and forgotten in field after field: in the law, in the conception of what constitutes the common wealth, in constitutional science, in morality, in the idea that society is based on contract, and, of course, in all the areas we've already discussed. And in this transition from a world based on the experience of fit, of appropriateness, to a world which I can't even name, a world in which words have lost their contours, what was once called common sense has been washed out. Common sense, as this term was used of old, meant the sense of what fits, what belongs, what is appropriate. It was by common sense, for example, that a physician understood the limits of what he could and should do. Today, we can think of a world of objects, of persons, of social constellations to which nothing corresponds. It is not only a wombless world, it is a world in which the idea of frontier, of limit, has a meaning which, I think, before Newton and Leibniz was inconceivable. Until their time, if you spoke of a limit, a horizon, the word itself implied that you spoke of a frontier leading to a beyond. A frontier with no beyond is something profoundly new, something which affects all our daily dealings, and makes us so different from all other persons, other cultures, worlds, languages. Even our poetry is arbitrary.

Our perception of speed provides another example. Even the Greeks could imagine that there might be something faster than a falcon, which was the fastest thing they knew, but they had no general concept of speed, figured as miles above time, miles per hour. When Galileo introduced this concept to the remains of the Florentine Academy or wrote about it to Kepler, his contemporaries were conscious of his creating a violently arbitrary relationship, which had not been there before. A friend of mine, Sebastian Trapp, has demonstrated this by analyzing a book on falconry written by the royal hand of the Holy Roman Emperor Frederick II [1194–1250].[4] This book is rich in words that describe the quickness, agility, and accuracy of the bird, but it never abstracts any general idea of speed from this performance or tries to compare the falcon with any other creature in this respect. Space and time could not be isolated and put into relationship in the way they are today. I recently read a beautiful study of time in Shakespeare which persuaded me that when Shakespeare says "Give me more space" he still means, Give me a few more hours to live. The distinction of space from time begins with Galileo and Kepler and implies a world which has no other side, a world in which there are no dead. In this new kind of world neither the vitality of nature nor the creative act of God make things what they are. This birthright is withdrawn, and things come to be what they are because of their genetic code, as we would say today.

IO

SCHOOL

The question under investigation here, the question of the origin and influence of Church-generated powers, has a history in my own life. I became aware of it as a mystery that I wanted to try to penetrate a little in the late 1950s. At that time I was acting as rector of the Catholic University at Ponce in Puerto Rico. And it happened that the man who two years later would be the U.S. State Department's chief organizer of John Kennedy's Alliance for Progress in Latin America was then the president of the island's Council of Education.[1] He was away somewhere. I was acting as his substitute. And I came to feel increasingly uncomfortable with the administrative and advisory power that this gave. Power had always been something that worried me, not because I rejected it, but because of its ambiguous taste. And so, possessing this power in educational matters on that little island of Puerto Rico, I had to ask myself, What is it that I'm involved in here?

At the time, so far as I know, the procedure of schooling had never been made an object of study in history, anthropology, or the social sciences generally. No one had thought it worthwhile to explore the origin of the strange assumption that people are born with the need for schooling. But, in conversation with a friend and colleague named Everett Reimer,[2] this question came up, and we were led to ask, What is schooling? So we tried to look at the institution in purely formal terms, leaving out people's intentions with regard to education. We defined as a school any established agency which gathers together, for a minimum period of four years, groups of more than fifteen and less than fifty people, of roughly the same age, around a person who has participated in such assemblies for many more years than they. And we observed that wherever we looked in the world, schooling seemed to involve a succession of four such periods, each one designed to eliminate more and more people. Four times around this circle and you achieve social privilege.

At the time I was asking, What is this? I was deeply involved in reading the anthropologist Max Gluckman, who wrote on African ritual.³ And I began to wonder what would happen if, instead of speaking about this as a social institution, or a service agency, I viewed it as a ritual. Gluckman defines a ritual as any well-established form of behaviour which leads those who participate in it to a certain belief. It's a procedure whose imagined purpose allows the participants to overlook what they are actually doing, that is, the idea that the rain dance will bring rain eclipses the social cost of organizing the rain dance and makes the dancers feel that if rain doesn't come then they ought to dance all the harder. Rituals, in other words, have an ability to generate in their practitioners a deep adherence to convictions which may be, internally, highly contradictory, so that somehow, the adherence to the belief is stronger than most people's capacity to question what they believe.

But, as a ritual, schooling is something very new. Rain dances are known among some people in the Southwest of the United States and among some of the tribal peoples of India, and I don't know where else; but I don't know of any rain dance which is worldwide. Schooling has been brought by missionaries during the last few generations to every corner of the world, and its procedures are followed among Inuit as much as among people in Holland, or in Westchester, the ritzy section of New York. So I suddenly had to ask myself, Is there any precedent for the successful spread of this ritual around the world? A ritual which has come to be taken for granted and which has generated a belief, a myth, which has become a matter of faith in spite of the stark contrast presented by its obviously deleterious effects.

Schooling was being promoted during this time, the pre-Kennedy years, as a way of providing equality within nations, and equality among nations — an impossible hope as the balance sheet of any country shows — but attachment to this hope was tenacious. When I later told my friend and neighbour Erich Fromm about my idea of schooling as a ritual, a myth-making ritual, he was so shocked he didn't want to see me for two weeks or three. The great psychoanalyst and social analyst, who as an old man still wore a red carnation to show his socialism, would not allow anyone to profane this sacred institution.

My attempt to speak about modern institutions in terms of rituals coincided in the early 1960s with the increasing awareness among social scientists studying development that institutions have both positive and negative effects, and that introducing schools or modern medicine into places seen as in need of development produced unavoidable negative effects. These people thought of schooling as a technique whose effectiveness ought to be assessed. I proposed that it be analyzed as a ritual because only then did it become evident that the major effect of these institutions was to make people believe in the necessity and goodness of what they were supposed to achieve. This cannot be seen from inside. Nor can it be seen when the present is examined "in the shadow of the future," as Zygmunt Baumann so beautifully says.[4] A firm stance in the past is helpful. Imagine trying to talk to a friend in the seventeenth century, or the twelfth century, or in antiquity, about contemporary institutions, and it becomes easier to perceive how intensely ritualized they are. Ritual generates belief, so I speak of *mythopoesis, poesis* being the Greek word for "making": myth-making ritual.

Now, in getting to this strange, idiosyncratic, questionable view which sustained me through the first twenty years of my intense reflection on the effects of development, I was aided by something more than the studies of Max Gluckman. When I became the president of the board governing all education in Puerto Rico, it wasn't as a social scientist, or even as an evil kibitzer into the social sciences. I came there as a man who, besides history and philosophy, had also studied theology, Roman Catholic theology of the most traditional and, if you want, somewhat obscurantist type, which, however, if you studied it properly, demanded from you an extraordinary foundation in the classics and in the Christian classics: the Fathers of the Church, the Scholastics, and the spiritual masters.

And in the study of theology, which is the attempt to penetrate the message of the Gospel intellectually, one field interested me particularly. You will have noticed the traces of it during our conversation. It is called ecclesiology, which is the theological study of the entity called the "Church." One can study the Church as an historical phenomenon. That is what, again and again, we have been doing. But one can also study it from the perspective of faith as someone who believes in the new possibility of facing each other indicated in the story of the Samaritan. One can look at the Church as a mystery of faith, and ecclesiology as the task of studying the object of faith which calls itself Church and considers itself to be the mystical body of Christ, with "mystical" meaning communal.

One branch of ecclesiology is the study of liturgy. Liturgy can be studied in terms of the history of rituals, folk processions, and blessings, or the aesthetics of altar implements; and, in that sense, it belongs within the history of mentalities and of performing arts. But it is not in that sense that liturgy is part of ecclesiology. Liturgy becomes part of ecclesiology when you understand the ritual as the womb out of which and within which the Church comes to be in the present. It is an unquestionable belief of Christian communities of the most different kinds that the Church as a community comes into existence in a *symposium*, in a drinking and eating together in memory of the Last Supper, which Christ celebrated and to which he gave an eschatological meaning, that is, a meaning related to time. When he celebrated that dinner, he called to the attention of his apostles that they were doing something which, in a sense, stands outside of time, which he intends to do with them in the home of the Father, meaning in the beyond, after not only the Resurrection and the Ascension into heaven but after *apocalypsis*, the end of the world as it is now. It is, therefore, the belief of Christians — and this is pretty widely shared, though differently interpreted by different sects — that the Christian community comes into existence by sharing the same bread. This is a *mythopoesis*, a belief-generating ritual. The ritual does more than merely remember a faith which we already have. When we celebrate that faith by sharing bread and sharing the spirit through the kiss of peace, the *conspiratio* of which we spoke, the social entity comes into existence. This idea has been present in ecclesiological thought since the second century. One could, therefore, jokingly say that ecclesiology is a social science twenty times older than sociology, if I put the beginning of sociology at the time of Durkheim [1858–1917] and Weber [1864–1920].

So my theological and ecclesiastical background led to suppose that this worldwide institution must have something to do with the Church, but at first I thought that I had stumbled on nothing more than a very vague analogy. But over the years of trying to understand how the idea arose that man needs magisterial revelations in order to know anything about any side of reality and that these are best administered in a strictly organized ritual, I came to think that the connection might be closer and more deeply determined. Why believe that human beings are born requiring institutional initiation into the concrete reality in which they have to fulfill their duties as citizens? Since the middle of the last century it has often been claimed that our word for education comes from the Latin *educare*, to lead out. But when I went back to classical Latin dictionaries, I found a sentence of Cicero's in which he uses the verb *educare* in connection with the suckling of infants. *Nutrix educat*, the wet-nurse educates, he says. For teaching he uses the verbs *docere* or *instruere*. So then I looked to see when *educare* was first connected with a male subject. And what did I find? For two hundred years after Christ, its subject was always a female with juicy breasts. Then came Tertullian, a Christian bishop in North Africa, who is the first ever to declare, according to my huge Latin dictionary, that men educate because bishops have breasts, to which Christians come to suck the milk of Christ: faith.

I had never thought much about education until destiny threw me into the situation I've already described in Puerto Rico. But the more I looked into what was happening, the more I felt sick to my stomach. Everyone was so certain that they acted for the good of these

impressionable young Puerto Ricans. Therefore, I couldn't help asking the question, How should I interpret the belief that people need
ritual of this kind, not just to grow up into competent persons, but
also to be capable of what they then called "citizenship" — that is, the
fundamental, ethical, and moral sense which is necessary to form a
community. And I was driven to the suspicion that I was standing in
front of a secularization of Catholic ritual. The Church made attendance at various rituals compulsory. It set out schedules of specific
days when attendance was required and defined the violation of such
prescriptions as sin. For the clergy the *breviarium*, the shortened form
of monastic prayers, was made obligatory by the Council of Trent
[1545–1563]. For the simple Christian there was the requirement
of going to Mass every Sunday — otherwise you go to hell — or of
going to confession once a year. The elaboration of this legal organization, and this legal imposition, which defined missing out on
services as a sin, immediately preceded the epoch in which the state,
the new Church-like state, as I called it earlier, began to introduce its
own rituals. And the easiest one to follow is education. It begins with
the idea that man is born in need of revelation about the world into
which he comes, revelation which can be handed down only by recognized catechists called teachers. And it goes on to take the
unbelievable form of four-years elementary, four-years middle, four-
years upper, and four-years college attendance. What the modern
college asks is attendance, the physical act of being there, just as you
have to be there for Mass, which gets us used to an intensity of ritual
behaviour for which I don't find precedents or comparable examples
in other cultures.

I don't want to speak further about education here but only to
show how I personally proceeded in trying to discover the origin of
this belief, unknown to other societies, that you need an organized
institution to make people competent to understand what is good for
them and their community, that knowledge does not come from living but from *educatio*, the milk of wisdom flowing from the breasts of
an institution.

In earlier talks I tried to make it plausible that the Christian message explosively expands the scope of love by inviting us to love

whomever we choose. There is a new freedom involved, and a new confidence in one's freedom. I also tried to establish that this new freedom makes a new type of betrayal possible. The way I was led to frame this hypothesis was by observing the modern mania for education and then concluding that the only way it can be explained is as the fruit of a 2,000-year institutionalization of the catechetical, or instructional, function of the Christian community, which has led us to believe that only through explicit teaching and through rituals in which teaching has a major part can we become fit for the community in which we ought to live.

I had begun, by the way, as a believer, a rabid fighter for the implementation of the law which said every Puerto Rican had to have at least five years of schooling. And I had carried my support to the point where I had opposed any further public money flowing into the university before enough money was in the public education system to implement that law. So I changed from a believer in schools into a man for whom social rituals, and the myths they generate, must be studied historically. But I want to warn, despite my earlier reference to Max Gluckman, that these modern myths should not be too easily identified or too quickly made analogous to the myths and rituals, past or present, which we know through ethnology. School is not just another rain dance. It's a rain dance whose universalization Erich Fromm took so seriously that he would break with one of the closest friends of his old age. Standing in front of this altogether strange and mysterious phenomenon in the 1950s, I did not yet have the terms for it. Foucault had not yet written of epistemic breaks.[5] But I would say now that I was contemplating an historical watershed which was of a deeper nature than most contemporary historians intend when they use the now common language of watersheds, breaks, and breakthroughs. And I believe that its origin lies in the Church's attempt to take what had begun as a personal vocation — a call to each one — and to try to control and guarantee it by giving it this worldly solidity and permanence.

II

FRIENDSHIP

Again and again during the last forty years I have been asked the question, Where do you stand? I have usually, at the beginning of any major lecture series, told my audience that I stand within the Christian faith, in order that they should be aware that my prejudices may differ from theirs; but otherwise I have trusted that people who seriously followed a semester, or several semesters of my teaching, would eventually become guests around my table and find out for themselves the way in which I try to proceed. Let me now, at the end of my life, make a little pencil sketch of where I think I have been standing.

I have to point out first of all that changes in the nature of the university, particularly during the last hundred years, have made this institution almost an enemy to the collegial procedure, which I've tried to cultivate. Yes, I have made my living out of the university, soberly milking that sacred cow and making my nest with the hand-outs I've received. I've never accepted a regular university job, but only a semester at a time at different institutions or at one institution — I've now been teaching at the University of Bremen for seven or eight years, and at Penn State for twelve. This has provided my friends and me with the wherewithal for a hospitable table. And a good tax lawyer found a way of making it credible to the IRS that a certain number of cases of ordinary but decent wine are my major teaching tool and can, therefore, be written off from taxes.

I was inspired by the *Symposium* of Plato. Plato's idea of *philia*, of love, as the way into knowledge has been a challenge because, from decade to decade, I have had to interpret it in new ways. But one conviction remained constant: friendship can never mean the same thing to me as it does to Plato. In the Greek city, virtue was understood as fitting behaviour. It was the *ethos*, or ethics, appropriate to a certain *ethnos*, or people. And such virtue was the foundation of friendship, what made it possible. Friendship was the flowering of civic virtue and its crown. It was only as virtuous Athenians that the guests at Plato's *sym-posium* — literally, "drinking party" — could love one another. This has not been my destiny as a wandering Jew and Christian pilgrim. I have not been able to seek friendship as something arising from a place and the practices appropriate to it. Rather the ethics that developed around the circle of my friends arose as a result of our search for friendship, and our practice of it. This is a radical inversion in the meaning of *philia*. For me friendship has been the source, condition, and context for the possible coming about of commitment and like-mindedness. For Plato it could only be the result of practices befitting a citizen.

This dramatic inversion makes it necessary for me to say a few words about the history of friendship. For Plato — and any other classical text would show the same — friendship presupposes an *ethnos*, a given here and now to which I belong by birth. It presumes certain limits within which it can be practised. In Athens, for example, being a free man would have been one such limiting condition. Then comes that major disturber and fool, that historical Jesus of the Gospels, with his story about the Samaritan, the Palestinian who is the only one who acts as a friend towards a beaten-up Jew. Jesus discloses a new unrestricted ability to choose whom I want for a friend, and the same possibility of letting myself be chosen by whoever wants me. This is often forgotten by people who portray modern "friendship" as just a further development of what Plato and Aristotle meant by this term. Jesus disrupted the frame that limited the conditions under which friendship could appear, and this led in the history of the West to the creation within the Church of new voluntary, self-chosen forms of life within which friendship could be practised.

Monasticism was certainly one of the ways, perhaps the main way, through which groups of freely chosen others came together and created conditions in which a spirit of community could flower. Within this lineage, there are many paths to friendship. Two contemporary examples which I have admired are the community of my friend Giuseppe Dozeti in Italy and the Catholic Worker communities established in the United States by Dorothy Day. I have seen it as my task to explore the ways in which the life of the intellect, the disciplined and methodical joint pursuit of clear vision — one could say philosophy in the sense of loving truth — can be so lived that it becomes the occasion for the kindling and growth of *philia*. (Let me use the word *philia*, in order to avoid the funny implications of the word friendship in different modern languages.) I wanted to see if it would be possible to create truly, deeply committed human ties on the occasion and by the means of common investigation. And I also wanted to show how the search for truth can be pursued in a unique way around a dining table or over a glass of wine and not in the lecture hall. If the expression "search for truth" makes people smile and think that I belong to some Old World, then very well, I do.

When I was younger, and was offered access to the lecture hall, the public forum, I grabbed it, but always with the idea of eventually bringing together those who took me seriously in more convivial circumstances. So when people approached after a lecture and asked, "May the three of us come to see you?" I could say, "Yes, but why don't you come when the other two, whom I would like you to meet, are also there?" And, in that way, the public occasion could be used to bring people together.

In this way one can foster the growth of an open group of people who are moved by fidelity to each other as persons and dare to maintain fidelity even if the other one becomes a heavy burden. But in order to pursue truth within the horizon of a "we" that is truly a plural "I," a "we" that is arbitrary, that is unique, that slowly emerges, that cannot be put into any class, then it is first necessary to shed a certain number of extremely sticky and persistent university-derived academic etiquettes, like the organization of knowledge into specialized and exclusive disciplines. It has been my experience that many of the people I meet who want to risk the style of research I've described will already have had considerable socialization, as one says, within a university and an academic milieu. For them disciplinary self-limitation may have already become a way of refusing conversation on what I really know and what really interests me with people outside the discipline, and this prejudice must be abandoned.

Let me say a little bit more about some of these deformations that my friends and I have tried to get beyond during the last forty-five years. The university is oriented towards disciplinary gatherings. People who know something about the history of ideas in one tradition tend to think that they can only advance in their knowledge within the circle of people who have the same training. I have tried to challenge them to put friendship above this prejudice, and to let this friendship motivate them to try to put into ordinary language the breakthroughs and insights that have become possible through their technical knowledge. This challenge goes further than just asking them to teach undergraduates — because undergraduate teaching can be just an introduction to their method — or just asking them to broaden their horizons to include other professionals. It rests on the conviction that things which are finally important must be capable of being shared with others whom I love first and then want to talk to. And this conviction will have a considerable impact on the way in which I assess and express my own insights.

I should also say that *convivium*, or *symposium*, the sharing of soup, wine, or other liquids, requires that at that table where we join, somebody must preside. And someone can only preside as a host when a threshold separates this table from the outside. The disappearance of thresholds in our world was brought vividly home to me not long ago by a Polish woman who attended my classes in Bremen. This woman was not what you would call an intellectual, but she had been coming regularly to my classes for five years. Once I spoke about the transformation of the idea of thresholds in history and particularly during the last thirty years. I pointed to the way in which walls have become permeable by many kinds of radiation from e-mail and faxes to telephones and television signals, and I suggested that the idea of privacy had been put into question, and the difference marked by a threshold muddied. "I get what you say, Professor Illich," she said in her heavy Polish accent. "I have lived now in Germany for thirty-five years. Germans are wonderful, lovely people. They never can come to visit you without bringing some gifts. But they don't stop at the threshold so that I may lead them in. Barely have I opened the door when they jump over the threshold, and I'm in my kitchen, finding a vase to put the flowers in. What do you do then?"

So, the table, or the rug on which we sit, must be distinguished from the commons, from the street outside. But this doesn't mean that the *convivium* should be understood as a private activity which stands opposed to a public sphere. Rather it's a personal activity. It's the creation, through sharing, of an inside, distinct from the outside. And this is made more difficult by the fact that the outside barely exists any longer as a true commons, that is to say, a space usable by people in various overlapping ways.

I've conducted this kind of inquiry for many years now with people I picked up at lectures, and I've learned that the presidency, the ability to lead somebody over the threshold, should not be the prerogative of one person only, but should be shared by friends. The possibility of meeting at the home of one of the hosts of Socrates has been weakened in our time; and for this reason the creation of a threshold, and the exercise of the power to bring someone over it, must acquire an entirely new significance. Some people speak about a new monasticism. I reject this, just as I reject the idea that a return to the true spirit of the university is possible. I think I've taken another road — to a place where fools can gather.

On the table, as you have noticed over the years, there is always a candle. Why? Because the text that shaped my understanding was *De Spirituali Amicitia*, a treatise on spiritual friendship by the twelfth-century Scottish abbot Aelred of Rievaulx. His father and his grandfather had been abbots of Rievaulx before him. His marvellous booklet on friendship is in the form of a dialogue with a brother monk, and it begins with the words "Here we are, you and I, and, I hope, also a third who is Christ." If you consider his meaning carefully, you understand that it could be Christ in the form of Brother Michael. In other words, our conversation should always go on with the certainty that there is somebody else who will knock at the door, and the candle stands for him or her. It is a constant reminder that the community is never closed.

So there must be, first of all, a threshold, and then a recognition that this threshold defines a space which is personal but never exclusive. A third requisite for the cultivation of the atmosphere I've been talking of is a willingness to accept discipline without having formally stated rules. The dishes have to be washed, and if fifteen more people than expected turn up for dinner, someone has to see that the soup stretches. And the question of how this is handled, and by whom, has to be settled without recourse to rules, because the moment you make rules you are already on the way to institutionalization. In the same way, academic conventions, covering, let's say, the form in which a citation is given, should be followed as something trivial but necessary. This was a major difficulty in the early 1970s, after the misunderstood anarchism of 1968. It's not so difficult to practise today.

So, to repeat, my idea was that the search for truth presupposes the growth of *philia*. This *philia* must find an atmosphere in which it can grow, and this atmosphere cannot be taken for granted as an outgrowth of civic virtue. It must be very carefully nonrestrictive. Always a candle ready, a candle lighted. God knows who comes to the door. Recently a guy came to the door and asked for money because he said he needed to call a locksmith. He wanted twenty dollars, and I said, "Let's give it to him." He came back a little later and told us not to worry, that he still hadn't been able to get into his apartment. Then he didn't come back for two days. Finally, he came just as we were sitting down to dinner, and it turned out that he not only had the twenty dollars but also some interesting ideas on the subject we were discussing.

Along this path I've been describing, I've had the luck to pick up friends, with whom conversations have now gone on for five decades. When these people have met each other, intense ties have frequently developed between them, and sometimes they have felt called to a deep revision of their views. Age cohorts, to my great surprise, are not decisive when people are careful in practising what I've been describing. I have seen friendships between people who could be grandson and grandfather become strong and fruitful. In the university, one would speak, hierarchically, of "my student." Here a truly rooted fidelity and commitment precedes the intellectual substance of the conversation.

It's a funny thing that speaking about one's life in recent times always implies a psycho-analysis, a search for unconscious undercurrents. I would like to speak about myself in my time, on my road, without inviting this impudence. Many people have considered the course of a life as a kind of "walking on foot," as in the Hindu world, or as a pilgrimage, so important still to Moslems. And my road has been one of friendship. A Christian monk of the Middle Ages said that living with others in community is the greatest penance one can undertake, but that is the way I have taken: to try to maintain fidelity and to bear one another's impossible way of being. You can't write the biography of a friendship — it's too deeply personal. Friendships run on separate ways that cross and run parallel and cross again.

ON KNOWING HOW TO DIE:
THE LAST DAYS
OF SAVONAROLA

Because what I am saying here about the Church can be easily misunderstood or misappropriated, let me tell you a story which I think displays a model attitude towards the Church, as well as the character of a man who knew in an extraordinarily beautiful way how to die. I'm speaking of Girolamo Savonarola, the Florentine monk and reformer who was executed as a heretic at the end of the fifteenth century. I had become interested in Savonarola when I was a boy of thirteen or fourteen, living in Florence, with that enthusiasm one can have at that age for rebels; but, then, in my seventieth year, I got a call from Paolo Prodi, a trusted and dear friend and the only historian for whom I feel the same esteem as I had for our mutual teacher Gerhart Ladner. Paolo called to say that the five hundredth anniversary of Savonarola's martyrdom was about to be celebrated in Pistoia. The gathering would mostly comprise historians of Florentine history between 1470 and 1510, but we have all decided, he said, that it would be ideal if you would preside over a final session of these historians and give the final talk on prophecy today. I felt very uncomfortable with this assignment, because there is an abysmal distance between me and the dozen or so first-rate historians who had been invited, but friendship for Paolo, as well as my gratitude to him as a teacher, made me stand to attention, bow my head, and say, "Yes, I will obey."

So I began to worm my way into the literature on Savonarola — thirty-two volumes of writings have survived and have just been published in a new edition — and the more I read, the more I was fascinated by this man. The other historians at this conference in Pistoia, when it finally happened, talked about Savonarola as a cultural figure, as an ecclesiastical reformer, or as a preacher in Florence. They were interested in the great praise heaped on him, despite the seeming contradiction, by Machiavelli, in why Ficino[1] had called him "the prince of hypocrites," in what he had done in his earlier life, or how he had conducted the final six or seven years of his public ministry and preaching. I concentrated only on his last day or last days.

Savonarola had become a politically impossible guy for the Medicis, who then ruled Florence, and they had to get rid of him. He spent fifty days in prison and underwent two major sessions of torture, one under the city government of Florence and one by the special emissary of the Pope. During this time in prison, as a result of the harsh treatment the Church administered to him, I see Savonarola as blossoming into a man who knew how to die. He had been a genius of rhetoric, a good — as far as I can judge — theologian, a careful reader of Holy Scripture, and one of the first effective champions of popular government. But during those fifty days he dictated two books, which go beyond these earlier achievements. With his body wounded, and his arm broken by torture, he dictated two interpretations of Psalms. These inspired the reforms attempted by Dominicans in southern Spain twenty years before Luther, and later had great influence in South America. One scholar has even claimed that Luther related his great experience of conversion to the true faith in the tower in sentences borrowed from Savonarola.[2] But more important for my purpose here is the way in which Savonarola understood the two faces of the Church. He died with signs of obedience to the Church which are public, unquestionable, and extraordinary, but, at the very same time, he recognized the Church as the nesting place for evil. And this was not just because Alexander VI, who was then Pope, had purchased the papacy, or because he had lived a wicked life, but because, in a much deeper sense, he represented the temptation of power within the Church.

Now, let me tell you about Savonarola's last day. He was condemned as a heretic. No proof of heresy was offered beyond the fact
that he would not desist from his claim that he was a prophet who
spoke under divine inspiration. Two other friars were condemned
with him because they had accepted Savonarola's claim and confirmed it in public. As a consideration of Florentine civility in 1498,
they were to be hanged before being burnt.

On the day of his burning, in the morning at Mass, he speaks in
a beautiful prayer of how sadness has invaded him, of how his
friends and everything he sees depress him. He comments on the
Miserere[3] and speaks of the abysm of his misery at having declared
the day before under torture that he was not divinely inspired when
he preached. I take it back, he says. I lied out of fear of torture, and I
want this to be known publicly. Let the abysm of my sinfulness dis-
solve in the abysm of your mercy.

Then he turned to his two brethren, two very different men,
Domenico, who had made swords in defiance of Savonarola, and
Sylvestro, who was terribly fearful and trembled at the idea of dying.
To Domenico he said, "During the night, it was revealed to me that,
when you're being led to your hanging, you should say, 'No, don't
hang me, burn me alive.' We are not masters of our own deaths. We
must be happy if we can die the death which God has destined for
us." And then he turns around to Sylvestro and says, "It's been
revealed to me that you want to make a statement about our innocence. Jesus, on the cross, didn't do it. And we won't do it." The two
friars knelt down, asked for his blessing, and obeyed.

They went out from the Palazzo de la Signoria in Florence on the
catwalk that had been constructed towards the gibbet. There they
were met by two Dominican friars who had been sent by the general
of their order to tear off their Dominican clothing so they wouldn't
disgrace the order by dying in their cowls. Savonarola said, "I won't
give it to you, but you can strip me." Then he went a step further and
met the special delegate of the Pope, who told him that he was being
condemned as a heretic and schismatic and — here's the nub —
excluded henceforth from the Church Militant and the Church
Triumphant, the Church on earth and the Church in heaven.

Girolamo Savonarola responded in his usual quiet, strong, unbroken voice, as the official observer of these proceedings noted. "You may exclude me from the temporal church, sir," he said, "but only from the temporal church. You don't have the authority to decree the second." He went a step further and there was the delegate of Pope Alexander, who had been sent as a special inquisitor to torture him and had done his job in the days before. He reconfirmed the judgement and took out a scroll by which the Pope conceded to the three condemned friars the grace of a perfect indulgence. All punishment in purgatory was suspended, according to this decree, and their innocence restored. Here the foolishness, not of Savonarola, but of the Church itself, reaches its high point. The decree ended with a question, Do you accept? And the last thing these three friars did was to bow their heads.

Now, either these are cowards, or they are people dominated by cultural assumptions in popular religiosity in Florence in 1498, or they are, in the fullest, the most glorious way, clowns, fools, who know what they are doing. I wish I could die that way.

13

THE AGE OF SYSTEMS

I argued earlier that the epoch of instrumentality, or the technological epoch, came to an end within the last twenty years. You can see the germ of this change much earlier, of course. It's present, for example, in Alan Turing's vision of a Universal Machine. But what I'm talking about only becomes visible in a full-blown way in an event like the Gulf War, a computer war which showed people at the same time their utter powerlessness and their intense addiction to the screen on which they watched it.

When I speak of the end of an epoch, of course, I'm not speaking about the end of its historical continuation. Epochs always overlap. So when Turing gave the name "machine" to the mathematical function that he had elegantly analyzed, he built a bridge between the new reality and the era that was actually ending and made it seem as if something explosively new was just a further stage, or perhaps the ultimate stage, in the evolution of technological society. Lots of great thinkers have fallen into that trap. In the Middle Ages, at the beginning of the technological era, Hugh of St. Victor and Theophilus Presbyter were the first to think of the implements proper to the various arts as something separable from the hands of the artisans who used them. But they did not realize the full novelty of what they were doing in creating, for the first time, a general idea of tools as means of production.

The epoch that Hugh began has now ended, because the computer cannot be conceptualized as a tool in the sense that has prevailed for the last 800 years. In order to use a tool, I have to able to conceive of myself as standing apart from the tool, which I can then take or leave, use or not use. Even something as up-to-date as the automobile is still a device in which I can seat myself, turn the ignition, and start. It might be objected that the car won't run without a road system, but I have driven the beast in the desert and know what a jeep is. Obviously the Model T sold by Henry Ford was a lot closer to a hammer than the modern Japanese product sold in the United States, which is already very much software within the hardware of roads, courts, police, and hospital trauma units; but, nevertheless, I am still able in front of the car to imagine a distance, a distality between me and the device. This becomes pure illusion when I create a macro in WordPerfect to organize my footnotes. As an operator, I become part of the system. I can no longer conceive of my relation to the grey box in the same way in which Theophilus Presbyter thought of a chisel.

So I want to distinguish first of all between society seen in the light, and in the shadow, of tools which remain separate from the one who uses them and the society of systems into which we have now slipped. One way of getting at the change we have undergone is by looking at what has happened to language. There has been an enormous increase in the last fifteen years in the availability of expert judgements on the effects of drinking beer or smoking or whatever it may be. People are inundated with instructions and help programs. And these instructions are not transmitted in the form of sentences, but through icons. I'm not speaking of holy images, of course, but of these innumerable minting stocks of public intercourse, which increasingly replace language. I'm speaking about the use of images in making arguments. Let me take an example: the population curve. Population is an icon of something moving, something which we know by now isn't stable, something which we have learned only too painfully is somewhat beyond our control. The devices available to control it are so horrible that they are tabooed from ordinary conversation. It's something about which experts can tell us. Even to say the word means submission to the expert who has gathered the statistics.

An icon, no matter whether it represents the population curve or some other administrative reality, is in a frame, which I haven't chosen but somebody else has chosen for me. This is not true of sentences. My sentences can potentially break the frame that you may want to impose on them. I have this extraordinarily beautiful freedom which is implicit in language, and which requires of my interlocutor the patience to allow his words to be turned around in my mouth. The icon fixes what it suggests. It produces a visual paralysis, which is interiorized. In Spanish "populating" was something that was formerly done in bed, and in older English one still populated a territory. But what is shown in the population curve has no connection with carnal intercourse. The word is a prison cell, or straightjacket, constructed by unquestionable experts; and what we call education, particularly higher education — as I have been able to observe in ten frightening years at Penn State University — forces people into this straightjacket. They become decent intellectuals who won't touch terms for which there is also a visual expression. The visual, the iconic representation determines the word, to the point that the word can't be used without evoking the icon. My friend Uwe Pörksen in a new book calls these icons "visiotypes."[1] A visiotype is the elementary form of this way of dealing with each other. Unlike a word it is unfit for predication, as I will try to explain. In English one can speak of a copula, which is the verb which joins the subject and the predicate, or object, of a sentence. The word has a wonderful hint of carnality, as if the subject and object of a sentence were mingled in the same way as a man and a woman in love. Visiotypes have no such relations with any predicate. They are fixed, static entities that stand outside the relativity of words. To speak in strict linguistic terms, they are connotative stereotypes. In this sense they are like those elemental sound bites which Pörksen wrote about in his earlier book on plastic words.[2] These are highly respected terms, few in number, the same in every modern language, which have innumerable connotations but no power to denote anything clear or specific. I prefer to call them amoeba words. They correspond to visiotypes and provide their only possible verbal equivalents. Ordinary words don't apply to visiotypes, and trying to apply them only creates confusion. They are not within the realm of personal knowledge. They include me, but I cannot include them in what I actually know.

We spoke earlier about the appearance of virtual spaces in the midst of the everyday. And I suggested, for the fun of it, that this was presaged, in the kiosks along Paris boulevards, by the appearance of stereoscopes, where you could look at the merchandise available in the brothels, gazing at it in a virtual space generated by two cameras, set apart by four times the distance between the two eyes. It heightened the reality of the pictured flesh, while making both the foreground and the background hazy, calling you to come and taste for yourself what would inevitably disappoint you. I borrowed this example from Jonathon Crary's good analysis of the introduction of visualized virtual spaces in everyday life. Crary says that sometime in the late 1970s the number of these virtual spaces exploded. I would add that each time you look at a visiotype, you contaminate yourself with the virtuality it carries within it. And I would also say that if I look at body history and particularly at the visualization of the contents of the pregnant uterus, I can locate the widespread appearance of these spaces thirty or forty years earlier.

I used the word "contaminate" here intentionally. One of the reasons we are having this conversation is because we want to walk in this world with the least possible contamination of our flesh, and our eyes and our language, and to be aware of how difficult this is to do. Language, above all, is threatened by the virtuality of this increasingly dominant visual manipulation of my thoughts — both my silent inner language and the public language in which I converse with others. I have to struggle to defend my senses from being pulled into a world of visiotypes. Otherwise, under the influence of a carefully programmed bombardment by visiotypes, I will begin to conceive of myself as *homo transportandus*, or *homo educandus* — a man standing in need of transportation or education.

Let me make a little parenthesis here concerning the history of technology. It is a commonplace now among historians of technology that people derive both their self-image and their conception of society from their tools. As far back as the Middle Ages, the idea of "the tools of the trade" was a precondition for the organization of guilds in this proto-industrial age. Think of the influence of the idea of "the means of production" via Marx in the period between 1850 and the Second World War. Or of the importance that the watch or the mechanical music box had in the late Baroque. Think of the transition from the clock on the tower, or the standing clock with its pendulum, to the watch that you could carry in your pocket. The obvious influence of these devices on ways of thinking leads easily to the idea that tools come first and changes in how we conceive of ourselves and our social organizations follow. But the general idea of tools had to be there before any particular action of tools could be recognized or accepted. So it's worth considering the possibility that the relation between techniques and concepts might be the contrary of what is now supposed by historians of technology. The attempt to model stereovision precedes photography by twenty years. Photography actualized the idea and put the stereoscope on your great-grandmother's desk for her enjoyment, but it did not begin it.

Don't think that I'm speaking about something terribly distant or academic. I found that in 1926 the American Educational Association insisted that an American school could not be considered up to standards if it didn't have at least as many stereoscopes as the number of students in its largest class and, at least, 700 sets of stereo stories on Greek gods and on chemistry, so that all children, even the poorest ones, would view reality through this window. But why am I telling you about it? Because I believe that the desire to achieve something very frequently precedes, often only by a generation or two, the creation of the tool that makes it possible.

Now to return to my main theme: There are two entirely different, and, I think, irreconcilable interpretations of our present predicament. In my writings of the 1960s and 1970s, I spoke of the modernization, or professionalization, of the client. I tried to show how the client forms his self-perception by interiorizing, as one so easily says, the school system, for example. You classify yourself, and submit to classification by others, according to the point on the curve at which you dropped out. In the same way you internalize your need for health care by claiming your right to diagnosis, painkilling, preventive care, and medicalized death. Or, by swallowing the car you paralyze your feet and have to jump into the driver's seat to go to a supermarket.

But sometime in the 1980s I began to think about these things differently. I realized that people were being absorbed or integrated into systems in a way that went beyond what I had at first thought. And I found the necessary rethinking very demanding. As long as I spoke of a successful university student as somebody who had swallowed the assumptions of the school system, I was still speaking of somebody who conceived himself as a producer and consumer of knowledge and, in some way, a citizen, somebody who could recognize his privilege as a citizen, and, by claiming a right to that privilege, provide grounds for its extension to everyone. As long as I thought about a person who had swallowed his need for analgesics, for freedom from abnormalities, for the prolongation of life, I was still thinking of someone who stood in front of large institutions with the idea, at least, that he could use them for the satisfaction of his own dreams or his own needs. But what of the person who has himself been swallowed by the world conceived as a system, a world represented or made present to his fantasy in a disconnected but seductive sequence of visiotypes? In this case the possibility of political engagement, and the language of needs, rights, and entitlements, which could be used during the 1960s and 1970s, ceases to be effective. All one can wish for now is to get rid of the glitches, as I think they are called in communication theory, or to adjust inputs and outputs more responsively. In the 1960s I could still speak plausibly about "the secularization of hope." The Good Society, the desirable future, lying behind the horizon, still invited aspiration. People still felt some power. Without the possibility of power it makes no sense to talk about responsibility, because, historically speaking, talk about moral responsibility extends only as far as my power, in some way, reaches. All the intense talk about responsibility in the 1960s was a reflection of people's belief, admittedly completely fantastic, in the power of institutions and of their possible participation within institutions. Powerful people could still enjoy a version of deeply secularized hope, a hope which took the form of belief in development, in betterment, in progress. In the new era, the characteristic person, and a type I have frequently encountered in the last few years, is someone who has been gathered by one of the tentacles of the social system and swallowed. For him this possibility of sharing in the bringing about of something hoped for is gone. Having been swallowed by the system, he conceives himself as a subsystem, frequently as an immune system. Immune means provisionally self-balancing in spite of any change in environmental conditions. Fantastic talk about life as a subsystem with the ability to optimize its immediate environment — the Gaia hypothesis[3] — takes on a gruesome meaning when it is used by someone who has been swallowed by the system to express his self-consciousness.

Let me make it simpler. You have children, and you told me once you have great difficulty imagining why they are so fond of branded clothes. Why wear a T-shirt decorated with an icon? To me this is a poetical way of speaking about a person swallowed by the system, someone who needs an icon, which I can touch when I want to obtain something, be it only attention from the other.

Now, at the centre of the context in which we speak stand those things I have to understand in order to practise, beyond Buber,[4] the I–Thou relationship — to face you and let myself be faced by your *pupilla*, your version of Ivan, which gives reality to me. I want to lay the intellectual foundation for an ascetical practice which will foster this relationship. And, there is definitely a difference between trying to face the romantic social do-gooder, the social democrat, or ecologist of the past in whom the ego does not yet reach for an icon and trying to face a really contemporary person, who pastes an icon on his breast and says, arbitrarily, "Hey, that's me."

What I have said today about icons brings to an end my searching and sometimes painfully stuttering inquiry into the Western history of iconoscepsis,[5] of doubt and hesitation before images into which my eyes might fall. In this history, the legitimization of *iconodulia*, devotion to sacred icons, is, for me, a major step forward. It allows me to search eternity and discover ultimate truth as a living body behind the threshold of the image. But *iconodulia* in no way excludes simultaneously the guarding of the eyes. The proscription of images in Judaism and Islam is intended, so far as I can understand, to prevent the face becoming an image, so that I will not look at you like a photographer fixing an image but remain constantly vulnerable to what looking at you in the flesh will reveal to me about myself. It invites me to be ruthless in tearing away the illusions, consolations, and fancies that make it possible to live with myself at this moment and to seek myself instead in what I find through your eyes.

One of the most serious steps away from the certainty that imagery, particularly imagery of the human face, is a major threat to our mutual presence, and to the possibility that you will find yourself in facing me, is taken with the mechanization of the image in photography. Widespread photography makes people forget how much images interfere with that ultimately indescribable gaze which reaches out on several levels simultaneously and, for the believer, into the beyond as well. Now the gaze can be conceived as that of the camcorder. The satellite view of the world can be taken as a real view, as if that were a possible human standpoint. People can become habituated to seeing in front of their eyes things which, by their very nature, are not in the order of the visible, trivially, because they are so small, smaller even than the wavelength of red light, or perhaps because, as long as they are living, they are below the skin, like the movements of my heart. They can learn to recognize figments, like the visual representation of quantities, or the so-called genome with its implication of command and control. And, by this habituation, we lose the everyday habit of placing our gaze on that which falls under our eyes. Iconoscepsis combined with the desert mentality of Jews and Moslems — "Thou shalt not make thyself an image" — therefore remain necessary complements to the extraordinary challenge which comes from the expansion of love made possible through the Incarnation, and through my belief in the Incarnation, because the recognition of this possibility is mortally threatened by kids learning in school to understand and use their eyes as camcorders.

We are moving into what I would call an a-mortal society. To illustrate, I would open a computer and show you what a crash means, the crash of a state. Or I would lead you into an intensive care unit where the brainwave monitor is on above the patient and is being watched for the moment when it goes flat. Or I would show

you the billboard that impressed me and several of my friends along
the road between Claremont and Los Angeles which shows brainwaves and then a flat line and then, in big letters, the name of an
insurance company. None of this has anything to do with death.
Dying is an intransitive word. It's something which I can do, like
walk or think or talk. I can't be "died." I can be killed. If a few seconds
or minutes are left, even then I can fully engage in saying goodbye.

   The art of dying is different in each society. This morning, literally this morning, just before you came in here, a Mexican woman
was here speaking about her poor sister who can't die because three of
her nine kids don't want to let her go, even though she's in pain. And
she recalled her father's death — how she had told him, "Daddy, you
can go in peace. I will take care of mother." She then told her two
brothers, "Don't get mixed up in this." And the man died, she told
me, in a beautiful way, with a radiant face. So I said, "Yes, let's take
him as our model." Now this might happen even under systems
assumptions. Anything can happen. Nevertheless a society — and it's
questionable whether I should even call it a "society" — a social system built on the assumption of feedbacks, of programs, and of lack of
distality between its immune subsystems and its entire functioning
eliminates mortality. Mortality is not the same thing as an immune
system with a limited probability of survival, or an immune system
not yet crashed. A person who has tried to establish the habit of virtuous action, so that living the right way becomes second nature,
incorporates in his action the knowledge of death. It may be the
step over the threshold into the world of the ancestors, or the reign of
Christ on the prairies beyond. Phillipe Ariès in his book on ways
of dying gives a beautiful account of different practices in different
parts of the world.[6] A person who constantly manages himself as a
system is totally impotent in front of the fact that he knows, just as
well as formerly, that life will come to an end.

   This condition of a-mortality is reflected in the demand that doctors now become executioners. To establish such a service would be a
remarkable certificate of national abulia. There are plenty of effective
ways of taking leave in every woman's cleaning cabinet. There are
more poisons around than ever before. Let the Hemlock Society take

care of instruction in self-use. I'm not speaking for suicide. I'm simply saying that the idea of institutionalizing it, and thinking people
incompetent to do it, is a recognition of national incompetence,
which is almost beyond imagination. The medical profession has
become an iatrogenic body factory, financed by tax money, and its
perversion is most clearly shown in this demand that doctors become
procurers of death for their patients. There were healers in all societies with various special competences. In most societies there were a
dozen different types of such specialists. Even here in this village, you
have different old women and men for different things which one
would call health care. The task was to enable a person to bear suffering, and to move, in some kind of peaceful way, towards death. In the
Italian city of Bologna, for example, during the period of the plague,
I have evidence that it was the candle makers and the sellers of
incense that were the ones who provided what one needed to die
appropriately.

    The idea that doctors should kill their patients on request is mon-
strous but easily explained. At a certain moment, and usually with the
support of our most venerable institutions, including religion, doctors, instead of taking care of patients, began to take care of human
lives. In *Medical Nemesis* I tried to show how this had already begun
to happen around the middle of the nineteenth century. Doctors were
then represented as taking the hypodermic and intravenous syringe,
which had just been invented, and using it to fight against death —
in one image a skeletal death figure is shown being thrown out the
door. From that moment on, doctors became life managers and, ultimately, producers of iatrogenic *somata* ["bodies"] and, of course, can
now be called on as executioners.

    I once wrote a letter — it will soon be published — to a nun
whom I have known since her girlhood and who is now in her old age
the superior of a beautiful contemplative community.[7] In this letter I
reflected on my friendship with a woman who confessed to me that
she intended to end her life. She told me that she had prepared herself for the next winter, and even chosen the spot under a tree where
she would like to go to die. She was alcoholic, but still very much
alive and clear, and said to me, Ivan, you are a chemist.[8] You should

know something about it. Tell me what poison to choose. She was a stubborn lady, I can tell you, not open to any arguments. And I know that she loved Johnny Walker's Black Label. So I wrote to my nun friend that I'm sorry that, at that moment, after bringing her to her home, I didn't go out, buy a bottle of Johnny Walker, and put it in front of her door in order to make her sure that what she had told me did not in any way interfere with our friendship, as she must have felt from the look on my face. I will in no way help in a suicide; but at least three times in my life I have had to tell someone, always different people — in my way of life, this happened — "I will not open the window for you, but I'll stay with you." And this position, of not helping, but standing by, because you respect freedom, is difficult for people in our nice society to accept. I have just recently had evidence of this difficulty in believing that somebody like myself would suspend judgement at the suicide of a friend. But to put the mark of betrayal on it seems to me outside of my competence.

Let me say a bit more finally about the iatrogenic body. One of the hallmarks of modernity is the progressive replacement of the idea of the good by the idea of values, as I've already said. The production and delivery of iatrogenic bodies to members of this society is part of this replacement of the sense of what is good and right and befits me and my interior balance of humours. The iatrogenic body is assessed by the reading of positive and negative values proceeding from an assumed zero point. It is *evaluated*. Look at the way patients in hospitals live their own charts. They are concerned about "Doctor, how is the pressure today?" not about how they feel today. Something very fundamental gets lost when I observe myself against values rather than feel myself as a bundle of miseries, in pain, half crippled, tired, but bearing all this. There are various accounts in various worlds of the past as to why and how I should bear it. In my world, it is bearing it as my cross. The cross doesn't cease to be something evil, even when I bear it. But as we said in our very first meeting, the cross is somehow paradoxically glorified by the belief that God has become man in order to bear it. This is not the glory of Constantine's *in hoc signo vinces*,[9] by which the cross becomes an instrument of power, but the cross as a sign of shame and of defeat, which the Son of God took upon himself.

We have spoken about evil already, and I have argued that an entirely unsuspected dimension of evil appears with the possibility of sin, which is betrayal of new and free love. The destruction of the possibility of shouldering the body is such an evil for me. But this aspect of evil is hidden from those who think only in values. They do not see the side of sin. Thinking about the body as a system, or a sub-system, is a way of hiding sin.

14

ENVOI

During the days that we have been discussing my hypothesis that modernity can be studied as an extension of Church history, I have again and again tried to show you that our present world can finally be understood only as a perversion of the New Testament. So, I do not believe, with some, that this is a post-Christian world. That would be consoling. I believe, though I'm hesitant about the term, that it's an apocalyptic world. At the very beginning of our conversations, we spoke about the *mysterium iniquitatis*, the mystery of evil, the nesting of an otherwise unthinkable, unimaginable, and nonexistent evil and its egg within the Christian community. We then used the word Anti-Christ — the Anti-Christ, which looks, in so many things, just like Christ, and which preaches universal responsibility, global perception, humble acceptance of teaching instead of finding out for oneself, and guidance through institutions. The Anti-Christ, or, let's say, the *mysterium iniquitatis*, is the conglomerate of a series of perversions by which we try to give security, survival ability, and independence from individual persons to the new possibilities that were opened through the Gospel by institutionalizing them.

I claim that the *mysterium iniquitatis* has been hatching. I know too much of Church history to say that it's now breaking its shell, but I dare to say that it's now more clearly present than ever before. It is, therefore, completely wrong to ascribe to me the idea that this is a post-Christian era. On the contrary, I believe this to be, paradoxically, the most obviously Christian epoch, which might be quite close to the end of the world.

The prophet of old was called into the desert — an extraordinary and unique vocation extending from Samuel down to Micah. In the first two generations of the Christian Church, from the little we know about it, prophecy was a necessary unfolding of the community's liturgy. There needed to be somebody who prophesied what was to come, which was not the Messiah but the Anti-Christ, the *mysterium iniquitatis*. This reality was then forgotten, or relegated to the status of those things about which we don't know enough to speak, and only occasionally touched upon by sectarians for 2,000 years. I am not trying to revive it. The vocation by which I try to live today I would call that of the friend rather than the prophet.

Let me tell you a story. I was recently in Bologna as a guest of Paolo Prodi. And it so happened that a boy for whose baptism I had been present sixteen years before was now being confirmed. And, as a good Italian family, the nine brothers and sisters gathered for the confirmation as they had for the baptism. One of them was Romano Prodi, Paolo's brother, who is currently the Prime Minister of Italy.[1] He was very happy to have me there and took me aside to talk. At one point in our conversation he asked whether something I had said was not a continuation of prophecy for our time. And I answered him, Romano, the time of prophecy lies behind us. The only chance now lies in our taking this vocation as that of the friend. This is the way in which hope for a new society can spread. And the practice of it is not really through words but through little acts of foolish renunciation. The guy understood me.

I have said that only faith can fully discern the mystery of evil. But I know that there are many who have experienced the horror of our time as something that they can't explain away, and that it would be cowardice to relegate to some locked corner of their heart. Those who are willing to face this horror as something unexplainable act as witnesses for a mystery. That this mystery is the *mysterium iniquitatis* does not make it less fit to be the entrance door into the entire mystery of the Incarnation. Out of the mouth of babes and sinners.

During these days with you I have frequently been disconcerted by my decision to dare this conversation with you — not the conversation which you and I for years have enjoyed, but with this extraordinary black box between us. Ten years ago, in State College, Pennsylvania, when we spoke about nonmysterious matters, you had to use your strength to carry your tape recorder into my room. Now you have this pocketable device. It has been a constant reminder of the new situation, the new stage of the world, in which we talk. This has allowed me to dare to engage in this conversation which has been, at many points, very real between you and me, and a continuation of other real conversations. And yet I marvel at your disciplined awareness, and am just as surprised at mine, that totally unknown people, perhaps after my death, will listen to these voices. I have often been tempted to give in to my fright at saying things which I can easily tell David Cayley to a microphone which will digitalize my utterance and bring it to the ears of people who cannot see our faces or the changes in your smile or frown. We have had with us a few very close friends, to each of whom I would have spoken differently, and their presence has been a reminder that I'm not reacting to an abstract questioner but to David Cayley, with whom a long mutual forbearance has established a unique and inimitable I–Thou perception.[2]

Ten years ago, when we were last caught in a similar situation, I explicitly refused to answer you personally when you asked questions. I took your questions as rhetorical and dictated to the microphone. Even this time, it is quite obvious that we both did what we could to preserve at least a veil of discretion. We were careful in our dance not to step on each other's feet and not to compromise third persons, except for one who always came up here. I leave it in your hands to make sure that my intention — I would not say of offering witness — but of speaking in gratitude and fidelity to the one behind this candle, which is burning here while I'm talking to you, was not a betrayal of his touching tenderness but a truthful statement chosen once in my life. I won't do it again.

This page intentionally left blank

II

Reiterations

And in the dark times will there be singing?
Yes, there will be singing about the dark times.

Bertolt Brecht, *For Posterity*

This page intentionally left blank

15

THE BEGINNING OF THE END

CAYLEY: I've read through my transcript of your talks of two years ago several times, and there are some points which I would like to try to clarify. In that conversation, you again and again reverted to the idea of the mystery of evil, which Paul first speaks about in his letter to the Thessalonians. Since that time I have had a chance to reread Paul's letters, and it seems to me that Paul is saying that the Incarnation is, so to speak, the beginning of the end. Something has happened that changes everything — irreversibly.

ILLICH: Yes, and he has this immensely consoling statement that he suffers whatever it is that he suffers — let's say it was epilepsy — in order to fulfill what is still missing and is, therefore, holding back the end.[1] To paraphrase Paul: Bearing the annoyance my neighbour causes me with humour and devotion might be just the last straw needed. By every instance in which one of us associates himself plainly with the suffering of Christ, he might just trigger the end. It's a gloriously consoling idea, and Paul claims — I believe legitimately — that this is a way in which I may look at the course of my own life. We might be contributing to it at this very moment.

I have this funny watch on my arm, with a moving part to indicate seconds. I used to wonder whether the next click might be the last. You know the story of the old Rabbi that Erich Fromm always told and retold. His wife said, I have to wash your socks. So he took off his shoe and gave her one sock. She said, can't you give me the second one? He said, no, I never get out of both shoes at the same time. I want to be ready when the Messiah comes.

CAYLEY: But what has changed with the Incarnation? Why is it the beginning of the end?

ILLICH: When Mary brought forth the Word of God in the flesh, something happened cosmically which, until that moment, had happened each time a woman proved to herself and others that her pregnancy was real by bearing the child she hoped for. The prophets were fulfilled. The stammerings of the prophets were legitimated in the only way that, until the twentieth century, a pregnancy could be legitimated — postpartum — because the kid is there. So that's the first thing that has changed. The second thing is that, from that moment on, any prophetic act or word is not only a hope but faith in the carnal presence of God. When I interpret twelfth-century texts for the graduate students, colleagues, and other regulars at my class, most of whom would regard what I just said as fantasy or ideology, they say, So you mean that Christians believe that a man is God. Now you're unlikely to hear Christians say this. I have listened to Catholics and Episcopalians, and they will generally put things the other way round — God comes first. But for Joseph the baby came first. Faith in the Incarnation can flower in our time precisely because faith in God is obscured, and we are led to discover God in one another. This seems to me important — more important than ever — because of the deepening obscurity which has been spread in recent years by those who claim that certain physical and mathematical features of the universe lead them to postulate, as a very fruitful hypothesis, a God — a constructed God — behind the Big Bang.[2] And I laugh, and I say, come, let's look at a crib — and I try to explain to them what a crib is — that there are many kids in many parts of the world where I have been whose mothers bundle them into a dirty coat on a street corner a few hours after their birth . . .

CAYLEY: You also argued in our earlier conversations that with the Incarnation, sin changed its meaning. And that is another point on which I wanted to invite you to say more.

ILLICH: In my opinion, Christ opened our eyes, in a unique and definite way, to the relationship between David and Ivan at this very moment. You can say between an I and a Thou, if you want to. I am increasingly certain that I can convince anyone whom you might bring up to me as an *adversarius* that there was nothing of this kind before Christ revealed it, though there might be things that look a little bit alike. Last time, if I remember rightly, we spoke about the Samaritan — a Palestinian, who doesn't worship at the Temple in Jerusalem — who walks down the street, sees a Jew lying there beaten, and turns to him. Like the Samaritan, we are critters that find their perfection only by establishing a relationship, and this relationship is arbitrary from everybody else's point of view, except the Samaritan's, because he does it on the call of the beaten-up Jew. But, as soon as this possibility is established, it can also be broken and denied. A possibility of infidelity, turning away, coldness has been created which could not have existed before Jesus revealed this possibility. So sin in this sense did not exist. Without the glimmer of mutuality, the possibility of its denial, its destruction, could not be thought. A new kind of "ought" has been established which is not related to a norm. It has a *telos*. It aims at somebody, some body; but not according to a rule. And it has become almost impossible for people who today deal with ethics or morality to leave out chatter about norms. They attempt to relate the "ought" to norms.

CAYLEY: In our earlier conversation you reacted strongly against my using the term "post-Christian" to characterize our time. You said, No, our age is not post-Christian, it is apocalyptic. And I would like to hear more about what you think it means to live in an apocalyptic world.

ILLICH: When I refused to designate our time as post-Christian, and insisted on its being apocalyptic, I did it as a would-be pupil of

Aquinas: *per fidem quaerens intellectum*, and *per intellectum quaerens fidem*, by faith seeking historical understanding of the time since Bethlehem; and, on the other hand, by intelligence seeking to understand the first and second Christian millennia. The world was changed forever by the appearance of a community — therefore a "here" and a "there" — based entirely on the contribution of each one, no matter what his rank, in the *conspiratio* of the liturgical kiss. A community was created by a somatic interchange and not by some cosmic or natural referent. When a "we" can come into existence as the result of a *conspiratio*, we are already outside of time. We are living already in the time of the Spirit.

One consequence is the appearance of a new type of evil which I call sin. It is thoroughly different from any non-good that can be framed in secular terms. It is also different from old ideas of the non-good as that which is disharmonious, not fitting, nonproportional. These terms are also insufficient to express the evil which is sin. Today I live in a world in which evil has been replaced by disvalue, negative value. We face something for which in German with its ease in combining terms I was able to coin the name diseviling (*Entbösung*) — I launched this word twenty years ago in Germany and it made people laugh. You can't have disharmony on a tempered piano; you can't have disharmonious buildings once you have lost the idea of architectural orders, as Joseph Rykwert has shown in his book *The Dancing Column*. So, within this apocalyptic period of two thousand years, we come first to diseviling; and then, in our time to something which for lack of a better word I would call misplaced concreteness, or perhaps mathematization or algorithmization, which Uwe Pörksen tried to describe with his idea of plastic words. During 1,500 years our entire social and political thinking were based on the secularization of the Samaritan, which means the technicization of the question of what to do when somebody in trouble suddenly surprises me on my way to somewhere else. Did I answer you?

CAYLEY: Well, let me see if I can paraphrase what you've just said: Diseviling, which occurs when the sense of proportion is lost, is a possibility that comes into existence only when Jesus expands the

horizon of the possible by the answer which he gives to the Pharisees
. . . You are saying that the whole post-Bethlehem era is apocalyptic
by definition.

ILLICH: Yes, but in modern usage this means some sort of disaster. To
me it means revealing, or unveiling. Our conversation of two years
ago, which we now want to try to deepen, deals with my hypothesis
that the corruption of the best is the worst. And it is part of this
hypothesis that the Church's attempt to give this worldly power,
social visibility, and permanence to the performance of ortho-doxy,
right faith, and to the performance of Christian charity, is not un-
Christian. As I understand the Gospels, with many others, it is part
of the *kenosis*, the humiliation, the condescension of God in becoming man and founding or generating the mystical body which the
Church understands itself to be, that this mystical body would itself
be something ambiguous. It would be, on the one hand, a source of
continued Christian life, through which individuals acting alone and
together would be able to live the life of faith and charity, and, on the
other hand, a source of the perversion of this life through institutionalization, which makes charity worldly and true faith obligatory. Now
why do I say this? Because I believe that the one way in which I can
look hopefully at what has happened during my lifetime is to say,
God's goodness and power shines more gloriously than ever in the
fact that he can tolerate — I'll come back to this word — the this-
worldliness of his church which has become the seed from which
modern service organizations have grown.

Let me put it in other words that are easier to understand. I, at
least, believe that I do not live in a post-Christian world, I live in an
apocalyptic world. I live in the *kairos*[3] in which the mystical body of
Christ, through its own fault, is constantly being crucified, as his
physical body was crucified and rose again on Easter day. I am therefore expecting the resurrection of the Church from the humiliation,
for which the Church itself must be blamed, of having gestated and
brought forth the world of modernity.

The resurrection lies behind us. What we now have to expect is
not the resurrection of the Lord, nor the bodily ascension to heaven

of our lady Mary, this strange girl whom I have not been able to help having as my ideal since I was boy. It's the resurrection of the Church; and, when I say I believe in the resurrection of the dead, and the life everlasting, the resurrection of the dead for me stands for the resurrection of the Church.

You came and said you wanted to talk to me about the *corruptio optimi quae est pessima* [the corruption of the best which is the worst], about the fact that wherever I look for the roots of something which is a modern certainty, I find that in the course of what we now call the second millennium it grew out of the Church and became, in my opinion, not a post-Christian reality, but a perverted Christian reality. The term post-Christian could be taken as implying a renewed innocence, in which evil becomes once again sinless and just plain evil. The way I judge and hope to accept modern institutions is not as plain evil but as sinful, as the attempt to provide by human means what only God calling through the beaten-up Jew could give to the Samaritan, the invitation to act in charity.

CAYLEY: Mircea Eliade, whom I used to read, speaks of the Christian "valorization of time." After Bethlehem, as you said earlier, time, for Christians, acquires a definite and irreversible direction, and is no longer cyclical. And this direction, according to Eliade, is preserved even in Christianity's modern secular descendants, like Marxism, which is still, in a sense, expecting the end. But, in the last fifteen years or so, people have begun to adopt the term postmodernity, which might suggest a return to cyclical time and the renewed innocence of which you just spoke.

ILLICH: If I rightly understand you, you are fishing for my reflections, or even feelings, about the mood in what is called postmodern poetry, novels, and philosophy, about what has happened to the temporal dimension, to temporality in the course of our lifetime. How has that passage, that mountain we came across in the 1970s, affected our sense of — I use the word for lack of anything better — timeliness and spatiality and frontier — the three inevitably go together. Now in order to speak about this transition, this transformation, the transmogrification to which you allude — we both know what you are alluding to even though we are not quite certain precisely what we are speaking about, and that's one of the difficulties in this particular conversation — in order to understand this transmogrification, I at least have to look at it historically. Where did it start to become what it is now? And once things are historical, once we claim that they have an end, at least in the mind, and the feeling, and the body and the breathing of some people, we already imply and assume that they have at some time had a beginning. Now the timeliness and spatiality and frontier which belonged to the certainties of existence in our youth, and much more in my father's youth, are of a kind for which the Middle Ages and the times before had no sense or taste. The simplest way of telling you about it might be to tell you about an international meeting of designers at which I was recently invited to give the opening speech. I took along two others in order to do it well. The meeting was held in a red plush theatre in Amsterdam. The organizers wanted to demand that henceforth all designers include in their designs the category of speed, because of the importance in our lives of slowing down. The twenty-first century must be slow rather than fast, it must belong to Slow but Better Workers — one of these millennial fantasies. And the argument I tried to make there was, I'm an historian, and I know that the very concept of speed is something that before Galileo wasn't there. When Galileo first conceived miles per hour, or more precisely distance in a given time, he knew that he was breaking a taboo by relating time and space to each other as distinct entities. The here and now, *hic et nunc*, related so intimately to each other that you could not speak of the one without speaking of the other. Galileo claimed that he could observe time apart from space. What news? Everybody knows that. No! He had the greatest of difficulty in making himself understood. Analysis of this idea of integration would require the invention of the infinitesimal calculus by Leibniz and Newton. Today the concept of time on which modernity based itself is in crisis in modern physics, in modern philosophy, and in modern biology. No question about this. But my point here is that the modern concept of time was already unrelated to lived duration, to the "forever" in the marriage vow, which doesn't mean "without end" but "now totally." In order to create the possibility of experiencing watch-less time in my classes, I ask that someone inform me when it's time for a toilet break. We have to engage in an asceticism which makes it possible to savour nowness and hereness, here as place, here as that which is between us, as the kingdom is. This is a most important task if we are to save what remains in us of the sense of meaning, of metaphor, of flesh, of touch, of gaze.

But here I find myself in a difficulty. Hunger for an ascetically cultivated sense of here is very intense, and from what I know of the waves of postmodernism to which you refer, it could be said that living that way is the mood of the new age. This hunger arises from a technologically produced mood of impotence in relation to the now. It has taken the place of the emphasis on planning and hope for the future which prevailed in the previous generation. But it tastes to me of abdication, of letting go, of indiscipline. What I want to cultivate, in myself, and with friends, is not impotence but powerlessness, a powerlessness which does not forego awareness of the here and now between the Jew and the Samaritan. Perhaps Thomas Aquinas can help clarify things. Thomas, in his unique and incredibly fragile way — I and some of my friends believe that Thomism is like a delicate vase, something glorious but apt to be broken when it is moved out of its time — Thomas insists very strongly that you can think about timeliness only when you distinguish time not just from eternity, which has no beginning and end, but also from a third type of duration which he calls *aevum*. *Aevum* is the type of survival and togetherness for which you and I are destined. It has no end but I know that it had a beginning even if I can't remember it precisely. I might have mentioned to you this man whom Gerhart Ladner made me love, Petrus Hispanus. Some medievalists take him as an example of the form which schizophrenia took in the Middle Ages, but Ladner pointed out the marvellous metaphors he uses. Petrus says that as people who live in the *aevum*, we sit on the horizon. The horizon is the line which divides us from nose to behind into two parts. One side sits in time, the other in the *aevum*. This is the sense I want to convey of our being a creature who lives in a now and forever which is contingent at every moment on the creative act of God.

And with this, the contemporary return to cyclical time, or to no time, or to living awake as if I were in a trance, has nothing in common.

CAYLEY: I hope you'll forgive my persistence, and, perhaps, my bluntness, but I want to keep pushing on what I get from the post-Resurrection New Testament: the sense that the end has begun and will soon occur . . .

ILLICH: I know you are struck by these guys with their happy trust that the light in the East would come tomorrow, and, if not tomorrow, the day after tomorrow; but, on the other hand, what a privilege to live in a time when our hope has lost its this-worldly, calendar, and watch-related scaffolding. We are in an age of scaffoldless hope.

CAYLEY: Recently I was looking at the Letter of James in the New Testament, and I read there that he who doubts is like the sea buffeted by waves.[4] He will have no friend in the Lord because he is of two minds, he is of a divided mind. Perhaps I don't know how to read this, but I would think that if I was of only two minds, in the circumstances in which I've grown up, I'd be doing well . . .

ILLICH: This has something to do with what Aelred says about friendship. What happens between the Jew and the Samaritan is a seed. When it grows up, it will be buffeted, and perhaps the stem will even be broken and it will never come to flower. What we hold on to is the seed. Not all friendships are beautiful or glorious or fully developed. That I leave to the psychologists. Faith, in its root, is a gift which demands my faith in my own faith. In its manifestation it can be terribly buffeted. And, if I understand James properly, I shouldn't glory in surviving my doubts. I should rather humbly, powerlessly hold on to the deep root in the heart. And so it is with love and charity. They are supernatural gifts. The difficulty is that 90 per cent of the people I am given to address would say, Oh God, what is that? And yet I think that people today are more capable than they were thirty years ago of understanding what I say when I talk about gifts which are like seeds, no matter what happens historically, biographically, to them. The apocalypse is the moment at which the meaning of my own life will be revealed to me. That's something totally different from autobiography, or, even worse, biography. Hagiographers once tried to pursue this mysterious historicity of each life. By now everyone is too much infected by psychology to be able to grasp this fleshy side of what's between me and you. Or, therefore, this scaffoldless hope.

CAYLEY: You spoke earlier about God's tolerance for the worldliness of his Church and said you would return to that word.

ILLICH: I did use that word. An hour later I'm not so sure I should have used the expression "God is tolerant." God is merciful. But mercy is something incredibly difficult to explain today. The Semitic languages have a word for it which comes from the root *raham*. When you look into the etymology, you'll see that it is related to the womb, and to Nature. The womb in the state of love, this is what *raham* means. The seventy rabbis who translated the Bible into Greek had great difficulty in finding a non-Semitic Greek equivalent, and they took the word *eleos*, which is tinged by pity, even for the Greeks. *Eleos* is something which Plato in a beautiful passage considers acceptable in women and kids, but not in mature men. And Aristotle corrects him and says, Unless these mature men act as lawyers and try to get pity from the jury for the accused. Alms, alms-giving, is an English way of saying *eleos*. It survives in the form of the English word eleemosynary, which comes to us via Latin. When I spoke about the tolerance of God, I really meant to speak about his *raham*. Five times a day, a good Moslem throws himself down towards the East, alone, with others who are also alone standing next to him, facing Allah. And in the first sentence of his prayer, the word *raham* appears twice.[5] After all we have said today, I at least am amazed. I could fantasize doubts which buffet me. Can one believe in the existence of somebody who has created the mess which I have described to you? The mystery that God still exists is indicated by naming him the merciful. After all, this is what we call sweet sorrow.

Is it possible that anyone who knows me, as only he knows me, would stand me? It's sweet because from there faith, hope, and charity can grow. Today we would speak about self-acceptance. I don't need a self in order to accept, in order to make an effort to accept the fact that he stands me.

CAYLEY: Let me say, finally, then, that as I understand it the mystery of evil — my Jerusalem Bible says the mystery of wickedness — is precisely the fall of the Church, it's precisely the creation of the Christian "religion."

ILLICH: Yes, it is instrumentalized, or instrumentally maintained, truth and charity . . . machines for doing one or the other.

CAYLEY: And do you think you're taking a liberty with Paul's intention in writing those words to the Thessalonians in interpreting them that way?

ILLICH: No, I don't think I take a liberty. God help me.

16

CONSCIENCE

CAYLEY: When you spoke about the origins of conscience you used the term *forum internum*, and I wonder if you could elaborate on why you chose that term.

ILLICH: Let me take you back to what is usually called the Constantinian peace, when the Church's legitimacy was recognized within the late Roman Empire. Technically speaking this was an imperial act by which those people who could show that they were recognized as supervisors or overseers — this is the literal meaning of *episcopoi* in Greek — would henceforth be recognized in the Roman Empire as having the status of magistrates. Now the Roman magistrate was not precisely an American judge, but to say they were given the status of judges is as close as one can come to the ordinary man's understanding today. One could appeal to them for justice. This must be kept in the background, this morsel of insight, in order to understand what happened hundreds of years later during the so-called struggle over investiture. In the high Middle Ages there was a controversy — to oversimplify a little — over whether the Emperor or the Pope had the last word in the appointment of bishops. For a hundred years at least, this was an important political and constitutional struggle. It was resolved with imperial recognition that the Pope had that privilege, that he was free, or at least highly independent, from the Roman Empire. In reality traces of imperial power remained. In a papal election — not the selection of a bishop but a papal election — just before the First World War the Austrian Hapsburg ambassador still had to give his okay.

But let's now look at the key issue — the way in which Gregory VII, whom one usually connects with the end of this struggle over investiture, attempted to confirm and crystallize the independence of the Pope's jurisdiction from the Emperor's jurisdiction. In order to understand his idea, you need to know a little of the history of technology. You'll forgive me, I'm sure, if I repeat myself, as I can't remember how much of this I told you last time. With the breakdown of the antique Roman Empire, Europe, especially the northern part of Europe, became a world of hamlets. It was only in the twelfth century, roughly speaking, that new European towns arose, and this was possible because of an extraordinary increase in the productivity of agriculture, which had begun a couple of hundred years earlier, and which has to do with horses. If I were lecturing to historians, I couldn't be that brief and would have to warn them of many pitfalls in my detailed judgements, but here I can say that antique horses were collared like dogs. They had to pull ploughs attached to a dog collar, and the more you pull on a dog collar the less air you get. So there was a braking effect as the gas pedal of the horse was pushed. Second, antique horses were not shod. They walked on their naked hooves, which is alright if you are ploughing in the dry areas around the Mediterranean, but when you take a horse with naked hooves into a northern soil, which is wet, the hooves very quickly become spongy. Then, in the tenth and eleventh centuries, at the same time the Emperor and the Pope were struggling over who names bishops, three technologies improved the power of the horse by a factor which is variously judged at between three and five times. One was shocing the beast by nailing on horseshoes. A second was the adoption of a collar that rested on the horse's breastbone and didn't constrict its throat. That horse collar came from Asia, where the Chinese had already solved the problem. And, third, horses were saddled. Stirrups, which made this possible, also came from Asia — they were first used five hundred years earlier in Bihar in India, then exported to China, where they became an important Chinese implement. Before this time, when armies of European Christians met the armies of the Arabs, they arrived on their horses and then dismounted to do battle because, unless you are sitting in a saddle tied to the horse's belly with your feet in stirrups, you will go down with your sword when you try to strike a blow with it. Only a hundred years later, the imperial European armies had to change the day of the imperial Diet from March to May, because only in May would there be enough greenery around to feed all the horses of the lords attending the Diet. So there was a major development in horse technology, which enabled hamlets to become villages. Peasants could now work fields three times as far from their homes as before. This allowed the size of settlements to increase, which in turn made possible the establishment of local parish churches.

The Pope had the brilliant idea of making the pastors of these new parishes his judges by making it a rule that at least once a year every Christian has to go to his own priest, *proprio sacerdoti*, to confess his sins. Otherwise he cannot go to Easter communion and he will be excluded from the Church. Every Christian has to go to accuse himself once a year to his own priest. The Emperor had his judicial system, highly accusatory, where the more powerful could drag the weaker ones in front of a judge. The Church would now have its own, and this splitting of the authority in charge of justice had to be given a name. So they began to speak about an ecclesiastic as well as a secular *forum*, or judgement place. Until then, the *forum* was the city centre. Now suddenly we have two centres of justice: ecclesiastic and secular.

It is important to point out here that people refused to go and confess their marital infidelities or their thieveries to the local pastor. The Pope did not succeed in making his law stick. What made it possible to require annual confession was the foundation of the first two orders of mendicants, the Franciscans and the Dominicans. These monks lived by begging and not by owning land, and, therefore, threw themselves on the mercy of the faithful rather than the toleration of a feudal lord. With their appearance, there were suddenly roaming confessors available. People could go to them and confess and remain within the Church without going to their own pastor.

This frustrated the Pope's attempt to establish territorial control. The mendicant orders made it possible to recognize that there is a *forum* distinct from the Emperor's without its being bound to the territorial network of the Church. So it's important to remember that the people wouldn't recognize the power that the Pope wanted to give his pastors . . .

CAYLEY: But surely the Pope did ultimately succeed. Didn't your congregation in New York come to you?

ILLICH: Yes, but they could go also down to the Dominicans. It stands in church law that you confess to your local priest. *De facto*, the Church has had to recognize that there are other ways of doing it. But the Pope did succeed in doing what I call criminalizing sin. Anybody who wants to know more about this has to go, for the moment, to Paolo Prodi. He is no longer the only man who has clear, solid historical insights on this subject, but he's certainly at the centre of the half-dozen people who in the last ten years have recognized that he has hit on something extremely important. Sin — we have spoken of this, but we can speak of it again — is an evil of a kind which could not exist except through the denial of grace. Sin is refusing to honour that relationship which came into existence between the Samaritan and the Jew, which comes into existence through the exercise of freedom, and which constitutes an "ought" because I feel called by you, called to you, called to this tie between human beings, or between beings and God. Sin, therefore, as a possibility which first has to be revealed, is something much more horrible than any evil which can be understood outside of Christianity. It is not frightening, and it is not simply disgusting. It is not in any sense offensive of a law. It is always an offence against a person. It's an infidelity. But, with criminalization, the sense of sin of the first millennium changes. It becomes the transgression of a norm because I must accuse myself before a priest, who is a judge, of having transgressed a Christian law. Grace becomes juridical. Sin acquires a second side — that of the breaking of the law. This implies that in the second millennium the charity, the love of the New Testament has become the law of the land and has put into shadow the more horrible side of sin which is that of the personal offence — against God, against my wife, against the woman with whom I broke my fidelity. This is what I mean by the criminalization of sin. The criminalization of sin makes it possible to speak about conscience. We too often forget that conscience, in the sense in which we have pangs of conscience and must act according to conscience, or, in a Kantian way, derive norms from conscience, because what I don't want done to me I shouldn't do to somebody else, that conscience in this sense is a product of the criminalization of sin, and that criminalization of sin can be plausibly tied to the twelfth century, and particularly to the Pope's attempt to expand the victory won in the struggle for investiture.

CAYLEY: Are there other aspects of the Gregorian reform, and not just the institution of confession, which are pertinent here? For example, Harold Berman in his book *Law and Revolution* writes extensively about the way in which the systematization of canon law during this period prepares the ground for what we now call our justice system.

ILLICH: Yes, there are several lines of evolution which link these changes in the medieval Church to the emergence of the modern state. At the period when the Church returned from Avignon to Rome at the insistence of St. Catherine, I would point to the creation within the Church of ministries, the Roman congregations, each competent to administer the law in a certain area. The idea of different secretariats for matters of faith, or for discipline, or for financial affairs, laid the foundations for the juridically distinct competences within the nation state. A state organized in this way is first attempted in France by Francis I around 1480 and is also very visibly forced on Spain by Isabella and Ferdinand in the years before Columbus, when the titled gentlemen with their swords were replaced in royal processions by lawyers with books and pens in their hands. But I would need six or seven colleagues, each following one of these lines and reporting back in two years, to do this subject justice; and, the way I feel at this moment, I will be happy just to get through today's conversation. So let me simply restate my basic idea.

My hypothesis is that today's certainties are, to a very high degree, the result of Western attempts to institutionalize the fundamental Christian idea that faith and charity and hope are not related to a norm but are interpersonal — a word I would like to use with great prudence. This general hypothesis — I do not present it as a thesis but as a hypothesis — allows me, Ivan, to understand — no, to notice — the abyss that lies beneath Kosovo, Auschwitz, universal cancerization through diagnosis, disembodiment — I could prolong the list. Western democratic ideas are an attempt to institutionalize an "ought" which by its very nature is a personal, intimate, and individual vocation. This must be accepted in order to understand that the evil too large to be grasped by my intelligence and feeling is really the door to an abyss of sin. The diseviling of which we spoke yesterday is a way of dealing with the impossibility of facing this abyss. This hypothesis — this view of history — by which I, Ivan, have tried to recognize the greatness of God does not depend on the final conclusions of any of the dozen of possible avenues of research on the threads which link the Church to the modern state. But I think you have a question.

CAYLEY: I would like to ask about one of these threads — the one which links conscience, as an inner forum where I can accuse myself, to the emergence of the citizen.

ILLICH: I am unable at this moment to give a short or pithy answer to your question; but let me think a moment — perhaps I'll succeed ... I did try to answer this question in a talk I gave in Bremen earlier this year. Have you had time to look at my Villa Ichon speech ...¹

CAYLEY: Yes, I've read it.

ILLICH: That was a speech of gratitude — the city of Bremen had given me its Culture and Peace Prize, a kind of honorary citizenship — and I took the opportunity to say something for which I wouldn't otherwise have found the occasion. I wanted to talk about *conspiratio*, and I couldn't imagine doing it in front of the groups who so often invite me: educators, lawyers, government or U.N. agencies. But, if Hanseatic citizens co-opt me into the citizenship of Bremen — a citizen of Bremen without any German citizenship — they almost force me to speak about the coming about of the very idea of citizenship that gives their gesture meaning. And there I could draw attention to what happened when Christians began to celebrate their communion: a "we" which also had the face of an "I," the body of Christ, came into being through a sharing of the breath of peace, to which each one contributed equally. This was a new class of societal event, one which could not be effectively compared to any which had previously existed. Unlike the Greek mysteries, for example, it was an extremely simple, open, everyday liturgical event. What came about — I tried to say in that Ichon paper — is a *conspiratio*. Historically it consistently turned into a *conjuratio*, a *conjuratio* to defend the *conspiratio*. *Conjuratio* means a swearing together, witnessed by God, by which men of the Middle Ages tried to give worldly stability to their peace and concord. And, consistently, the *conjuratio* remained, while the *conspiratio* was forgotten, or relegated to second place, or reduced to a symbolic handshake. What I had to say about the citizen I tried to say there.

CAYLEY: What is the alternative to conscience, if I can put it that way?

ILLICH: It seems amazingly difficult for my auditors and pupils to conceive of conscience as anything other than an appeal to a norm. The norm might be exogenous, given by a law, or endogenous in a Kantian or post-Kantian way. So, as far as I can understand, conscience and norm are inextricably bound together and mutually dependent. The Samaritan did not act out of conscience. How should one call what he acted out of? Paul speaks of love, faith, and hope.

CAYLEY: Why is a new kind of anxiety the destiny of a man or woman of conscience?

ILLICH: During the night I couldn't sleep, so I read from A to Z a sociological treatise on the anthropology of the bedchamber, and I thought about this. Anxieties that threaten the peace of sleep have always existed, the author claims, but these anxieties must not be confused with what, in German, are called *Gewissensbisse*, "bites" of conscience. Medieval Latin also has this expression. It is something new which conscience introduces. Angst, narrowness, anxiety, is in a deep sense communally felt, and is therefore community creating. In the Roman breviary, in the compline, the night prayer said when it is already dark, before complete silence begins, it says, *vigilate, fratres*, watch out, brothers, because the devil, like a hungry lion, turns around and looks for whom he might devour. The cultivation of such anxiety is extremely helpful, I think, in creating a strong sense of fraternity and commonality in front of the unspeakable — none of us knows how to say it exactly. Pangs of conscience can be experienced only by an individual. The more he is detached from the community, the more he can become afraid of acting or not acting according to a norm. Conscience is experienced in the darkness of your inner chamber. It creates, and reinforces, the experience of individualism, an experience not of solitude but of loneliness. The fear and the awe that can be felt by someone who has a cultural matrix within which to understand his lack of understanding is something very different than the anguish of the scrupulous. So is the sense that actions have effects which go beyond those which you can see, and therefore you worry.

I say this as somebody who believes in the value of meditation, Christian, Buddhist, whatever you want, on evil, on hell, on the devil. This is too strong, perhaps, for the poor conscience-stricken individual who now roams the streets, and I am afraid, in discussing something like this, that people might misunderstand. They might think that I'm preaching fire-and-brimstone sermons and so trying to generate conscience. But ritual exorcisms do not do that. There's another of those lines that I'd like to have somebody pursue.

17

THE CROWNING GLORY

CAYLEY: At the end of the Gospel of Matthew the risen Christ appears to disciples and says, "All authority in heaven and on earth is given to me. Go and make disciples of all nations, baptise, teach, teach them all the commands I gave you." That is what is written there. But, when I first knew you, you were engaged in a crusade against the missionary activity of the Church, if that's a good description of your campaigns of the early and middle 1960s . . .

ILLICH: No, it is not, and I reject your imputation that in the 1960s I took a stand against the missionary activities of the Church. That was the time of development mania — the years of Kennedy's Alliance for Progress. Those were the days of the foundation of the Peace Corps in America, and of comparable organizations in Germany, France, and other countries. They would send people to South America to help them to shake off the shackles of underdevelopment. Those were the days when an American manipulator, journalist, and priest, who had glorified the missionary activities of the American Maryknoll Fathers in China, found a new vocation for this Catholic missionary order by inveigling Pope John XXIII into signing a document in which he asks North American bishops and religious superiors to send 10 per cent of their ordained or trained priests or trained nuns to South America, the new mission field of the Church. This man also wrote a paper, which he then had signed by the Vatican authorities, creating, as a parallel to the secular Peace Corps, an agency called Papal Volunteers for Latin America. And I denounced this as an obvious, easily understandable caricature, as a *corruptio* of the mission given by Jesus to his apostles. This was a mission carried out by a Catholic institution imbued with American values which kept the star-spangled banner behind the altar in every church and justified the do-goodism called development by claiming it as a missionary activity. I was amazed, but not surprised, at the degree to which my stance was taken as anti-Americanism and interpreted either as a bowing to Latin American distrust of the powerful neighbour to the north or as service to world Communism. For what other reason, at the height of the Cold War, would you be against sending not only young Americans but Christian Americans to South America for missionary purposes? This skilful, simple-minded, brutal use of what, at the end of the 1950s and the McCarthy period, was a rather innocent and dull American Catholic Church to reinforce American cultural domination in South America and, in this way, lead South Americans to modern values — exactly those values which I believe are a corruption, initiated by the Church itself and later secularized, of Christian mandates to love — became for me a model around which I could discuss with individuals whose well-meaning generosity attracted them to this enterprise the question of *corruptio optimi*. Is that clear enough?

CAYLEY: It's very clear, and I never meant to say that . . .

ILLICH: You don't have to excuse yourself. We both know that we are in a shadow battle on radio.

CAYLEY: But what does Christ's commandment mean to you?

ILLICH: Forgive me for being personal . . . Doing what the two of us are doing at the moment.

CAYLEY: And as Paul did when he came with nothing but the shirt on his back and stood in the square telling the Athenians the good news about the Resurrection . . .

ILLICH: . . . Yes, and the Athenians said you can tell us another time.

CAYLEY: And would that also be your answer to the question posed in Sushako Endo's novel *Silence* which we have sometimes discussed? [In the novel a young Portuguese missionary priest in Japan is forced to choose between martyrdom and stepping on an image of Christ as a sign that he has renounced his mission. The priest finally chooses to desecrate the image; and Endo, himself a Christian, leaves hanging the question of whether this may not have been the more "Christian" option at a time when Japan had just awoken to the profound cultural threat posed by Christian mission. — Ed.]

ILLICH: I think so. I did not trample on John XXIII's face, but I was accused of doing so, when I referred to a study by the Harvard Business School which had come to the conclusion that, from an organizational point of view, the Catholic Church was a model of effectiveness and efficiency worthy of emulation by U.S. Steel. I paraphrased that study in an article called "The Vanishing Clergyman,"[1] where I said that the Roman Catholic Church had become the largest international corporation.

CAYLEY: When we discussed proportionality, you told the story of how alarmed the Chinese intelligentsia became over the teaching of Matteo Ricci, the first missionary to learn Chinese and establish himself in China, when they realized what a corrosive effect his doctrine of a master in heaven might have on people's sense of proportion . . .

ILLICH: . . . because it introduces an imbalance. If there's a master in heaven, there should be a master on earth too.

CAYLEY: But could the Good News have been preached without the destruction of proportions?

ILLICH: My answer is, Yes; but it was not God's will. Just as he allowed the sin of Adam and Eve with all its consequences, he accepted the founding of a church which is in this world, even though it is not of this world, and, therefore, will also be a sinful church. Let me explain. During the two years since our last recorded conversation, the issue which you touch upon here has been central to my reflection, teaching, and study: Does the Good News inevitably lead to the destruction of the sense of proportion? And I would say that it has been preached, at least to this one believer, me, Ivan, in such a way that proportions might have been preserved. When I reflect on the history of proportionality, I see that nothing can exist without being dysymmetrically proportional to something else and that this dysymmetric proportionality is the reason for the existence of both. And in this light, what is revealed to us in the parable of the Samaritan is a new kind of proportionality. When they ask Jesus, Who is my neighbour? he answers, He to whom you as a free human being establish your personal proportionality by turning to him in love, and inviting him to the mutuality of love which one usually calls friendship. The Samaritan story makes me understand that I am "I" in the deepest and fullest sense in which it is given to me to be "I" precisely because you, by allowing me to love you, give me the possibility to be co-relative to you, to be dysymmetrically proportionate to you. I see, therefore, in love, hope, and charity the crowning of the proportional nature of creation in the full, old sense of that term. Nothing is what it is except because *convenit*, it fits, it is in harmony with something else, and I am free to choose with whom, or, better, to accept from whom I want, to whom I let myself be given, the possibility of loving. The call of charity, *agape*, which the Samaritan hears, does not destroy proportionality but rather elevates it to a level which formerly was not perceived. It goes beyond Plato and Aristotle, and beyond the Greek mysteries. It says that your *telos*, your end purpose, the goal of your being, is in an other whom you freely choose.

CAYLEY: Can you explain why and how you use the term dysymmetric and what you mean when you say things exist through their complementarity — that here engenders there, and this, that?

ILLICH: Gladly, but first let me tell you a story. I have this lovely teacher, who died in '42 — 1142 — Hugh of St. Victor, and in his *De Sacramentis*, a book he left unfinished, he comes to the question, Why did God create Adam and Eve? It's amazing what these guys had the guts to want to figure out. Their curiosity was daring and, at the very same time, humble in a way in which our generation can't quite follow them, or I, at least, can't. And he comes to the conclusion, Because he had to give to Adam something that he could grasp, in every sense, something which was totally different from him, and different in such a way that he could be wounded by that difference, that he would be vulnerable to that difference. So he created Eve to give Adam a sense of how Creation and God relate to each other. Woman and man are God's masterpiece, Hugh claims, because they are two entities whose proportionality is constitutive for both. Early on, I described this relation as asymmetrical. This was a term people could understand, and I hoped it would convey the sense of difference, the sense of a relation that can never quite be grasped, or that slips away when it is grasped. But later on I was called on to correct myself by my mathematical friend Kostas,[2] who pointed out that the word asymmetrical didn't mean what I wanted to say. So I said, Well, in mathematics one calls this dysymmetrical. It is not lacking symmetry, asymmetrical, but it is dysymmetrical, different entirely though almost the same.

CAYLEY: So, corresponding but not the same . . .

ILLICH: . . . corresponding in everything, but in everything slightly off the mark. In German I have a simple way of expressing it: *rücken* means move, *verrücken* means moving off mark, out of focus. Now people who are *verrückt* are crazy — you know it from Yiddish. So God created a world which is, in the supreme form, to say it in Yiddish, *verrückt*. And that's the essence of the world which God has created. [laughs]

CAYLEY: And in what sense do you use the word constitutive?

ILLICH: Take away, deny, the otherness of the other, and both cease to be what they are. Both lose what they really are. I can still see my old friend Erich Fromm's face lighting up when I told him that sex is what remains when gender is lost. I get you, he said, you want to speak about sex as something which circulates in two bodies with different plumbing . . . Yea — all mystery ceases. Sexualize this relationship, tell them they are two sexes with different characteristics, and you destroy the basic idea of genderedness, of mutual engendering.

CAYLEY: And to this sense of proportionality which exists, presumably, everywhere . . .

ILLICH: . . . according to the old seemingly so . . .

CAYLEY: . . . the Gospel might have been a crowning glory.

ILLICH: Yes, in that marvellous statement of Hugh of St. Victor's you have the anthropological basis of the Christian message. That's what we discussed in State College ten years ago.

CAYLEY: The anthropological basis?

ILLICH: The love of which I speak is an expression of proportionality as gift and choice. It finds its supreme expression, Hugh says, in the fact that our human constitution demands, as Hugh says, that there be both Adam and Eve. And that's why it can happen between you and me.

CAYLEY: So you're saying that the Samaritan's response to the Jew in the ditch crosses a boundary, but doesn't necessarily destroy or efface this boundary?

ILLICH: It liberates from the ethnic boundary without destroying it. It expands hospitality beyond the ethnic boundary. But to go back to where we began, when you bring American college boys to Peru to show people how to really dig wells, you enact a caricature — a fantastic caricature — of what we are talking about.

18

FROM TOOLS TO SYSTEMS

CAYLEY: In this conversation I'd like to revisit the question of tools, and your claim that they acquire a distinct and independent existence only after the twelfth century.

ILLICH: A little while ago, I spoke about Father John Considine, the Maryknoll priest who convinced John XXIII to enlist the Church in the Alliance for Progress. The idea of these missioners was to help these poor people, and to help meant to provide those people with means, with tools, that they didn't have — with electricity, penicillin, decent legal devices, instrumentally conceived knowledge. This was taken for granted. It's as difficult to put an epistemic parenthesis around concepts like instrument, tool, device, technique, as it is to put a parenthesis around norms or rules in ethics. As soon as we speak about conscience, someone will invoke norms according to which a conscientious man ought to act. And as soon as we speak about help, as a result of my love for you, my benevolence towards you, we will think about my empowering you by providing you with some device or technique. Now what we discussed two years ago was the fact that the very idea of the tool as a special type of causality has an historical beginning, that the idea of the tool takes mature shape in Scholasticism in the late eleventh and early twelfth centuries. Almost absurdly, but correctly, we then spoke about the discovery that angels who are pure spirits require tools, which are planets, in order to act as

God's governors in the ordering of the world. We can consider
the time between the century in which I am so much at home, the
twelfth century, and today, by speaking of it as the epoch of technique
or tool-making — "tool" meaning something that incorporates,
materializes, or formalizes a human intention, and can be picked up,
or not picked up, by a person who wants to pursue the goal that corresponds to this intention. It is marked by its belief in the
omnipresence of instruments: eyes are instruments for seeing like
cameras, concepts are epistemic devices, laws are tools for the ordering of society. Thirty years ago it was very difficult to make anybody
even doubt the fact that the word "tool" refers to a natural category
without which we cannot intelligently think. Even the body becomes
a tool for the soul, or for the person, and, more importantly, the individual organs become specialized devices to perform specialized
functions within the body. It becomes difficult for anyone except
heretics and homeopaths — and you notice how difficult it is for
medicine to swallow the existence of homeopaths — to conceive
of medical help except as the provision of instruments which interfere
in the malfunction of some organ. The fact that this instrumental way
of perceiving the world around us, and ourselves, has an historical
beginning is especially clear in the case of physicians because with
them a noninstrumental mentality survived much longer than it did
with lawyers, and philosophers, and theologians, and moralists, and
natural scientists, of course. As late as the eighteenth century the
typical doctor did not do any tests on patients. It was the great
Frenchman Laënnec[i] who heard something nobody had ever heard
before when he made a roll of newspaper into a proto-stethoscope
and listened to the waves in the ocean of a pregnant woman's belly. It
seems crazy, but in our Western society counting heartbeats is something which appears only in the nineteenth century. The doctor never
sought — until Paracelsus, which is a few hundred years earlier — for
the cause of disease in a person. He listened to a sick person, and to
what nature was telling that person — through his pains, through his
difficulty in breathing, through his anguish, through his bleeding, or
through his other juices. The doctor knew sick people; but the idea of
what medical history calls entitive diseases, diseases as distinct enti-

ties, measles rather than scarlet fever, the idea that such things exist, is post-Reformation. The possibility of really in some way defining them hardly begins before the eighteenth century. Therefore, in the case of medicine you can see very clearly what a change was implied and brought about by the instrumental mentality. All traditional doctors — in the Hippocratic tradition as much as the Galenic — believed in people, their patients, telling them about their nature. Nature was experienced, was felt, was smelled, was tasted by people; and the physician was trained to feel the circumstances of the individual in front of him who, in his human condition, had been caught in some mess, in something contrary, which nature was trying to heal. It was as if the physician were participating in a Greek tragedy, and, like the spectator in the Greek theatre, reached out through *mimesis*, sympathy, which became feeling the other. The idea of health didn't exist, but only of nature being more or less capable of constantly healing itself; and what he did as a doctor was, through counsel, through sympathy, through the power of the word, the healing word, and perhaps through ground corals or mercury pills, which were highly poisonous, as we would say today, to encourage nature, to reinforce nature to perform its own healing act. Today we can hardly think that way about the function of the doctor. We always think that he uses some tool of his profession, to do something to the system, or the subsystem in the patient, which he knows about, and not the patient. Therefore I find in medicine, in the history of medicine, an extraordinary possibility of speaking about the transformation in self-perception, and therefore also in the ego, brought about by the certainty with which we accept the instrumental relationship of help and assistance.

CAYLEY: You have also argued also that this technological era is now over.

ILLICH: Yes . . . If any respectable, academically trained biologist, microbiologist, medical technician, or diagnostician were sitting here with us, he would say, Illich, we have turned back, we have taken a major step back from this entirely technological and instrumental view of the human being. We now consider the human being as a system, that is, as an extraordinarily complex arrangement of feedback loops. And the fundamental characteristic of that system is to seek its own survival by maintaining an informational balance which keeps it viable. That's the way they think about this rose here, and you, and the cosmos. Each is a system that maintains informational balance. The age in which instrumentality was a key that increasingly opened all doors lasted from the twelfth century to sometime during the lifetime of my audience. There's nobody in my audience without one foot in the age of instrumentality. And they are barely aware of the fact that they have passed over into the age of systems, which I just described, in which you can't speak about the instrument any more. This computer here on the table is not an instrument. It lacks a fundamental characteristic of that which was discovered as an instrument in the twelfth century, the distality between the user and the tool . A hammer I can take or leave. It doesn't make me into part of the hammer. The hammer remains an instrument of the person, not the system. In a system the user, the manager, logically, by the logic of the system, becomes part of the system. As Heinz von Förster[2] said to me when we first began to discuss this thirty years ago, a man walking a dog is a man–dog system — a cyborg, one would say today. Therefore, I would strongly stress that within our lifetime we have left the epoch during which the instrument dominated self-awareness, world-awareness, and philosophical explanation of the world and language. But to interpret this as a return to the lived and felt body would be an extraordinary mistake. The systems analyst imputes to the patient what he or she is, and in a way that goes beyond what was possible under the domination of shadow tools. The system analytic doctor imputes ever more complex feedback loops, most of which, if not all of which, he recognizes only on the basis of probabilities. In the body perception of which I spoke earlier, the doctor behaves like a good theatre audience at a tragedy — through the complaint of the patient, he receives, gathers, and grasps the touching singularity of the sensual self-perception of the person sitting in front of him. The systems analyst is therefore the opposite of the Galenic or Hippocratic doctor.

19

EMBODIMENT AND
DISEMBODIMENT

CAYLEY: What is the connection between your interest in body history and your understanding of the Gospel?

ILLICH: Let me begin by telling you why I became so interested — twenty-five years ago — in understanding what people meant in past times when they spoke about body. As an historian, never mind as a theologian, you just can't get around the idea that Christianity, faith, the New Testament, whatever you want to call it, begins with *verbum caro factum est*, or *logos sarx egeneto*.[1] If you look the Greek word *logos* up in the dictionary, you'll find that it means proportion or proportionality or fit before it means what we call a word. The word of God was the relationship of God to himself, as theologians later on said. But whatever is meant by this message, *sarx* quite obviously means flesh. So there is something funny about even having to raise the question, What does body have to do with Christianity and Church? It's fundamental. But it's not the *soma*, the whole of the body, that is spoken of, but its fleshiness. The absolutely unique and crazy newness of the New Testament consists in God's word becoming flesh in the womb of a little girl, of a very young woman.

In order to get into the mood for talking to you this morning, David, I may have done the wrong thing. During a pretty sleepless night I picked up my Sergio Quinzio. Quinzio was a strange man from Pistoia,[2] a contemporary of mine. He was a man who had the scholastic preparation to be a sergeant in the financial police of Italy, but when his wife died and his daughter was an adult, he retired to become a hermit. He studied Greek and Latin and became a non-scholastic, nonacademic, high-level thinker. Before he died — we never got together physically, unfortunately — he sent me his little book about the mystery of God's failure, and about the difficulty of accepting the existence of a God who fails in his intentions and who has, as far as we can judge it, limits to his omnipotence.[3] It is a book which weaves together very carefully translated passages from the New and the Old Testaments with passages from Nietzsche — because, in my opinion, the scandal of Christians believing in an omnipotent God has never been treated as intensely, as violently, and in as beautiful language as by Nietzsche. Nietzsche says, I can't accept an omnipotent God when I look at the world as it is. He says this for reasons of pride. Sergio Quinzio, this strange, hardly known Italian ruminator, says it out of deepest humility and a spirit of prayer and adoration. When Paul speaks about the word being enfleshed, or incarnated — we still speak about the Incarnation, the enfleshment — he speaks about the emptying out of God, of God emptying himself out. The Greek word is *kenosis*.

In earlier conversations I've indicated a number of possible research themes. Each of them already has a scholarly foundation, but none of them has been developed in the direction in which I would like to see it flower. An example is my suggestion that an understanding of the consequences of the criminalization of sin is a foundation for understanding the Western world. Our contemporary perception of self, of human relationship, so-called inter-personal relationship, has been deeply corrupted. When norms are brought into the "ought" through the criminalization of sin, the glorious side of the encounter between the Palestinian and the Jew is hidden. What the Lord told the Pharisees with this story was this: it is open to anyone who walks down that road to move away from the road and establish a relationship, a fit, a tie, with the man who is beaten up. To do so corresponds to the nature of two human beings and permits this nature its full flowering. The Samaritan has the possibility of establishing a proportion, a relatedness to the other man which is entirely free and conditioned only by his hope that the beaten-up Jew will respond to it by accepting this relationship. No doubt, as I said yesterday, the Samaritan parable was scandalous for the Pharisees to whom it was presented, because the Master told them who your neighbour is is not determined by your birth, by your condition, by the language which you speak, but by you. You can recognize the other man who is out of bounds, culturally, who is foreign linguistically, who, you can say by Providence, or pure chance, is the one who lies somewhere along your road in the grass, and create the supreme form of relatedness which is not given by creation but created by you. Any attempt to explain this "ought" as corresponding to a norm takes out the mysterious greatness from this free act.

But, Ivan, you may say, I didn't ask you to go back to the Samaritan but to explain to me what Christianity has to do with the body. And I told you first about the extraordinary words with which the whole story begins: that God didn't become man, he became flesh. I believe, as I hope you do, in a God who is enfleshed, and who has given the Samaritan, as a being drowned in carnality, the possibility of creating a relationship by which an unknown, chance encounter becomes for him the reason for his existence, as he becomes the reason for the other's survival — not just in a physical sense, but a deeper sense, as a human being. This is not a spiritual relationship. This is not a fantasy. This is not merely a ritual act which generates a myth. This is an act which prolongs the Incarnation. Just as God became flesh and in the flesh relates to each one of us, so you are capable of relating in the flesh, as one who says ego, and when he says ego, points to an experience which is entirely sensual, incarnate, and this-worldly, to that other man who has been beaten up. Take away the fleshy, bodily, carnal, dense, humoural experience of self, and therefore of the Thou, from the story of the Samaritan and you have a nice liberal fantasy, which is something horrible. You have the basis on which one might feel responsible for bombing the neighbour for his own good. This use of power is what I call the *corruptio optimi quae est pessima*. What is most glorious but remains, as a possibility of thinking and experiencing, always somewhat in the shadow, somewhat in the clouds, is corrupted into a very clear and powerful ideal of democracy.

God's love is in the flesh, and the relationship between two people, the mystery of the Samaritan, is inevitably a mystery of the flesh. This becomes very difficult to explain, or even to say, in our generation, during which I believe an extraordinary process, and an extraordinary history of disenfleshment of our perceptions, our concepts, and our senses has reached a high point. It has become very difficult, I know from experience, to write about the enfleshment of God during the late twentieth century. Funnily, the first great difficulty in speaking about it is connected, for anybody who knows history, with a certain monk, Berengarius,[4] at the beginning of the high Middle Ages, who was interested in the interpretation of the Eucharist. Christians, following the teaching of the Lord, generated and celebrated their "we," in a ceremony that had two high points: one, of which we have already spoken, was the *conspiratio*, the sharing of their spirits by a mouth-to-mouth kiss, which went under the euphemism of peace; the other was the *comestio*, the sharing of the same bread and wine, which, in their opinion, since this was a commemorative service, were really the body and blood, the alive flesh, of God. There is probably some historical foreshortening involved in claiming that nobody ever questioned this experience; but it is the case that for a thousand years hundreds of thousands of faithful went through it in innumerable ceremonies of celebration of the Eucharist, and then suddenly, precisely at that moment where I see the great break which we discussed in terms of criminalization of sin, the experience became problematic. Is this bread which we share really the body of Christ? How can this be? How can something which looks like bread be flesh? Face it. There seems to have been no difficulty for simple faithful or for theologians for a thousand years, and suddenly it became an issue, which was resolved purely philosophically by going back to the teaching about categories in Aristotle and saying the substance is changed but everything that is visible of the substance, which can be smelled, tasted, touched, has the characteristics of bread.

This was an important crisis within Christianity, and yet for eight hundred years after Berengarius — the guy with whose name one would usually connect doubts about the real presence of Christ in the Eucharist — the understanding of flesh seems not to have changed in the encounter between doctor and patient. That is why I was so happy, through writing *Medical Nemesis*, to have gotten into the study of the history of medicine, because there is sufficient documentation to allow this encounter between doctor and patient to be studied. Now if I think of such a medical encounter today, it usually has a shape, which would have been unthinkable until my generation. I call up the doctor and say, Doctor, I feel terribly tired. Well, Mr. Illich, first you must go to the lab and have a blood test of such type, and a urine test of such type, and excrements of such type, and, when you come here, my assistant will make, because you're an old man by now, a cardiogram, and let's hope he stops there. And then he'll look at the results and tell me what's happening with my body. If he's a very well-trained modern doctor, he may go further and say, I'll give you a few direct and indirect psychological tests as well, because you are not a body only, you are a psycho-physical being. From earliest childhood on, it is in this way that we are trained, or our mothers are trained, to think about what we are made of and what the stuff is that sits there and smiles or sighs. Nothing of this can I find in eight hundred years of history of the medical encounter. The one thing the doctor wants from the patient is that he tell him stories. He doesn't have to solicit them because the patient will begin and say, "You know, doctor, I'm so terribly tired, and I knew that this would be coming now I'm a seventy-year-old man. Once, when I was a boy, I walked along a cemetery wall during the night, and it was afterwards that I felt this fatigue for the first time. Now, to say the truth, I feel completely sandy, washed out, dry. I can't connect with my bowels and have to ask for a second or third cup of coffee or something even better than coffee." The doctor, as I suggested yesterday, had to learn to accept that the flesh was something that was summed up in the experience of it, in the experience of materiality, in the experience of stuff, in the stuffiness, the gestalt, the shape of the stuffiness of the guy sitting in front of him, which he, through hearing the story and watching the man's behaviour, language, gestures, way of sitting, diet, could grasp. This sense of the body which is totally that to which the

word ego, I, points, that which I make present in a conversation when
I say, I say to you, I believe . . . that body, during the last fifty years,
in my opinion, has been profoundly obscured, the ability of perceiving it maligned, and its remainders transformed into symptoms
which a doctor, if he is a good specialist, somewhere on the border of
psychology, can classify. I have therefore come to the conclusion that
when the angel Gabriel told that girl in the town of Nazareth in
Galilee that God wants to be in her belly, he pointed to a body which
has gone from the world in which I live.

   I can study this disembodiment of the modern *soma* particularly
well in medical interviews, but I can also study it by reflecting on the
way in which my feet are disembodied when I move mainly on my
behind. I was struck by the waitress in a quick food shop on the way
from Philadelphia to State College who presented me with a choice of
vitamins and other inputs which a man of my age and my constitution
would need. And I remember when I invited an historian of the body
whose writings had impressed me to State College. When he got
there, he sat seven or eight of us down in a circle and said, Now, in
order to be able to study body history, we first must visualize our interior. You know something about where you heart is and where your
liver is from the charts in grammar school, now we'll feel our liver, and
we'll feel and visualize and taste our heart, as if he were taking us on
a trip through the innards of some mechanical device. And, in the
most intense way, I think, this disembodiment happens through what
we call risk awareness. If anybody should ask me what is the most
important religiously celebrated ideology today, I would say the ideology of risk awareness — palpating your breast, or the place between
your legs, in order to be able to go to the doctor early enough to find
out if you are a cancer risk. Why is risk so disembodying? Because it
is a strictly mathematical concept. It is a placing of myself, each time
I think of risk, into a base population for which certain events, future
events, can be calculated. It's an invitation to intensive self-
algorithmization, not only disembodying, but reducing myself entirely
to misplaced concreteness by projecting myself on a curve.[5]

   You asked me to speak about why it seems to me important, in
relation to Christianity, to understand what the historical, the

epochal sense of body is. And my answer is, because I know from my conversations with people whom I meet, to whom I want to talk about the Incarnation, or the carnal side of faith, hope, and charity, trust in your word, hope in your answer, love, that the majority have no more sense of body. Or, if they do speak of body, it is in the New Age sense of a body which is an ideological construct interiorized through certain psychological techniques with which the person identifies.

CAYLEY: Is there a sense in which this disembodiment is a corruption of the possibilities inherent in God's becoming flesh?

ILLICH: . . . I would like to find a pithy way of answering, but there's a difficulty involved in the fact that you are recording a radio show. I'm constantly aware of the mercenary side of the relationship between the two of us. I'm being used for a show, by a good madam . . .

CAYLEY: You flatter me . . .

ILLICH: . . . You're the only one whom I've trusted enough to do such a thing, but it certainly has something to do with disembodiment that you'll take snippets of this and make some glorious work out of my boxed, canned voice, perhaps even after my death. I feel uneasy because I know that all people will get is what you can catch in your microphone.

Your question can be best answered with a story, but a story as an historian would tell it. The story will also allow me to shorten things, caricature things. People today take hospitals for granted and tend to forget that until about 120 years ago, hospitals were places where you put people when they had to die. The idea that you go to the hospital to be repaired and sent back is that new. People are even more surprised when I tell them that antiquity didn't know anything like hospitals. There were certain temples where you could sleep at the feet of the statue of a god which might heal you in a religious way, but hospitals were not there. The Christian West found out about hospitals among the Arabs during the Crusades. By the eighth century the

Arabs had developed the *maristan*, a place where Galenic doctors
could gather people affected by certain diseases. It made it easier for
them to teach their novices how to deal with wounds, provided a
convenient place to treat people, and allowed them to experiment
with drugs. That's an Arab idea. No one, strangely, had had that idea
in Western Europe. People tell me it can't be true, but it's true. One
of the Arab doctors whom I love, Al-Razi [865–925], was the head of
the hospital, the *maristan*, in Baghdad. He wrote the first treatise I
know of on doctor-induced diseases. But the Christians found out
about this institution only during the Crusades, and one usually says
that the first Western hospital is founded in the year 1102 or 1103.

This first hospital was completely different from the Arab hospital and was really based on a religious idea. There had been very wet
weather during the late eleventh century for years in a row, and therefore ergot had invaded the grain fields. Ergot is that black
mushroom, which is a rather powerful poison and is still used today
in medicine, in very light doses, for serious hemicrania, or migraine.
What happened then was that lots of people ate bread infected with
ergot, and ergotism became endemic. Thousands of people were suffering from it. Modern doctors have never seen this disease. What it
looks like is best studied in paintings, the glorious paintings of the
Passion by Matthias Grünewald, which were painted for one of these
ergot hospitals in Alsatia. That is, the first Christian hospital was
founded for those to whom God had given the marks of ergotism,
and who, if they wanted, could decide to answer God's call and join
what was called the order of St. Anthony. It's as if a contemporary
person took a positive HIV test as a special call from God to join an
order dedicated exclusively to the treatment of people who had the
same vocation and therefore a somewhat similar course towards death
in front of them. This affliction was taken as a bodily sign from God,
which opened to the sufferer a very special and glorious way of caring for the dying and then dying himself in the community bodily
established through this most painful drying off and withering away
of the limbs. For 200 or 300 years there was never a doctor connected
with a hospital, though doctors were around at that time. Within a
generation of the founding of the first such hospital, there were in

southwestern Europe at least 160 of these monastic centres dedicated to a special way of approaching the hour of death, liturgically celebrated. The Grünewald pictures show you how the hospital wards were arranged so that people could look at the Passion of Christ when they celebrated the Eucharist. It took hundreds of years before hospitals developed into repair centres, and it happened very largely through the generosity of small groups of Christians banding together, consecrating their lives in community to charitable action with some medical competence. As medical supervision increased, there developed the idea that the nuns or merciful brothers should be merely the administrators and the servant personnel for doctors practising medicine, hospital medicine, which particularly in the last two centuries became increasingly a medicine focusing on the medically diagnosed and imputed body. I don't know if this is one line by which you can see how the attempt to find a loose institutional form, in order to facilitate in a very special way mutual caring, could grow into a caring institution which provides the service of care, and how this is deeply connected with the creation of the basis for the modern imputed body.

CAYLEY: Does a belief in the resurrection of the body in some way open the door to disembodiment?

ILLICH: Let me try to answer in this way. You referred yesterday to Paul the Apostle, speaking on the *agora* in the midst of that fabulous architecture of Athens.[6] The Athenians listened with interest, as they would to any wandering peddler of good news, until Paul came to talk about the resurrection. Then they told him, Listen, it was very nice, but stop it for the moment and talk to us about this another time. How intuitively right these Athenians were. From what I know of their medical texts and the light these texts throw on the philosophical texts of this Hellenistic period, I would say that these Athenians had a pretty strong fleshy sense of something when they said "I." They knew how their different statuses, their professions, their activities, their diets, and their celebrations all influenced the humoural, flowing, gooey, sensitive, touchy feeling that they referred to when they said "I." And here was this guy Paul who not only believed in his vocation as a Samaritan but who also knew something about the resurrection of the enfleshed word. His sense of the flesh had exploded to include the enfleshed God; and, wherever he visited, he celebrated the mystery of this enfleshment. And, therefore, he could innocently say to the Athenians that, as a consequence of the coming of our Lord, Jesus Christ, we now have a flesh which we will feel again, as we do not feel it in sleep, and will not feel it in death. It will be given back in a glorious way. Paul — I'm elaborating now — could speak about the eternity of the flesh, of his flesh, because he had celebrated the Eucharistic mysteries often enough to take it for granted that the flesh is that which God, the word of God, has assumed. The Athenians said, No, now you are touching on something whose meaning for you we can feel from the way you speak, but, for us, it has none.

You cannot speak about the Resurrection except as already implicit in the Incarnation. And the Resurrection is the proof of the Incarnation. Only God's flesh is capable of resurrecting, of being resurrected; and I am destined for resurrection, hopefully on the right side, precisely because I'm enfleshed through my acts of charity, and through my doxological celebration of the enfleshment. Paul speaks about the *cosmos*, about a new heaven and a new earth which is a new relationship between the two, a new proportionality, a new *cosmos* which in Greek means *vis-à-vis*, lined up in front of each other, facing each other in a new and glorious way. Creation, through the Incarnation, will perdure. It has a beginning. It is not eternal like God, but it has no end. This is what I referred to earlier by Thomas's term *aevum*, a now which is also forever, in which heaven and earth are facing each other, and therefore the flesh which is already in heaven and the flesh on earth will somehow be glorified together. But I'd rather not speak about things about which I understand so little, but which I enthusiastically believe and claim the right not to have to defend.

20

CONSPIRATIO

CAYLEY: Ivan, I would like to ask you today to say more on the subject of *conspiratio*, the kiss of peace, which you spoke of in our conversation of two years ago and again in recent days.

ILLICH: Let me try and answer in terms of citizenship, because when we ended our conversation a few days ago, I was evasive on this subject. We tend to assume that our ideas about democracy, our democratic certainties, derive in some way from Greek politics, from the idea of the *polis*, which was translated by Cicero as *civitas* and then elaborated during the Reformation and afterwards into what we assume about the citizen today. This involves an oversimplification because, in Athens, you were born out of the city, not into the city. The city was conceived as a womb, or as an aspect of nature. Nature was always conceived according to this womb figure, and Athenian citizens were bound to each other by having come from the same womb, and having therefore the obvious purpose of acting according to the needs and the characteristics of the city, of Athens. Citizenship, as belonging to this "we," was in no way something which you established by your own will. In later Roman times, through Cicero's elaboration of the idea of the citizen, there were possibilities of being adopted into the city. One such adoptee of whom we've often spoken was Paul, a Hellenistic Jew who could nonetheless say, I'm a Roman citizen. What has strangely been overlooked, and very frequently, by people who have tried to retrace the history of our political concepts and particularly that of the citizen, is its Christian derivation. The Eucharistic gathering in the very first Christian centuries explicitly claimed to establish a new "we," a new plural of the "I." This "we" was not of this world. It didn't belong to the world of politics in the Greek sense, or of citizenship in the *urbs*, in the Roman sense. These guys got together for a celebration which had two high points, one of them called *conspiratio*, and the other one *comestio*. *Conspiratio* mustn't be translated too easily into English as conspiracy because *spiritus*, spirit, ghost, the supreme form of inwardness, Holy Spirit, was the meaning which informed the word *conspiratio* and not the sense we give it today of a bunch of rebels trying to subvert the political community. This *conspiratio* was expressed by the mouth-to-mouth kiss, *osculum*. *Osculum* is one of three possible Latin words available for what in English would translate as kiss. There's *basium*, in French *baiser*, the most frequently used old Latin word — it's really a Celtic word which came into Latin — and *suavium*, which makes you think of President Clinton. *Osculum*, which says mouth-to-mouth, was only used as a legal device. A man departing for military service could go before a judge and call his pregnant woman and kiss her in front of this magistrate. He thereby said that the fruit, if it should be born, would be recognized by him in his absence as his child. The Christians adopted this symbolism, which might in a faint way also have been used in some mystery cults — I'm not going into this — to signify that each one of those present around the dining table contributed of his own spirit, or, if you want, the Holy Spirit, which was common to all, to create a spiritual community, a community of one spirit. They then sat down and shared the same meal of which we spoke yesterday when we also touched on the Eucharist. This simple dinner table was their central liturgical function, the function at which *ecclesia*, calling together — that's what the term means — took on body and soul. Slave and master, Jew and Greek, each contributed equally to making the community to which, through his contribution, he could then belong.

The idea of this embrace preceding the communion remained in the Roman liturgy, and in most liturgies, throughout two millennia.

But by the fourth century, when the Church was established and made legally acceptable, bodily contact of this peculiar kind was already suspect, and its name was changed from *osculum* to *osculum pacis*, and finally to *pax* alone.¹ So when, as an historian, you read texts of the fourth to the twelfth century, and it is said that people came together to establish the *pax* or to give the *pax* to each other, you have to ask yourself whether they are still speaking about the *osculum pacis*, about this kiss as a ceremonial preparation for joining in the same plate, the same food.

Now, what does this have to do with citizenship? Again I take my lead from my teacher Gerhart Ladner, in a book which he was unable to finish before he died. This ceremony gave its participants the idea that community could come into existence outside of the community into which they were born, and in which they fulfilled their legal obligations — a community in which all those who are present share equally in the act of its establishment. It's interesting that even within the history of the Christian liturgy this idea began to be shocking by the high Middle Ages. It seemed to contradict the feudal ideal of the time with its hierarchical assumption about how society comes into existence; and, by the tenth century, the mode of performing this ceremony had changed. Anybody who knows Eastern or Roman liturgy, and quite a few other liturgies, knows that even now, or even into our twentieth century, the priest, instead of sharing the peace with everybody, kisses the altar, as if taking something from the altar which stands for Christ, and then hands it down to the others. The priest's kiss, since the twelfth century, has been handed down from the altar. Not only have kiss, and *conspiratio*, moved into the background, and *pax* into the foreground, but during the thirteenth, fourteenth, and fifteenth centuries an instrument was developed called an *osculatorium*, a kissing object. You can see it in museums, sometimes made of beautiful wood with precious stones. The priest would kiss it after kissing the altar and then hand it down to the community so that it could make its rounds through the church.

So, the Christian practice of establishing a bodily community through an equal contribution of everyone of the spirit within, this total innovation, remained, in some faint way, valid and meaningful throughout two millennia, but not for the purpose of establishing a *conspiratio* around the Eucharistic table, but with the idea of creating a modern society bound by a social contract. What is established in the *conspiratio* is, in the strictest sense, non-worldly, in spite of its somatic, its bodily depth. It is a celebration of the statement, You are in this world but not of this world. During the period of the Gregorian reform the attempt to establish, legalize, and formalize the *conspiratio* reached a high point. Just as we spoke of Prodi's idea of the criminalization of sin, we can also speak at the same time of a very explicit attempt to back up the *conspiratio*, this spiritual union in which each one's breath has the same weight, and make it into a *conjuratio*. How would you say it in English?

CAYLEY: A conjuration, but it wouldn't make any sense any more because conjure has taken other denotations.

ILLICH: Well, in this case, it refers to an attempt to give the Church this worldly solidity and clarity and definition and to create, through legal, contractual means, a social body entitled to recognition as an equal by the Emperor and the civil law. At the same time as sin is being criminalized, the Church is being made into a separate, legal entity. The civic forum in which one seeks justice in a legal sense is paralleled by a new ecclesiastic forum which acquires increasingly contractual characteristics. Now perhaps you can see why, in order to understand the general idea of *corruptio optimi quae est pessima* as it applies to the political, it is necessary to observe throughout history this fading of the *conspiratio*, and the monumental elaboration of the *conjuratio*, or contractual arrangement. You can see it in the case of marriage. Christians got along for a thousand years without knowing that marriage is a contract between a man and a woman. The idea was unthinkable, and nobody would have thought about it that way. There might have been a type of contract between two families who wanted, let's say, to share certain lands and used a daughter from one house and a son from the other to effect it. But it was only in the twelfth century that the idea that the substance of marriage is a contract between this man and that woman appeared. In fact, it occurs for the first time in the writings of my friend Hugh of St. Victor. The mystery of marriage was understood to be based on a *conjuratio*, a contract, and then the contract was made the substance of a sacrament and lifted into the sphere of the divine in order to give this unbelievable idea credibility with people.

21

ACROSS THE WATERSHED

CAYLEY: You have often said to me that the world, in our time, has crossed a watershed. And I would like to ask you once again to expand on the nature of this change.

ILLICH: An example of the change I'm talking about can be seen in the use of the word responsibility. Responsibility, as defined in tort actions, has a respectable past. Responsibility as a moral obligation, or as a feeling which should influence ethical judgements, is something which appears at the beginning of our century. You can look it up in the *Oxford English Dictionary* and its supplements, and you'll have to rely mainly on the supplements. Twenty years ago — even ten years ago still, but let's say twenty years ago — among the people with whom I usually deal — that's, of course, a very peculiar type of people — it was impossible to question their responsibility for the children with hunger-blown-up bellies whom they saw in the ads of the children's funds. They felt responsible, and they were scandalized when I talked to them about responsibility being the soft underbelly of fantasies about power, and told them that the responsibility they felt was a way of justifying their sense that, because they were from a rich country, they had some power to plan, to organize, to change the rest of the world. During the last few years — I'm speaking from experience — I have been able to make people laugh at themselves for having fallen into this trap and believed in this kind of responsibility. A new sense of impotence is around. The future, in this earlier period, was subject to planning, designing, and policy-making. In fact, the very idea of policy-making and policy execution belongs to the period after the Second World War. You couldn't have spoken about it in the language which the *Oxford Dictionary* recognized before the war. It needed the new language of the Harvard Business School. But now all this is receding very fast. It still finds expression in terms of the United States bombing Milosovic, or Qaddafi, or Iraq into the recognition of the human rights of their own citizens. It still nourishes the new book by Rostow[1] about the need to maintain American police power worldwide as a condition for the survival of democracy. But the people who speak to me, as opposed to those who spoke to me twenty years ago, recognize a fallacy in this thinking. They recognize that they are in front of a world, not the future world but the present world, which is built on assumptions for which they haven't found the appropriate names yet. I could also illustrate this by speaking about health care, about education, about urbanism. I speak with people who are beginning to understand that the language about the organization of power prevalent between 1950 and 1980 has no hold on reality any more. And this is true whether they are people who come from an attempted philosophy of power structure — let me say, Michel Foucault — or if they come from the Rostow corner. Foucault assumes that power exists along the same lines on which science after 1840 constructed the idea of energy in the physical world. Power in the social domain corresponds metaphorically with energy in the physical domain. Twenty-five years ago, in spite of my great admiration, when I argued this, to Foucault's face but also with others, people considered me evil, David. Now there is a recognition that we cannot help but renounce power, not because of a Gandhian or Christian spirit of renunciation of violence, but because the power which we sought ten or twenty years ago reveals its own void, its own illusory characteristics.

We have spoken already about disembodiment. Disembodiment, which really seems at first sight absurd — to speak about disembodied people — is reaching a second level which I can only call algorithmization or mathematization. People annihilate their own sensual nature by projecting themselves into *abstracta*, into abstract notions. And this renunciation of intimate uniqueness through the introjection and self-ascription of statistical entities is being cultivated with extraordinary intensity by the way in which we live. This has to be explored. The consequence is an insensibility not only to myself but to you. In the Gospel story of the Samaritan, as I told you yesterday, it says that the Samaritan felt moved in his belly, in his entrails — *splágchnon* in the Greek. That the Samaritan felt touched in his innards would probably be the most respectable way of saying it in English. Luther in his German translation uses the verb *jammern*, which even in Toronto, not only in New York, you might know from Yiddish because "yammer" is a Yiddish way of complaining. He felt a sense of dis-ease in his belly when he looked at that Jew in the ditch. That beaten-up one provoked in him a bodily sense of dis-ease. This dis-ease was a gift from the other. Theologians call this grace, or sanctifying grace, but I don't want to go into that. The Samaritan understood that this guy was in a peculiar state of misery. I am carefully avoiding saying that he was in need of something. If I attribute needs to myself and to others, all I can give is need-satisfaction, and that really doesn't have to be personal, that doesn't have to come from me. That would probably come with more effectiveness, efficiency, and competence if we were to call in the right professional, or let the right agency do it.

We are in a situation in which the disembodiment of the I–Thou relationship has led into a mathematization, an algorithmization, which supposedly is experienced. It has seemed to me during the last couple of years that the main service I still can render is to make people accept that we live in such a world. Face it, don't try to humanize the hospital or the school, but always ask, What can I do, at this very moment, in the unique *hic et nunc*, here and now, in which I am? What can I do to get out of this world of needs-satisfaction — that's why I used the image of the flying fish[2] — and feel free to hear, to sense, to intuit what the other one wants from me, would be able to imagine, expects with a sense of surprise, from me at this moment? I think that many people have very reasonably withdrawn from trying to improve the social agencies and organizations for which only twenty years ago they felt responsible. They know that all they can do is to try, by negative criteria, to diminish the impact and the hold of this idea on their milieu, in order to be increasingly free to behave an-archically as human beings who do not act for the sake of the city, but because they have received the ability to respond as a gift from the other.

The credibility of the world that based itself on citizenship, on responsibility, on power, on equality, on need, claim, and entitlement — the credibility of these as ideals to which it is worthwhile to consecrate your life is declining, and, in my opinion, very fast. Most people see this as a serious danger, which it is, to the survival of a democratic order. I want to suggest the possibility of seeing it as the end of an epoch, just like the Roman Empire at the time of Augustine, and as an entirely new access/credibility/ease of moving into the world of *conspiratio*, knowing that it can't be contractually insured, that it's a renunciation of insurance.

CAYLEY: The most common way of naming the current sense of being at a watershed is as the inception of postmodernity. May I again ask how are you disposed to that way of speaking?

ILLICH: When I first heard it, and again and again when that word was thrown into my face, I of course thought of the struggle, the dispute, the minuet played between the *antiqui et moderni* in the Renaissance. It has something of *déjà vu* about it. On the other hand the word is usually used to reflect the widening awareness, and the deepening awareness, that the assumptions, the axioms, the rules taken for certain, for natural, for unquestionable during a rather long period, have, some twenty–thirty years ago, begun to give out. Therefore it reflects the awareness that something along the lines which I just exposed might be happening. But I want to be very careful not to be identified as somebody who is a postmodernist, because the term has been pretty effectively appropriated by a certain type of literary criticism, extending then into anthropology and ethnology and then picked up by politicians, by movements, to indicate some kind of legitimacy which the language of the social sciences could preserve and maintain under entirely new conditions. So I don't see why I should say more than, Watch out, when you listen carefully to me, you will be angry if you are a postmodernist. Postmodernism is incredibly disembodying.

22

GRATUITY

CAYLEY: I'd like to conclude with your reflections on living in what I remember you once calling "a world immune to grace." What practices, what dispositions are necessary to live with faith in a world which is itself a perversion of faith?

ILLICH: We ended our last conversation with your request that I interpret that which quite commonly today is called the beginning of postmodernity. I've explained why I don't want to be pulled into the discourse that goes under that title. Another way in which I can speak, as an observer and an historian, about the threshold over which many people had the sense of having passed in the early 1980s, is to call it the end of the age of dominant instrumentality. This makes sense only when you look at the concept of *instrumentum*, "tool," as an historian of ideas — something we have already discussed. Together with Professor Carl Mitcham and others, I am by now pretty certain that the idea of the tool, in the narrow sense, is something which appears only in the high European Middle Ages. Just to repeat and sum up: when Plato or Pliny talk about tools, or devices, they call them *organon*. They call the hand an *organon*, the hammer an *organon*, and the hammering hand an *organon*. The tool is an extension of the human body. In the twelfth century we notice that an increasing awareness appears, partly under Arab influence, that certain material objects can incorporate, can be given

human intentions. The intention to do something can pass from the
hand into the hammer. The hammer can be seen as something made
for hammering, and the sword something for killing, no matter if the
hammer is taken in hand by a craftsman, or by a little girl, or by a mill
— it's that way that in the twelfth century they begin to speak about
it. The sword can serve for killing, or for war-making, no matter if he
who touches it is a noble born to the sword or any peasant trained to
the sword. I believe this distinction between tool and user is characteristic of the epoch which I claim came to an end with the 1980s.
There is a distance — I use the specific term "distality" — between
the hand, the operator, and the instrument that performs the task.
This distality disappears again when the hammer and the man, or the
dog and the leash held by the man, are conceived as a system. You can
no longer say that there is a distance between the operator and the
device, because according to systems theory the operator is part of
the system within which he operates and regulates.

Now, why do I begin by once more calling to your attention my
reflections on the age of instrumentality and my claim that it has
come to an end? With the increasing dominance of instrumentality
during this 800-year period, it became certain, obvious, natural, that
wherever something is achieved, it is achieved by means of an instrument. The eye is perceived as an instrument for recording what's
before me, the hand is conceived and spoken about as an instrument
shaped by evolutionary development. Love is an instrument for satisfaction. Just as it becomes almost unthinkable that I should be
guided by an "ought" that is not determined by some kind of norm,
so it becomes unthinkable that I should pursue a goal without using
an instrument for that purpose. In other terms, instrumentality
implies an extraordinary intensity of purposefulness within society.
And hand-in-hand with the increasing intensity of instrumentaliza-
tion in Western society goes a lack of attention to what one
traditionally called gratuity. Is there another word for the nonpur-
poseful action, which is only performed because it's beautiful, it's
good, it's fitting, and not because it's meant to achieve, to construct,
to change, to manage? You asked me to speak about a grace-less
world, and it seems to me that the traditional word for the opposite

of the purposeful act is the gratuitous act. In German I invented the word *Umsonstigkeit*, for no purpose at all, and it seems to have stuck, though it's in no dictionary.

So it is my strong belief, and I can back it up by referring to many important thinkers and authors of our century, that one aspect of modernity was the loss of gratuity. One of the profound reasons for this is that with the Enlightenment, philosophers largely stopped speaking about ethics and morals as the search for the good and increasingly spoke instead about the valuable. The replacement of the good by the valuable we have already discussed. The valuable always implies some relationship to effectiveness, to efficiency, therefore to device, to tool, to purpose. It has become very difficult at the end of the modern time to imagine actions which are good and beautiful without in any way being purposeful. What I meant when I spoke to you about the absence of a sense for grace referred to this absence of a sense for gratuity. To go back to our main image, our guiding *topos*, the Samaritan, the Samaritan acts because his action is good, not because this man can be saved or not saved, not because this man needs medical attention, or needs food, but because, imagining that I am the Samaritan, he needs me. What the beaten-up Jew's presence evokes in the Samaritan's belly is a response which is not purposeful but gratuitous and good. And I claim that the recovery of this possibility is the basic issue we are discussing here — the possibility that a beautiful and good life is primarily a life of gratuity, and that gratuity is not something which can flow out of me unless it is opened and challenged through you.

CAYLEY: The end of instrumentality, the recognition that when I walk my dog, I constitute a man–dog system, has been taken by many as a liberating perspective, as an overcoming of alienation, in which I see myself once again as part of the world, and as part of nature. I at first, when younger, took systems theory as liberating . . .

ILLICH: . . . Bateson . . .¹

CAYLEY: . . . Bateson, etc. So why do you see it so differently?

ILLICH: Well, my first answer, from my belly, would be, I'm the master of that beast. It's not Mr. Dog. I once needed a dog to defend me, and I treated the beast which I had to train to watch and defend me as Mr. Dog. I had to give him up because that's not the way you deal with a beast. But, on a deeper level, I would simply say that I can't be resumed into a system. I am not a system, neither an immune system, which is an independent subsystem in the world-system, nor fully absorbable in that which can be analyzed by systems analysis. Systems analysis would explain love, charity, as a feedback; and, in fact, I've recently read some theological nonsense by reputable people explaining what special kinds of feedback go on when you engage in acts of faith, hope, and charity. These people have lost the concrete sense of themselves as this mysterious thing which we are, an "I" which is somatic — my whole *soma* is "I" — free and independent. Systems theory is a good instrument for analysis of certain things, but, unless you draw limits to it, you have the gooiest outlook which ever has been invented . . . Draw three boxes and four arrows to show how they inter-relate with each other.

CAYLEY: So how can one live gratuitously in a world like this?

ILLICH: Friends, friends . . . gratuity, just so, for the fun of it, for your sake . . .

CAYLEY: Does this require a certain asceticism?

ILLICH: Well, *ascesis* is the old word for training, for repetition. I would say what is required is a word which is difficult to pronounce today — virtue — repeated acts of faith, hope, and love which slowly create in you, psycho-physically, an ease in performing them; and, in order to sustain yourself in a disciplined way, *ascesis*, self-training, is of a certain importance, although it has to be said again that training for our contemporaries always implies instrumental purposes, which is not what I'm taking about. It's strange that in modern Californian English it's easier to speak of *yoga* than of *ascesis*, but what the word *ascesis* meant for 2,000 years is something like what *yoga* now signifies in our Western world.

CAYLEY: You suggested earlier that a new possibility has been opened by the ending of the age of instrumentality . . .

ILLICH: I think so. In this world I couldn't find a better situation in which to live with those I love, and those are exactly people who are overwhelmingly aware of the fact that they have passed beyond a threshold. And because they are no longer so deeply imbued by the spirit of instrumentality, or of futility, they can understand what I mean by gratuity. I do believe that there is a way of being understood today when you speak about gratuity, and gratuity in its most beautiful flowering, is praise, mutual enjoyment; and what some people, such as those who propose a new orthodoxy,[2] discover, is that the message of Christianity is that we live together, praising the fact that we are where we are and who we are, and that contrition and forgiveness are part of that which we celebrate, doxologically.

CAYLEY: With praise . . .

ILLICH: Yea.

CAYLEY: I have no more questions.

ILLICH: Thank you.

CAYLEY: Do you have any more answers?

ILLICH: I hope nobody takes what I said for answers.

This page intentionally left blank

NOTES

Epigraph

This quotation is taken from Muska Nagel, *A Voice . . . Translations of Selected Poems by Paul Celan* (Orono, ME: Puckerbrush Press, 1998), 83.

Foreword

1. "The Corruption of Christianity: Ivan Illich on Gospel, Church and Society," *Ideas*, CBC Radio, January 3–7, 2000. Available in audio or transcript from *Ideas* Transcripts, Box 500, Station A, Toronto, ON, Canada, M5W 1E6.

Preface

1. David Cayley, *Ivan Illich in Conversation* (Toronto: House of Anansi Press, 1990), 242–43. Illich had also broached this idea earlier in our conversation (213–14). The interview was recorded for CBC Radio's *Ideas* and became the basis for a series of five one-hour programs called "Part Moon, Part Travelling Salesman: Conversations with Ivan Illich," first broadcast in early 1989. These programs are available in audio or printed transcription from *Ideas* Transcripts, Box 500, Station A, Toronto, ON, Canada, M5W 1E6.

2. As a man at home in medieval Latin, Illich often used the old Latin adage *corruptio optimi pessima* as a shorthand for this idea, but it is a proverb that can be found in many forms, from Aristotle to Aquinas to Shakespeare. "'Tis the most certain sign the world's accurst," says Sir John Denham in his *Progress of Learning*, "That the best things corrupted are the worst."

3. CIDOC began life as the Center for Intercultural Formation, a training institute for priests, persons in religious orders working in Latin America, and lay persons, soon grew into what amounted to a free university, hosting seminars which attracted reform-minded thinkers from around the world.

4. "The Corruption of Christianity: Ivan Illich on Gospel, Church and Society,"
    Ideas.

5. From the address given by Celan at the reception of the Literature Award of
    the Free Hanse City of Bremen, January 20, 1958, printed as an epilogue to
    Muska Nagel, *A Voice . . . Translations of Selected Poems by Paul Celan*, 221.
    Another interesting coincidence tying Illich to Celan is the fact that in 1998
    Illich was also given an award by the city of Bremen, its Culture and Peace
    Prize, in recognition of his contribution to the city during his years of living
    and teaching there.

6. Lee Hoinacki heard the story from Illich and retells it in *Death Is Not Dying,*
    forthcoming.

7. This interview is, so far as I know, unpublished.

Introduction

1. Dalmatia lies on the Adriatic Sea opposite Italy. It was then part of Yugoslavia
    and is now part of Croatia.

2. The details are unclear to me, but in David Cayley, *Ivan Illich in Conversation,*
    80, Illich says that, until the time of his grandfather's death in 1941, his father's
    status provided "diplomatic protection" for his family. Bribes were also paid to
    the Nazis, and, on one occasion, young Illich himself carried a payment to an
    official of Hermann Göring's ministry.

3. "The Germans had decided to use a scorched earth policy in Italy as they with-
    drew, and they were taking the livestock. I was able to get information from the
    German command about where they would be requisitioning cattle, and I
    would get the cattle off to the mountains where the Germans couldn't find
    them. It wasn't tremendously heroic activity, but since then . . . resistance has
    come naturally." From an unpublished interview with Doug Lummis, recorded
    in Japan in the winter of 1986–87.

4. "Part Moon, Part Travelling Salesman: Conversations with Ivan Illich,"
    Ideas, 3.

5. David Cayley, *Ivan Illich in Conversation*, 88–89.

6. Francine du Plessix Gray, "The Rules of the Game," *The New Yorker*, April 25,
    1970, 80.

7. Ivan Illich, *Celebration of Awareness: A Call for Institutional Revolution* (Anchor
    Books, 1971), 30, first published by Doubleday, 1970.

8. These words appear in the introduction to a little essay called "The Eloquence
    of Silence," in Ivan Illich, *Celebration of Awareness*. It is one of Illich's most
    luminous statements of his faith.

9. Ivan Illich, *Deschooling Society* (Penguin Books, 1973), 50, first published by
    Harper and Row, 1971.

10. Ivan Illich, *Celebration of Awareness*, 165, 152.

11. Illich's addresses to the Church during this period are to be found in Ivan Illich, *Celebration of Awareness*, and in a partially overlapping volume, Ivan Illich, *The Church, Change and Development* (The Urban Training Center Press, 1970).

12. David Cayley, *Ivan Illich in Conversation*, 98.

13. Francine du Plessix Gray, "The Rules of the Game," 44.

14. The essay appears in both Ivan Illich, *Celebration of Awareness*, and Ivan Illich, *The Church, Change and Development*.

15. Ivan Illich, "The Powerless Church," in *Celebration of Awareness*, 87–94.

16. Ivan Illich, *Celebration of Awareness*, 87.

17. Ivan Illich, "The Powerless Church," 90.

18. David Cayley, *Ivan Illich in Conversation*, 100–101.

19. Ibid., 102.

20. Ibid., 103.

21. Ivan Illich, *Celebration of Awareness*, 58.

22. Francine du Plessix Gray, "The Rules of the Game," 62.

23. Illich tended to downplay, and certainly never dramatized, the physical danger he faced during this period, but there is a brief account of his "being shot at and beaten up with chains" in David Cayley, *Ivan Illich in Conversation*, 120–22. Illich was appalled by the Church's silence about torture in Latin America, and, in the fall of 1970, wrote an open letter to the Pope censuring his silence and imploring him to condemn torture and terror as means of government. It was published in *Commonweal*, September 4, 1970, 428–29.

24. Illich rarely spoke of these events in later years. When I first interviewed him in 1988, he dismissed the whole affair as "some silly Roman business." But there are journalistic accounts from the time. The most detailed is du Plessix Gray's "The Rules of the Game." Also informative are Edward B. Fiske, "Vatican Curb Aimed at Cultural Center of Reform Advocate," *New York Times*, January 23, 1969; Edward B. Fiske, "Religion: Illich Goes His Own Way," *New York Times*, February 2, 1969; Edward B. Fiske, "Head of Cultural Center Tells of Secret Hearing in Vatican" *New York Times*; and Edward B. Fiske, "Illich Makes Public Classified Paper of 'Inquisition' That Preceded Church's Move Against Institute in Mexico," *New York Times*, February 4, 1969.

25. This is a paraphrase of one of the sayings from the Sermon on the Mount, Matthew 5:40.

26. Cardinal Seper was a former archbishop of Zagreb and actually spoke in his native Serbo-Croatian, a language Illich also knew from childhood.

27. Fyodor Dostoevsky, *The Brothers Karamazov*, vol. 1, trans. David Magarshack (Penguin Books, 1958), 308.

28. From a letter to Sergio Mendez Arceo, the bishop of Cuernavaca, quoted in Edward B. Fiske, "Vatican Curb Aimed at Cultural Center of Reform Advocate," 1–2.

29. This letter is quoted in Francine du Plessix Gray, "The Rules of the Game," 91. Illich had remained assigned to the archdiocese of New York since his years in Incarnation Parish, and, during all those years, the Archbishop of New York, Cardinal Spellman, had encouraged and protected him. As late as November 1967, after the Archbishop of Puebla had written to Spellman complaining about Illich, Spellman had responded with unequivocal support. "Illich is a priest of excellent standing in my diocese," he wrote back, "in every way obedient." Two weeks after he wrote this letter Spellman died. Illich's troubles began before the year was out.

30. Lee Hoinacki, "Why Philia?" an unpublished talk by Illich's old friend at a symposium in memory of Illich, Pitzer College, Claremont, California, March 2004.

31. David Cayley, *Ivan Illich in Conversation*, 99.

32. Lee Hoinacki, "Why Philia?"

33. Ivan Illich, *Deschooling Society*, 48.

34. David Cayley, *Ivan Illich in Conversation*, 119–20.

35. Ivan Illich, *Deschooling Society*, 18.

36. Ibid., 55.

37. Ivan Illich, *Energy and Equity* (Harper and Row, 1974), 30–31.

38. Ibid., 23.

39. Ibid., 76.

40. Ivan Illich, *Limits to Medicine: Medical Nemesis: The Expropriation of Health*, (Penguin, 1976). Lest there be any confusion, *Limits to Medicine* was the primary title of the Penguin edition of *Medical Nemesis* from which I am quoting. It refers to the same book.

41. Ibid., 49.

42. Ibid., 133.

43. Ibid., 272.

44. See, for example, Thomas Frank and Matt Weiland, eds., *Commodify Your Dissent: The Business of Culture in the New Gilded Age: Salvos from the Baffler* (New York: W. W. Norton & Co., 1997).

45. Ivan Illich, *Limits to Medicine*, 270.

46. Ivan Illich et al., *Disabling Professions* (Marion Boyars/Burns and McEachern, 1977).

47. Ivan Illich, *Deschooling Society*, 112.

48. Ivan Illich, *Limits to Medicine*, 270.

49. Ivan Illich, *Tools for Conviviality* (Harper and Row, 1973), 27–28.

50. Tom Blackwell, "Healthcare Premium Will Have to Triple: Study," *The National Post*, July 30, 2004, A1.

51. A full account of why CIDOC came to an end can by found in David Cayley, *Ivan Illich in Conversation*, 202–204.

52. David Cayley, *Ivan Illich in Conversation*, 119.

53. Ibid., 132.

54. Ivan Illich, *Gender*, (Pantheon, 1982), 177.

55. Karl Polanyi, Conrad M. Arensberg, and Harry W. Pearson, eds., *Trade and Markets in the Early Empires* (New York: The Free Press, 1957). Other notable influences on Illich's thinking at this time were Karl Polanyi, *The Great Transformation* (Boston: Beacon Press, 1957); Louis Dumont, *From Mandeville to Marx: Genesis and Triumph of Economic Ideology* (Chicago: University of Chicago Press, 1977); and Elie Halevy, *The Growth of Philosophical Radicalism* (Boston: Beacon Press, 1955).

56. Ivan Illich, *Shadow Work* (Marion Boyars, 1981), 29.

57. Ibid., 24.

58. Ibid., 57–58.

59. In David Cayley, *Ivan Illich in Conversation*, Illich describes how novel his use of the word *gender* was at the time he wrote: "When I used the term *gender* in 1980, and told my publisher Pantheon, that I wanted to write a book with that title, they told me that the only thing anyone understands as gender is the article you put in front of a noun. . . . Then I went . . . to the library . . . and looked at feminist literature. It was all a question of sexism. Sex and gender were used identically. A few people had begun to speak about the social aspects of women's behaviour as gender and their physiological differences as sex. One year after my book was published, in 1983, the two major indices for scientific literature in the United States introduced, for the first time, as a new word in the subject index *gender*." 181.

60. Ivan Illich, *Gender*, 81.

61. He describes the book in these terms in an introduction to a German re-issue in 1995: *Genus* (Munich: C. H. Beck, 1995), revised introduction to the second German edition, 1995.

62. David Cayley, *Ivan Illich in Conversation*, 182.

63. Ivan Illich, *Gender*, 179.

64. In this sense, Illich's argument in *Gender* resembles his earlier critique of schooling. Feminism, by and large, pursues equality but opens the door to an unlimited competition for goods that are bound to remain scarce by definition. So long as the pursuit of more continues, some will inevitably have less, and equality will prove to be a will-of-the-wisp.

65. *Feminist Issues: A Journal of Feminist Social and Political Theory* 3, no. 1 (Spring 1983).

66. See, for example, British historian Keith Thomas, "Back to Utopia," *New York Review of Books* 30, no. 8 (May 12, 1983).

67. Illich made an interesting remark about his style when he was talking to me about his friend Paul Goodman: "Goodman once said to me, 'I have never

written a line unless I was sure either that I had said it or would say it as it's written.' And that impressed me, of course, because I've never written a line which I have the feeling I could have said." Illich wrote with wit, penetration, and a poet's feel for the aura of the words he chose, but he certainly lacked the fluid, conversational ease that was one of the hallmarks of Goodman's prose.

68. Bookstores tend to file Illich in sociology, but he neither had nor accepted any comfortable academic niche, and his works range across a dozen conventional categories from anthropology and economics to philosophy and theology.

69. Ivan Illich and Barry Sanders, *ABC: The Alphabetization of the Western Mind* (Random House Vintage Books, 1989), first published by San Francisco: North Point Press, 1988.

70. Illich first adopted the English word *conviviality* when he wrote *Tools for Conviviality* in 1973. It was a word not much used at the time, and, when it was, it suggested the atmosphere of a cocktail party, more than the heightened mutual presence that Illich wanted to evoke. But he made the word his own and gave it the denotation of playful austerity that I hope to indicate here.

71. See Barbara Duden, *The Woman Beneath the Skin: A Doctor's Patients in Eighteenth Century Germany* (Cambridge: Harvard University Press, 1991); and Barbara Duden, *Disembodying Women: Perspectives on Pregnancy and the Unborn* (Cambridge: Harvard University Press, 1993).

72. Ivan Illich, *H_2O and the Waters of Forgetfulness: Reflections on the Historicity of "Stuff"* (Berkeley: Heyday Books, 1985).

73. Ibid., 11.

74. Ibid., 7. According to the ancient Greek story from which Illich drew his title, the waters of the river Lethe washed memories from the feet of the dead, thus turning them into mere shadows, and then carried the memories to the well of Mnemosyne. There mortals blessed by the gods could approach and listen to the Muses sing what had been and what would be. "In this way," Illich says, "the world of the living is constantly nourished by the flow from Mnemosyne's lap through which dream water ferries to the living those deeds that the shadows no longer need." 31.

75. Ivan Illich, *In the Vineyard of the Text* (Chicago: University of Chicago Press, 1993), 3.

76. Steiner uses this term for a type of solitary, disciplined, attentive submission to the authority of books that he believes is now fading to the margins of Western societies. He makes the argument in "The End of Bookishness," *Times Literary Supplement* 8 (July 16, 1988): 754.

77. Ivan Illich, *In the Mirror of the Past: Lectures and Addresses 1978–1990* (Marion Boyars, 1992), 172. The essay from which I'm quoting, "A Plea for Lay Literacy," parallels and supplements Ivan Illich, *In the Vineyard of the Text*.

78. See, for example, Marshall McLuhan, *The Gutenberg Galaxy: The Making of Typographic Man* (Toronto: University of Toronto Press, 1962).
79. *New York Times*, Wednesday, December 4, 2002.
80. *The Times*, Thursday, December 5, 2002.
81. *El Mostrador*, December 3, 2002.
82. All of Girard's works are relevant to this claim, but I would particularly recommend *Things Hidden Since the Foundation of the World* (Stanford University Press, 1997) as providing the best summary.
83. Hans Blumenberg, *The Legitimacy of the Modern Age* (MIT Press, 1985).
84. Ivan Illich, "Hospitality and Pain," (lecture), 1. This lecture is one of Illich's few explicit treatments of the theme of the present book. It is the earliest of a collection of essays and addresses, created between 1987 and 1998, which has so far appeared only in French, under the title *La perte des sens* (*The Loss of the Senses*), trans. Pierre Emmanuel Dauzat, Fayard Librarie, and Arthème Foyard, Paris, 2004. English publication is now being arranged. Meanwhile, the English versions of most of these essays — and all but a few were originally written in English — are available on the Internet at http://www.pudel.uni-bremen.de, a website established and maintained by friends of Illich's with his blessing. Many of these writings are germane to what Illich says here. Of particular note are "The Cultivation of Conspiracy," also available in Lee Hoinacki and Carl Mitcham, eds., *The Challenges of Ivan Illich* (Albany: State University of New York Press, 2002); "Health as One's Own Responsibility: No Thank You!"; "To Honour Jacques Ellul"; "Posthumous Longevity: An Open Letter to a Cloistered Community of Benedictine Nuns"; and "Philosophy . . . Artifacts . . . Friendship."
85. Luke 10:25–37.
86. Short quotations, when not otherwise noted, are taken from the text that follows.
87. On the breaking of religious rules, see Matthew 12:1, Mark 2:23, and Luke 6:1; on the primacy of the family see Matthew 12:48 and Mark 3:33.
88. On this point, I see a strong resemblance between Illich's argument and the Kierkegaard of *Fear and Trembling*. Dietrich Bönhoffer in his unfinished *Ethics* also makes the point that Christianity can never be reduced to a system of rules.
89. David Cayley, *Ivan Illich in Conversation*, 268. Here Illich shows an affinity with, among others, Karl Barth. In his *Church Dogmatics*, Barth portrays revelation as "the abolition of religion" and denounces the attempt "to foist a human product into the place of his Word, to make our own images of the One who is known only where He gives Himself to be known," Karl Barth, *Prolegomena to Church Dogmatics*, vol. 1, Part Two of *The Doctrine of the Word of God* (Edinburgh: T. T. Clark, 1956), 308. The entire discussion runs from 280–361.
90. Romans 7:6.

91. John 1:14.

92. Deuteronomy 30:19.

93. James Alison, *The Joy of Being Wrong: Original Sin Through Easter Eyes* (New York: Crossroads Publishing, 1998). This book was very helpful to me in interpreting Illich.

94. John 15:22–25.

95. See p. 189.

96. Colossians 1:14.

97. These are the words of the Communion service as they appear in the Anglican Book of Common Prayer.

98. 2 Thessalonians 2. The New Testament attributes this letter to Paul, and so, in the present book, does Illich. Current New Testament scholarship holds that the letter was probably written in the early second century, sixty years after Paul's time. Illich likely knew this, and simply followed convention in referring to Paul as the author. Since I didn't know it until recently, I never asked him.

99. This is a Greek word used in theology to signify the self-emptying of God implied by his Incarnation.

100. See p. 179.

101. Klaus Baier is a Lutheran pastor, a writer, and a teacher at the University of Oldenburg in northern Germany. He was acquainted with Illich during Illich's last years, and Baier's lively interest in the ideas expressed in my radio series "The Corruption of Christianity" helped persuade Illich to authorize the publication of this book. It was he also who pointed out the similarity between Illich's argument and Karl Barth's on the question of Christianity as a religion. See note 89.

102. Ivan Illich, *Shadow Work*, 59–60.

103. See p. 57.

104. Unani medicine, which is still a living tradition in Moslem countries, descends from the Hippocratic school of ancient Greece. It also contains, via Avicenna (980–1037), elements of Aristotelian philosophy. The balance of humours is its key idea.

105. Unrefined opium, despite its fearsome reputation as the raw material of morphine and heroin, is quite mild when smoked in moderation.

106. Colossians 1:24.

107. Ivan Illich, *Limits to Medicine*, 138.

108. David Cayley, *Ivan Illich in Conversation*, 123.

109. G. W. F. Hegel, *The Phenomenology of Mind*, trans. J. B. Baillie (New York: Harper Torchbooks, 1967), 79. Hegel quotes this as a folk saying; but, since I heard it first from him, I give him the credit.

110. Maurice Merleau-Ponty, "Eye and Mind," trans. Carleton Dallery, in *The Primacy of Perception*, ed. James M. Edie (Evanston: Northwestern University Press, 1964), 160–61.

111. "Health as One's Own Responsibility: No Thank You!"
112. Ibid.

Chapter 1: Gospel

1. Romans 8:22.
2. Luke 10:25–37.
3. The Center for Intercultural Documentation, first called the Center for Intercultural Formation, was the institute that Illich founded and directed in Cuernavaca, Mexico, between 1961 and 1976.

Chapter 2: Mysterium

1. This statement is exceptionally vulnerable, even in the present context, and may require some clarification. God, insofar as we can conceive of God, cannot be bound by time. God must therefore contain foreknowledge, rather than finding out as humans do by blind experiment. For Illich, this implied that the perverse consequences of the Incarnation must somehow have belonged to God's intention. He once remarked to me in conversation, "The Absurdistan, or hell-on-earth, in which we live is something Jesus must have foreseen, and it must therefore have been his intention in his founding of the Church." That's the mystery. A mystery is not a puzzle we haven't worked out yet. It is something that our thought, by its nature, cannot penetrate. So Illich speaks here of "an intense temptation" to "curse God's Incarnation" not in order to threaten blasphemy but in order to dramatize the unique, mysterious, world-devouring character of the evil he is trying to describe.

Chapter 3: Contingency, Part 1: A World in the Hands of God

1. Aristotle uses the term to describe any proposition that may be true but is not true in and of itself, that is, it is true only if some other proposition is true.
2. Duns Scotus — Duns the Scot — was a Franciscan philosopher/theologian who lived from 1266(?) to 1308.
3. St. Bonaventure lived from approximately 1217 to 1274. He was a Franciscan philosopher/theologian and an influential shaper of the Franciscan tradition in which Duns Scotus also worked. St. Francis of Assisi lived from 1182(?) to 1226.
4. Illich took part in a seminar directed by Jacques Maritain, when Maritain was ambassador to the Vatican and Illich a student at the Gregorian University.
5. Nature is called the birth-giver.

Chapter 4: Contingency, Part 2: The Origin of Technology

1. Theodor Litt, *Les corps célestes dans l'univers de saint Thomas d'Aquin* (Löwen, Paris, 1963).

Chapter 5: The Criminalization of Sin

1. Illich wrote a good deal about the appearance of what he called "the visible text." See particularly Ivan Illich, *In the Vineyard of the Text*; Ivan Illich and Barry Sanders, *ABC: The Alphabetization of the Western Mind*; and "A Plea for Lay Literacy," in *In the Mirror of the Past*.
2. Jack Goody, *The Development of the Family and Marriage in Europe* (Cambridge University Press, 1983).

Chapter 6: Fear

1. The original operating system for IBM-style computers and the foundation, before it was replaced by Windows, of the Microsoft empire.
2. A Norwegian criminologist, and an old and dear friend of Illich's. The international conference Illich refers to took place in Oslo in 1995. Its purpose was to call attention to the growing number of prisoners in all Western countries as a grave political emergency. For me, this conference was the starting point for a ten-hour radio series, "Prison and Its Alternatives," CBC Radio, 1996, and later a book, *The Expanding Prison: The Crisis in Crime and Punishment and the Search for Alternative* (Toronto: House of Anansi, 1998).
3. In 1951 Illich moved to New York and took a position as a curate in Incarnation Parish in upper Manhattan in the area just north of the George Washington Bridge. He has told the story in David Cayley, *Ivan Illich in Conversation*, 84–85.

Chapter 7: The Gospel and the Gaze

1. Barbara Duden is a professor at the University of Hanover. It was in her hospitable and often teeming household in Bremen that Illich lived when he was in Germany. She and Illich worked closely together during the last twenty years of his life, and this collaboration is expressed in her writings. In English see Barbara Duden, *The Woman Beneath the Skin*; and Barbara Duden, *Disembodying Women*.
2. Gérard Simon, *Le regard, l'être et l'apparence dan l'optique de l'antiquité* (Paris: Éditions de Seuil, 1988).
3. Evil be to him who evil thinks — an old French proverb.
4. George M. Foster, "The Anatomy of Envy: A Study in Symbolic Behaviour," *Current Anthropology* 13, no. 2 (1972): 165–202.
5. Alain Besançon, *L'image inderdite: Une histoire intellectuelle de l'iconoclasme* (Paris: Fayard, 1994).
6. Exodus 20:4.
7. Jonathon Crary, *Techniques of the Observer: On Vision and Modernity in the Nineteenth Century* (MIT Press, 1990).

Chapter 8: Health

1. "What are you doing at the moment?" "I'm occupied with health."
2. Illich offers an alternate etymology of *educare* in Chapter 10.
3. In 1997 the United States Supreme Court decided two cases bearing on a patient's right to choose death. Six moral philosophers filed an *amicus curiae* brief in these cases. They were John Rawls, Judith Jarvis Thomson, Robert Nozick, Ronald Dworkin, T. M. Scanlon, and Thomas Nagel. See "Assisted Suicide: The Philosophers' Brief," *New York Review of Books*, March 27, 1997.
4. Chicago pediatrician Robert Mendelsohn was a friend of Illich's and the author of *Confessions of a Medical Heretic* (Chicago: Contemporary Books, 1979).
5. Fra Domenico was one of the friars executed with Savonarola in Florence in 1498. Illich tells the story in Chapter 12.
6. See, for example, D. Banerji, *Poverty, Class, and Health Culture in India* (New Delhi: Prachi Prakashar, 1982).
7. Acts of the Apostles 17:16–34.
8. A version of Illich's article for *The Lancet* appears in *In the Mirror of the Past: Lectures and Addresses* 1978–1990 (Marion Boyars, 1992).

Chapter 9: Proportionality

1. As Illich explains in Chapter 17, he adopted this possibly unfamiliar but more accurate term in preference to asymmetrical because he wanted to describe a relation between things which are different yet still symmetrical.
2. Jacques Gernet, *A History of Chinese Civilization* (Cambridge University Press, 1982).
3. Illich is drawing here on the work of his German colleague and friend Matthias Rieger. For more on Rieger's work see http://www.pudel.uni-bremen.de.
4. Sebastian Trapp presented the paper Illich is referring to at a meeting on "Speed" organized by the Netherlands Design Institute and held in Amsterdam, November 7–8, 1996.

Chapter 10: School

1. When John F. Kennedy was elected President of the United States in 1960, he called his aid program for Latin America the Alliance for Progress.
2. Everett Reimer was then the chairman of Puerto Rico's Human Resources Planning Commission
3. See, for example, *Essays on the Ritual of Social Relations* (Manchester University Press, 1962).
4. Zygmunt Baumann is Emeritus Professor of Sociology at Leeds University and a prolific theorist of modernity and postmodernity.
5. French historian/philosopher Michel Foucault used this term to signify historic shifts in what people think they know. Illich once defined an epistemic break as

"a sudden image-shift in consciousness in which the unthinkable becomes thinkable." See "The Shadow Our Future Throws," an interview with Illich in *New Perspectives Quarterly* 6, no. 1, (Spring 1989): 20–26.

Chapter 12: On Knowing How to Die: The Last Days of Savonarola

1. Niccolò Machiavelli (1469–1527) and Marsilio Ficino (1433–1499) were both Florentines and contemporaries of Savonarola. Machiavelli was a statesman and political philosopher, Ficino a humanist scholar who revived the tradition of Plato.

2. Martin Luther relates in one of his "table talks" that he was studying in the tower of the Black Cloister in Wittenberg when he broke through to what he believed was the true understanding of God's righteousness.

3. The Miserere is Psalm 51 (Psalm 50 in the Vulgate), which begins "Have mercy on me, O Lord . . ." It has often been set to music.

Chapter 13: The Age of Systems

1. Uwe Pörksen, *Weltmarkt der Bilder: Eine Philosophie der Visiotype* (Stuttgart: Klett-Cotta, 1997).

2. Uwe Pörksen, *Plastic Words: The Tyranny of a Modular Language*, trans. Jutta Mason and David Cayley (Pennsylvania State University Press, 1995).

3. The Gaia hypothesis, first advanced by British scientist James Lovelock, holds that life as a whole constitutes a homeostatic, or self-regulating, system. See James Lovelock, *Gaia: A New Look at Life on Earth* (Oxford University Press, 1979).

4. Jewish scholar Martin Buber (1878–1965) was the author of *I and Thou*. This book distinguished the free, personal relation that Buber called I–Thou from the self-serving or instrumental relation that he named I–It. (His first translator used the archaic "thou" as the only way of capturing the sense of *du* in Buber's original *Ich und Du*.)

5. The terms *iconoscepsis* and *iconodulia* are defined and explored in Chapter 7.

6. Phillipe Ariès, *The Hour of Our Death* (Oxford University Press, 1982).

7. The essay is called "Posthumous Longevity: An Open Letter to a Cloistered Community of Benedictine Nuns." It has not yet been published in English. See Introduction, note 84.

8. Illich had a keen interest in chemistry during his youth.

9. "In this sign you conquer." According to the historian Eusebius, the Emperor Constantine saw a vision in which the cross appeared in the sky with this legend. Constantine was the first Roman Emperor to profess Christianity and begin the establishment of Christianity as a state religion.

Chapter 14: Envoi

1. This was recorded in 1996. At the time of writing, Romano Prodi is President of the European Parliament in Strasbourg.

2. During the recording of these talks and the interviews that follow, Illich and I were sometimes alone and sometimes joined by friends who listened in. Present at different points were Jacques Barzaghi, Valentina Borremans, Jerry Brown, Kate Cayley, Samar Farage, Lee Hoinacki, Carl Mitcham, Matthias Rieger, Jean Robert, Silja Samerski, and Sajay Samuel.

Chapter 15: The Beginning of the End

1. This statement comes from Paul's Letter to the Colossians 1:24.

2. Illich is referring here to the so-called Anthropic Principle. This is an updated version of what was once called the argument from design. It holds, briefly, that the requisite conditions for life on earth are so unlikely to have arisen by chance that a creator is the only reasonable hypothesis. Illich found this an abominable theory because it put deduction in the proper place of revelation.

3. *Kairos* is one of the Greek words for time. In New Testament Greek, and in subsequent Christian writing, it stands for the moment of revelation, the moment of grace and opportunity. When Jesus predicts the destruction of Jerusalem in Luke 19:44, he tells his listeners that it will be "because you did not recognize the *kairos*," which the Jerusalem and King James Bibles render as "the time of your visitation."

4. James 1:6–8.

5. *Bismillahi rahmani rahim*: In the name of Allah, the most gracious, the ever merciful.

Chapter 16: Conscience

1. Illich's talk appears as "The Cultivation of Conspiracy" in Lee Hoinacki and Carl Mitcham, eds., *The Challenges of Ivan Illich*. See Introduction, note 84.

Chapter 17: The Crowning Glory

1. This essay appears in *Celebration of Awareness* and in *The Church, Change and Development*.

2. Kostas Chatzikyriakou, a friend and sometimes colleague at Penn State.

Chapter 18: From Tools to Systems

1. René-Théophile-Hyacinthe Laënnec (1781–1826).

2. Heinz von Förster (1911–2002) was one of the founders of cybernetics.

Chapter 19: Embodiment and Disembodiment

1. The Latin and the Greek for "The word was made flesh." John 1:14.
2. A town near Florence.
3. Sergio Quinzio, *Mysterium Iniquitatis: Le encicliche dell'ultimo Papo* (Adelphi, 1995).
4. Berengar of Tours (999–1088).
5. Silja Samerski, one of Illich's collaborators during his last years, has investigated the disembodying character of risk awareness by studying encounters between pregnant women and genetic counsellors. For more information see http://www.pudel.uni-bremen.de.
6. The story of Paul and the Athenians is told in The Acts of the Apostles 17:16–34.

Chapter 20: Conspiratio

1. *Pax* means peace. The *osculum pacis* is the kiss of peace.

Chapter 21: Across the Watershed

1. W. W. Rostow, *The Great Population Spike and After: Reflections on the Twenty-first Century* (Oxford University Press, 1998). This is the only book of Rostow's that was new at the time Illich was speaking, so I assume it is the book to which he is referring.
2. The flying fish, which belongs to the air and the water at once, is an old emblem used by Christians to signify a stance which is in the world but not of it.

Chapter 22: Gratuity

1. Gregory Bateson (1904–1980) was one of the pioneers of systems theory.
2. This refers to the contemporary theological movement known as "radical orthodoxy." Illich and I had been discussing one of its foundational texts, Catherine Pickstock, *After Writing: On the Liturgical Consummation of Philosophy* (Oxford: Blackwell Publishers, 1997). See also *Radical Orthodoxy: A New Theology*, ed. John Milbank, Catherine Pickstock, and Graham Ward (Routledge, 1999).

INDEX

ABC: The Alphabetization of the Western Mind (Illich), 26
Abelard, 88
Absurdistan, 239*n.*
adultery, criminalization of, 87, 91–92
Aelred of Rievaulx, 18, 150–51, 183
aevum, 182, 214
age of systems, 77, 157–68, 226, 227–28
age of technology, 77, 157–58, 201–3, 225–26
Al-Haytham, 115–16, 117
Alighieri, Dante, 66
Alison, James, 32, 36
Alliance for Progress, 5, 6, 194, 201, 241*n.*
Al-Razi, 212
American Educational Association, 161
amoeba words, 158–60
a-mortal world, 122–23, 164–66
angels, perceived as tool users, 74–75, 201–2
Anthropic Principle, 243*n.*
Anti-Christ, 34, 60, 61, 80. *See also* mystery of evil
apocalypse, as revelation rather than catastrophe, 43, 100–101, 179, 184
apocalyptic world, 169–70, 177–80
Aquinas, St. Thomas, 67–68, 116, 214
  misrepresented by modern scholars, 74
  views on contingency, 67, 69, 74, 134
  views on timeliness, 182
Ariès, Phillipe, 165
Aristotle, 71–72, 184, 239*n.*
asceticism
  emphasis on moral use of eyes, 108–9
  as precondition for gratuity, 228–29
Augustine, St., 54, 66

Baier, Klaus, 36, 238*n.*
Banerjee, Debabar, 123
Barth, Karl, 237*n.*
Bateson, Gregory, 227
Baumann, Zygmunt, 141, 241*n.*
Berengarius, 208–9
Berman, Harold, 190
Besançon, Alain, 110–11
blessings, separated from sacraments, 78–79
Blumenberg, Hans, 29, 64–67, 68
body
  felt, 129
  history of, 104–5, 127, 160, 205–11, 213–14
  iatrogenic, 107, 129, 167–68, 209–10
  resurrection of, 213–14

Bonaventure, St., 66, 239*n.*
Bönhoffer, Dietrich, 237*n.*
"bookish reading," 26, 236*n.*
books, evolution of design, 27–28
The Brothers Karamazov (Dostoevsky), 9–10
Buber, Martin, 163, 242*n.*

canon law
  codified, 190
  separated from civil law, 89, 90
Catherine, St., 190
Catholic Church. *See* Roman Catholic Church
causa efficiens, 72, 73, 74–75
causa finalis, 72
causa formalis, 71–72
causa instrumentalis
  dependence on contingency, 73
  as precondition for age of systems, 78
  as subcategory of *causa efficiens*, 72, 73
causa materialis, 71
cause
  ceases to be basis for modern world-view, 77–78
  changing meaning of, 72–73
  types, 71–72
Celan, Paul, xvii–xix, 232*n.*
Celebration of Awareness (Illich), 8, 16–17, 232*n.*
Center for Intercultural Documentation (CIDOC), 10, 18, 231*n.*, 239*n.*
Center for Intercultural Formation (CIF), 4–5. *See also* Center for Intercultural Documentation (CIDOC)
charity
  as act of free will, 31–32, 33, 50–52, 197
  institutionalization of, 33–34, 37, 54–56, 58, 145, 180, 189–90, 191
Chatzikyriakou, Kostas, 37, 198
Christian Church. *See* Christianity, Roman Catholic Church
Christian icons, 112–16
Christian teachings
  emphasis on the relationship, 52, 53–54, 177
  resistance to codification, 36
  threat posed to traditional ethics, 30–31, 47, 51

Christianity
anthropological basis of, 199
corruption of, 33–34, 36, 47, 56–57, 61, 106
early ritual, 6, 33, 85–86
first encounter with iconoscepsis, 113–14
legitimized by Constantine, 33, 54, 186, 242n.
renunciation of worldliness, 50, 57–58, 98–99
as *symposium*, 6, 33, 142–43
See also Roman Catholic Church
Christie, Nils, 240n.
Chrysostom, St. John, 54
Church Dogmatics (Barth), 237n.
Church law
codified, 190
separated from civil law, 89, 90
CIDOC. *See* Center for Intercultural Documentation
circle of fifths, 134–35
citizenship
ancient view of, 215
basis in idea of conscience, 92–93, 191–92
Christian view of, 216
clergy
juridical role of, 89–90, 186, 188
professional, 6, 8, 37
clinical iatrogenesis, 15, 125
collegiality, universities as enemies of, 146–47, 148–49
communication, through icons, 26–28, 158–60
complementarity, 22, 132–34, 197–99
computers, difference from all previous tools, 157–58
confession
becomes a juridical act, 89–90, 188–89
circumvented via mendicant orders, 91, 188–89
value of, 90–91
conscience, 186–93
alternative to, 192
as basis for citizenship, 92–93, 191–92
as inner forum, 27, 90
made possible by criminalization of sin, 190
spawns new kind of anxiety, 192–93
spawns new sense of self, 98–99
Considine, John, 194–95, 201
conspiratio, 6, 33, 85, 142–43, 178, 191–92, 208
de-emphasized by Church, 216–18
as new form of citizenship, 215–16
Constantine, 33, 54, 242n.
contingency, 64–70
Aquinas's views on, 67, 69

broadening scope of, 66, 73–75
defined, 65
effect on idea of complementarity, 132–34
Franciscans' views on, 66–67, 68
as precondition for modernity, 67–68, 70, 73, 75
as uniquely Christian concept, 65–66, 133, 196
contractual society, 86, 88
contrition, 33, 53, 54
Cooke, Archbishop Terence, 10
Copernicus, 64
The Corruption of Christianity (CBC Radio), xvii
cosmos
effect of contingency on perceptions of, 73–75
as gift from God, 65–66
perceived as governed by angels, 74–75, 201–2
Council of Trent, 92, 144
Crary, Jonathon, 119, 160
Crucifixion, 49–50, 58
cultural iatrogenesis, 16, 18, 37–40, 165–68
cybernetics, 40–41
cyclical time, 180–83

da Vinci, Leonardo, 118
Dallas Institute of Humanities and Culture, 25
Dalmatia, 232n.
The Dancing Column (Rykwert), 178
Daniélou, Jean, 54–55
Dante, 66
Dawson, Christopher, xv
Day, Dorothy, 148
De Esse et Essentia (Aquinas), 67–68
De Motu Cordis (Harvey), 124
De Sacramentis (Hugh of St. Victor), 198
De Spirituali Amicitia (Aelred), 150–51
De Varies Artibus (Presbyter), 73
death, art of, 153–56, 165–67
The Death of Nature (Merchant), 69
Delumeau, Jean, 93–94
Denham, Sir John, 231n.
Descartes, René, 68, 136
Deschooling Society (Illich), 3, 11–13, 17, 76–77
"development decade," 5, 6, 20, 194–95, 201
devil, embodiment of, 98
Didascalicon (Hugh of St. Victor), 26, 73
"disabling professions," 11–18, 37
diseases
as distinct entities, 110, 122, 146–47, 202–3
proliferation of, 123

34654001R00154

Made in the USA
Lexington, KY
17 August 2014